Physical Education and Sport Studies

Advanced Level Student Revision Guide

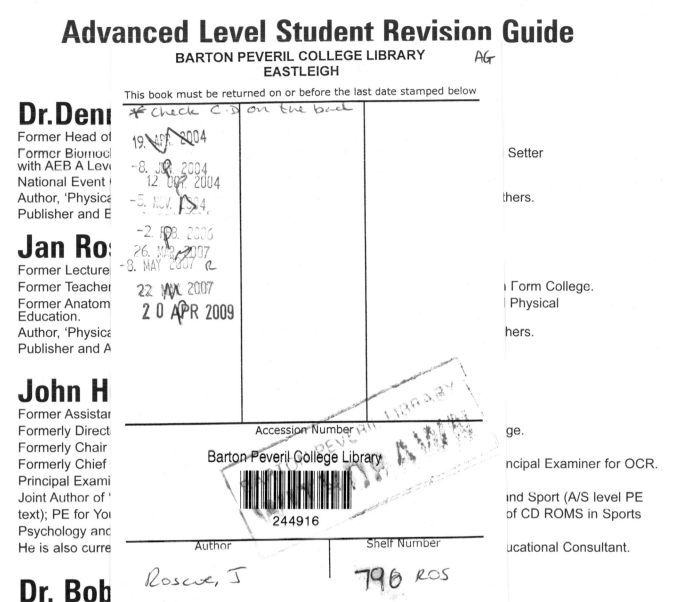

Dr. Denn...
Former Head of...
Former Biomech... Setter
with AEB A Leve...
National Event...
Author, 'Physica... ...thers.
Publisher and E...

Jan Ros...
Former Lecture...
Former Teacher... ...Form College.
Former Anatom... ...Physical
Education.
Author, 'Physica... ...hers.
Publisher and A...

John H...
Former Assistar...
Formerly Direct... ...ge.
Formerly Chair...
Formerly Chief... ...ncipal Examiner for OCR.
Principal Exami...
Joint Author of '... ...and Sport (A/S level PE
text); PE for Yo... ...of CD ROMS in Sports
Psychology and...
He is also curre... ...ucational Consultant.

Dr. Bob...
Former Principal Lecturer in Physical Education, Madeley College of Higher Education
Former Lecturer in Physical Education, Worcester College of Higher Education;
Former Chief Examiner, Question Setter for Contemporary Issues, History of Sport and Comparative
Studies in PE, Reviser and Practical Moderator with AEB A Level Physical Education;
Former Principal Examiner for OCR A Level Physical Education, OCR Revisor and Senior Moderator;
Currently Question Setter for OCR Synoptic Papers. Education Consultant.
Author, 'Physical Education and the Study of Sport', A Level PE Text, Teachers' Guides, and many others.

Dr Frank Galligan
Former Lecturer in Physical Education Worcester College of Higher Education.
Former member of MEG Regional GCSE Physical Education Subject Group, and Examiner with AEB A Level
Physical Education,.
Research associate for De Montfort University at the International Centre for Sports History and Culture.
Former examiner for OCR A Level Physical Education, question reviser for Edexcel A2 / AS level Physical
Education.
Executive member of British Society of Sports History, Editor of Philathletic Newsletter.
Author, 'Advanced PE for Edexcel', and Teachers' Guides. Education Consultant.

Jan Roscoe Publications

First published as 1 901 424 20 0 in 1998 by Jan Roscoe Publications
                           Holyrood 23 Stockswell Road
                           Widnes
                           Cheshire
                           WA8 4PJ
                           United Kingdom

                           0151 420 4446
                           0151 495 2622 fax
                           jroscoe@rapid.co.uk e-mail

A Catalogue record for this book is available from the British Library

Reprint January 1999.
Reprint January 2000.
Second edition January 2001 - 1 901424 32 4
Reprint September 2002.
Third Edition April 2003.

ISBN   1 901424 94 4

Cover designs by Helen Roscoe.

Published via QuarkXpress 4.1, CorelDraw 10.410, and Adobe Illustrator 9.0

Printed and bound by Poplar Services
                           Poplar House
                           Jackson Street
                           St Helens
                           WA9 3AP

                           01744 23363
                           01744 451242 fax

INTRODUCTION

Examination courses in Physical Education and Sport Studies have now become established within the post-16 curriculum and are a very popular and successful part of school, college or higher education.

This new edition has been written to address the change in content and style of AS / A2 Physical Education and Sport Studies programmes which commenced in September 2002.

Physical Education and Sport Studies courses are multidisciplinary in nature, covering anatomy and physiology, exercise physiology, biomechanics, skill acquisition, sports psychology, contemporary studies, comparative studies, global issues and historical studies. These subject areas have generated a substantial quantity of specialist literature each with its own specific language. At times you may be overwhelmed by the amount of material covered in a one or two year examination course. 'Physical Education and Sport Studies Advanced Level Student Revision Guide' addresses the problem of dealing with copious notes. What makes this new student resource unique is that this single package consists of hard copy summary pages (as in previous editions) and a CD ROM which contains all this material coded as to syllabus and year.

The CD ROM consists of a menu whereby a student can select their specific exam board (AQA, Edexcel or OCR) and then access the course material and attempt exam questions (which can be printed off in exam style format) that link to the relevant content. Full answers to the questions are also provided. Materials are presented in a concise and visual approach for effective and efficient revision.

The final chapter of the book looks at the latest style of question which links together different parts or modules within a course. Different styles of 'synoptic' question are favoured by different exam syllabuses, and so on the CDROM we give examples of each style of question (and answer).

Modern terminology, nomenclature and units have been used wherever possible. At the end of the book there is a comprehensive index available for easy reference.

Although this revision book is directly aimed at students preparing for Advanced Level (AS or A2) Physical Education and Sport Studies, it should also provide an invaluable resource for BTEC / GNVQ Sport Studies / Science courses.

HOW TO USE THIS REVISION GUIDE

The ideal use of this Revision Guide would be to purchase it at the start of the course and relate each of the summary pages to the specific areas of the syllabus as an aide memoire. The inclusion on the CDROM of summaries, specific questions and full answers provide a means of self-testing, complete with navigation guide enabling you to browse with ease. This CD Rom is syllabus specific. Don't be tempted to find out the answers before attempting a question.

In reality, whole examination questions contain a much broader content than those given in this guide. Examiners will attempt to examine more than one area of the syllabus within the context of one full question and therefore it is important that you revise all aspects of your syllabus.

The main use of the Revision Guide should be during the final revision period leading up to your examinations, as it should help you to understand and apply concepts i.e. link summary content with examination question.

The aim of this Student Guide is to provide an aid that enhances syllabus analysis, and to raise your level of success in examinations.

THE QUALITY OF AUTHORS

In order to create for the student a product of high quality, we have brought together an expert team of writers, who have considerable experience in teaching 'A' Level Physical Education, who have written past and current examination syllabuses, who have set and marked examination questions within this subject area and taught at revision workshops throughout the UK. Much of the material within this book has been thoroughly student tested.

We hope that this Revision Guide will prove useful to staff and students. Jan Roscoe Publications will welcome any comments you would wish to make about the book's utility or layout. Thank you for using our work.

Dennis Roscoe
Jan Roscoe.

ACKNOWLEDGMENTS

We would like to thank the authors for their cooperation and adherence to our demanding deadlines, Poplar Services for their patience in allowing us to experiment with new software and linking our work to their computers, and the JRP staff, Linda Underwood, Joanne Pierce, Ian Lowthian and Susan Street for working hard in the background while I put this book together, Helen Roscoe for her contribution as cover designer, proof reader and indexer, and Kelly Thomas for her contribution in creating the index.

Dennis Roscoe
Editor.

Contents

Chapter 9 - Global Issues
Frank Galligan

Chapter 10 - Synoptic Question and
Analysis Framework
Bob Davis, Jan Roscoe,
Dennis Roscoe, John Honeybourne,
Frank Galligan

Index

THE SKELETON

ANATOMY and PHYSIOLOGY

APPENDICULAR   &   AXIAL
- Shoulder girdle   - Skull.
- Hip girdle   - Vertebral column.
- Leg and arm bones   - Ribs & sternum.

- Names of major bones.

SKELETAL FUNCTIONS
- Lever system.
- Surface area for attachment of muscle.
  tendons and ligaments.
- Shape.
- Support.
- Red / white blood cell manufacture.
- Stores fats and minerals.

TYPES OF BONES & PRINCIPAL FUNCTIONS
- Long :   e.g. femur : lever.
- Short :   e.g. carpals : strength and lightness.
- Flat :   e.g. pelvis : surface area for muscle & tendon
                   attachments, cranium : skull protection.
- Irregular :   e.g. vertebrae : protection of spinal cord,
                   patella (sesamoid) increases mechanical
                   advantage of quadriceps tendon.

BONY FEATURES
- Protrusions   For example, tibial tuberosity / iliac spine.
- Depressions   For example, bicipital groove.
- Function of these features is to increase surface area for
  attachment of ligaments and muscle tendons.

BONE TISSUE - structure and function of :

CARTILAGE
- Hyaline : smooth, solid matrix (forms joints).
- White fibro : tough and slightly flexible (between
  vertebrae).
- Yellow elastic : soft and elastic (ear lobe).

PERIOSTEUM
- The periosteum is an outer protective covering.
- Which provides attachment for muscle tendons and ligaments.
- Deeper layers are responsible for growth in bone width.

Haversian system
basic structure of
compact & spongy bone
101

←— 0.5mm —→

LS of long bone

hyaline cartilage

compact bone

periosteum

spongy bone

102

JOINTS

ARTICULATION
- A place where two or more bones meet to form a joint.
JOINT TYPES
- FIBROUS or immovable : for example, between bones of the cranium.
- CARTILAGINOUS or slightly moveable : for example, vertebral discs.
- SYNOVIAL or freely moveable :

F/E	= Flexion/Extension
Ab/Ad	= Abduction/Adduction
R	= Rotation
C	= Circumduction

JOINT TYPE	MOVEMENT RANGE	eg. BODY PLACE : ARTICULATING BONES
Ball & socket	3 axes F/E Ab/Ad R C	Hip : femur, acetabulum of pelvis. Shoulder : scapula, humerus.
Hinge	1 axis F/E	Knee : femur, patella, tibia. Elbow : humerus, radius, ulna.
Pivot	1 axis R	Spine : Atlas : odontoid process of axis (turns head side to side). Elbow : proximal ends of radius and ulna.
Condyloid	2 axes F/E Ab/Ad = C	Knuckles joint of fingers : metacarpals, phalanges. Wrist : radius, carpals.
Saddle	2 axes F/E Ab/Ad = C	Joint at base of thumb : carpal, metacarpal.
Gliding	a little movement in all directions	Centre of chest : clavicle, sternum. Spine : articulating surfaces. Wrist : carpals. Ankle : tarsals.

STRUCTURE & FUNCTION OF A TYPICAL SYNOVIAL JOINT

- Synovial fluid (S) (lubricates joint, maintains joint stability).
- Synovial membrane (M) (secretes synovial fluid).
- Capsular ligament (C) (joins bones of the joint).
- Articular or hyaline cartilage (A) (prevents friction between bones).
- Bursae (prevent friction and wear between a bone and a ligament
  or tendon which glide against each other).
- Pads of fat (cushions joint, acts as shock absorbers).
- Menisci (help bones fit together better to stabilise the joint).

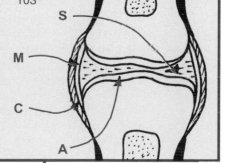
103
S
M
C
A

MAJOR ACTIVE MUSCLES INVOLVED IN SPORTS TECHNIQUES

body part / joint	movement pattern	active muscles
SHOULDER GIRDLE	elevation	upper fibres of trapezius, levator scapulae.
	depression	lower fibres of trapezius, pectoralis minor.
	rotation / adduction	serratus anterior, rhomboids.
SHOULDER JOINT	adduction	pectoralis major, anterior deltoid, corocobrachialis, latissimus dorsi.
	abduction	posterior deltoid, supraspinatus.
	flexion	anterior deltoid, pectoralis major, corocobrachialis.
	extension	latissimus dorsi, posterior deltoid, teres major.
	medial rotation	subscapularis, pectoralis major, latissimus dorsi.
	lateral rotation	teres minor, infraspinatus.
UPPER ARM / ELBOW	flexion	biceps brachii, brachialis, brachioradialis.
	extension	triceps brachii, anconeus.
RADIO-ULNA PIVOT	supination	supinator, biceps brachii.
	pronation	pronator teres, pronator quadratus.
WRIST	extension	extensor carpi ulnaris, carpi radialis brevis, extensor digitorum.
	flexion	flexor carpi radialis, flexi carpi ulnaris.
	adduction	extensor carpi ulnaris.
	abduction	extensor carpi radialis, longus, brevis.
TRUNK / SPINE	flexion	rectus abdominus.
	extension / hyperextension	erector spinae (sacrospinalis).
	internal flexion	internal obliques, external obliques, quadratus lumborum.
HIP JOINT	flexion	iliopsoas, quadriceps, pectineus, sartorius, tensor fascia latae.
	extension	hamstrings, gluteus maximus.
	adduction	adductor longus / magnus / brevis, pectineus, gracilis.
	abduction	gluteus maximus / medius / minimus, sartorius, tensor fascia latae.
	medial rotation	gluteus minimus, tensor fascia latae.
	lateral rotation	gluteus maximus, psoas major, sartorius.
KNEE JOINT	flexion	hamstrings group - biceps femoris, semimembranosus, semitendinosus, sartorius.
	extension	quadriceps group - rectus femoris, vastus medialis, vastus intermedius, vastus lateralis.
ANKLE	plantar - flexion	gastrocnemius, soleus, tibialis posterior
	dorsi - flexion	tibialis anterior, peroneus brevis.

RELATIONSHIP of MUSCULAR SYSTEM to SKELETAL SYSTEM
- Names of major muscles in relation to joint action.
- Attachments :
    - Tendons attach muscle to bone to transmit muscle force.
    - Ligaments attach bone to bone.
    - Periosteum provides attachment for muscle tendons and ligaments.
FUNCTION OF MUSCLES
- Antagonistic muscle action :
    - Agonist is the muscle that actually contracts to move the joint.
    - Antagonist is the muscle that relaxes in opposition to the agonist.
    - Fixator holds joint in position which stabilises the origin of the prime mover.
    - Synergist holds body position so that the agonist can operate.

Movement Analysis, example : curling a bar:
    Agonist = biceps, antagonist = triceps, fixator = deltoid, synergist = trapezius.

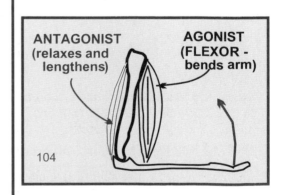

ANTAGONIST
(relaxes and
lengthens)

AGONIST
(FLEXOR -
bends arm)

104

BODY PLANES AND AXES

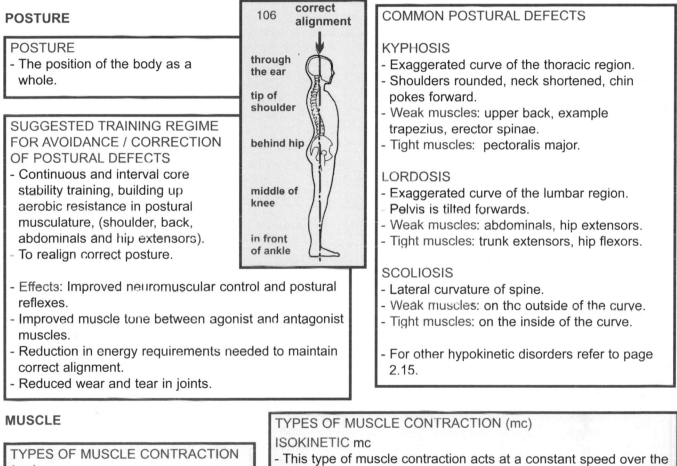

BODY PLANES & AXES

Plane   - an imaginary flat surface running through the body.
Axis of rotation - an imaginary line about which the body rotates or spins, at right
                           angles to the plane.

PLANES :

Frontal   - divides body into front and back sections : abduction, adduction,
                          lateral flexion.
                        - whole body movements include cartwheel.
Sagittal   - divides the body into left and right sections : flexion, extension,
                          dorsiflexion plantarflexion.
                        - whole body movements include somersaults, pole vault take-off,
                          sprinting.
Transverse   - divides the body into upper and lower sections : medial / lateral rotation, supination, pronation
                          whole body movements - twisting / turning, spinning skater / discus / hammer / ski turns.

As a student you will have to identify the major planes and axes in physical activity.

105

sagittal frontal
transverse

POSTURE

106 **correct alignment**

POSTURE
- The position of the body as a
  whole.

**SUGGESTED TRAINING REGIME
FOR AVOIDANCE / CORRECTION
OF POSTURAL DEFECTS**
- Continuous and interval core
  stability training, building up
  aerobic resistance in postural
  musculature, (shoulder, back,
  abdominals and hip extensors).
- To realign correct posture.

- Effects: Improved neuromuscular control and postural
  reflexes.
- Improved muscle tone between agonist and antagonist
  muscles.
- Reduction in energy requirements needed to maintain
  correct alignment.
- Reduced wear and tear in joints.

through
the ear

tip of
shoulder

behind hip

middle of
knee

in front
of ankle

COMMON POSTURAL DEFECTS

KYPHOSIS
- Exaggerated curve of the thoracic region.
- Shoulders rounded, neck shortened, chin
  pokes forward.
- Weak muscles: upper back, example
  trapezius, erector spinae.
- Tight muscles: pectoralis major.

LORDOSIS
- Exaggerated curve of the lumbar region.
- Pelvis is tilted forwards.
- Weak muscles: abdominals, hip extensors.
- Tight muscles: trunk extensors, hip flexors.

SCOLIOSIS
- Lateral curvature of spine.
- Weak muscles: on the outside of the curve.
- Tight muscles: on the inside of the curve.

- For other hypokinetic disorders refer to page
  2.15.

MUSCLE

**TYPES OF MUSCLE CONTRACTION
(mc)**

ISOMETRIC mc
- This is the muscular contraction where
  the tension developed occurs with no
  change in length of the muscle.
- Otherwise known as a static
  contraction or position.
- Improves muscle strength at fixed joint
  angle.
- Does not develop aerobic fitness.
- Can be done anywhere.
- Examples : rugby scrum, tug of war,
  chins - holding bent arm position.

TYPES OF MUSCLE CONTRACTION (mc)

ISOKINETIC mc
- This type of muscle contraction acts at a constant speed over the
  full range of motion, therefore the tension developed by the
  muscle is over the full range of motion.
- Needs special hydraulic weights machine = expense.
- Develops aerobic and anaerobic fitness.
- Strength is developed over the full range of motion but movement
  at a constant velocity may not assist strength development at the
  speed of motor recruitment required for a specific sports activity.

ISOTONIC mc
- Here muscles contract at a speed controlled by performer.
- Motor unit recruitment is at the speed required for the specific
  sports activity.
- Develops aerobic and anaerobic fitness.
- Most physical activities are isotonic.

MUSCLE (continued)

TYPES OF MUSCLE CONTRACTION (mc)

Isokinetic and isotonic muscle contraction can be :

CONCENTRIC mc
- This is muscle action involving the shortening of muscle fibres whilst developing tension, as origin and insertion of active muscle move towards each other.
- Example : Chins - use of biceps brachii in upward phase.

ECCENTRIC mc
- This is muscle action involving the lengthening of muscle fibres whilst developing tension as origin and insertion move away from each other.
- Example : Chins - use of biceps in downward phase.
- Can result in DOMS (delayed onset muscle soreness), possibly due to structural damage to muscle membranes.

PLYOMETRIC
- Work occurs during for example bounding exercises in which maximum effort is achieved during eccentric mc.

TRANSMISSION OF NEURAL IMPULSE
- This is an electrochemical process.
- Action potential (A) is initiated when Na^+ are allowed to diffuse into the axon of motor neurone.
- This depolarises (D) the axon to a critical point known as the 'all-or-none law'.

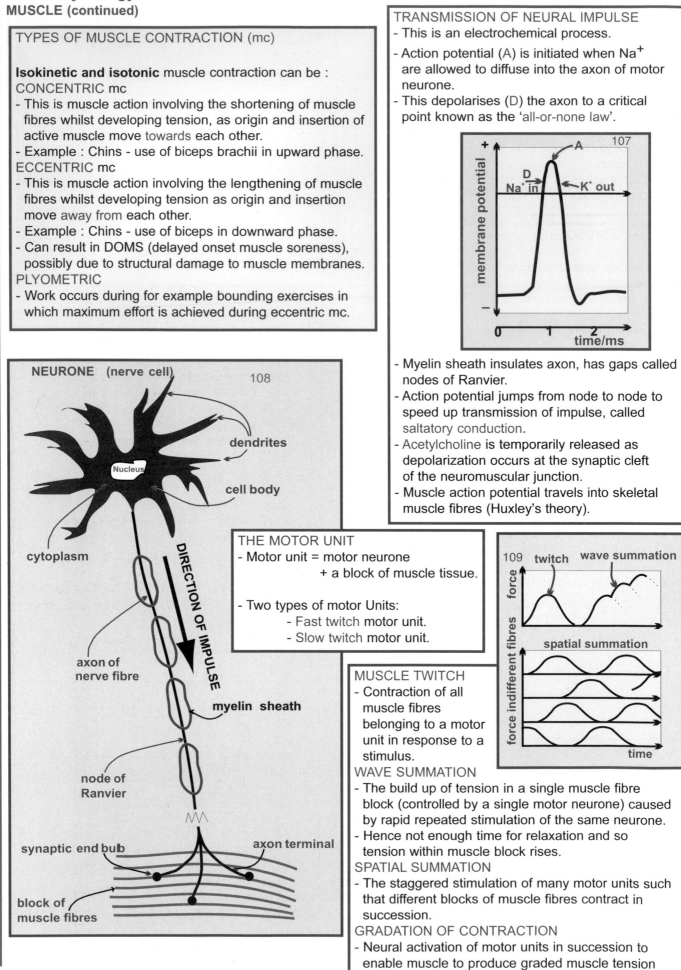

- Myelin sheath insulates axon, has gaps called nodes of Ranvier.
- Action potential jumps from node to node to speed up transmission of impulse, called saltatory conduction.
- Acetylcholine is temporarily released as depolarization occurs at the synaptic cleft of the neuromuscular junction.
- Muscle action potential travels into skeletal muscle fibres (Huxley's theory).

NEURONE (nerve cell) 108

dendrites

Nucleus

cell body

cytoplasm

DIRECTION OF IMPULSE

axon of nerve fibre

myelin sheath

node of Ranvier

synaptic end bulb

axon terminal

block of muscle fibres

THE MOTOR UNIT
- Motor unit = motor neurone + a block of muscle tissue.

- Two types of motor Units:
  - Fast twitch motor unit.
  - Slow twitch motor unit.

109 twitch   wave summation

force indifferent fibres / force

spatial summation

time

MUSCLE TWITCH
- Contraction of all muscle fibres belonging to a motor unit in response to a stimulus.

WAVE SUMMATION
- The build up of tension in a single muscle fibre block (controlled by a single motor neurone) caused by rapid repeated stimulation of the same neurone.
- Hence not enough time for relaxation and so tension within muscle block rises.

SPATIAL SUMMATION
- The staggered stimulation of many motor units such that different blocks of muscle fibres contract in succession.

GRADATION OF CONTRACTION
- Neural activation of motor units in succession to enable muscle to produce graded muscle tension (i.e. from weak to strong).

MUSCLE (continued)

MOTOR-NEURAL FIRING PATTERNS
- Stimuli are transmitted to different motor units which do not necessarily work in unison.

CONTROL of COORDINATED MOVEMENT
- The cerebellum compares intended movement with actual movement.
- If a difference is detected, cerebellum sends impulses to appropriate motor units which produce a correction.
- Control is achieved by increasing or decreasing the number of motor units operating.

SKELETAL MUSCLE
Fasciculus
- is a bundle containing muscle fibres.

Muscle fibre
- is a muscle cell containing myofibrils.

Long myofibril
- consists of a chain of contractile protein filaments
- actin and myosin.

Sarcomere
- is the functional unit of the muscle fibre, Voluntary or Neurogenic muscle.

SHAPES OF MUSCLES
- There are two major muscle shape categories.

PENNATE
- Limited range of movement.
- Very strong.
- For example, the pectoralis major.

FUSIFORM
- Perform a large range of movement quickly.
- Not very powerful.
- For example, the biceps brachii.

MUSCLE CELL STRUCTURES
- Motor Unit consists of a motor neurone and all the muscle fibres it stimulates.

HUXLEYS SLIDING THEORY OF MUSCLE CONTRACTION
- A neural impulse travels via a motor neurone to the motor end plate to create a muscle action potential.
- This muscle action potential triggers the release of Ca^{++} from the 'T' vesicles (located within the sarcoplasmic reticulum).
- Ca^{++} bind to the troponin molecule (on the actin filament) causing it to change shape by neutralising the tropomyosin and exposing the myosin cross-bridge binding sites on the actin molecules.
  - Mitochondria enable aerobic ATP regeneration.
  - ATP attaches itself to binding site on the cross-bridge releasing energy :

$$ATP \overset{ATPase}{======>} ADP + P_i + energy$$

  - Myosin cross-bridges swivel towards the centre of sarcomere (called the power stroke).
  - This draws the actin filaments past the myosin filaments (attach, detach, reattach of cross-bridges = ratchet mechanism).
- Contractile strength is dependent on cross-bridges formed.

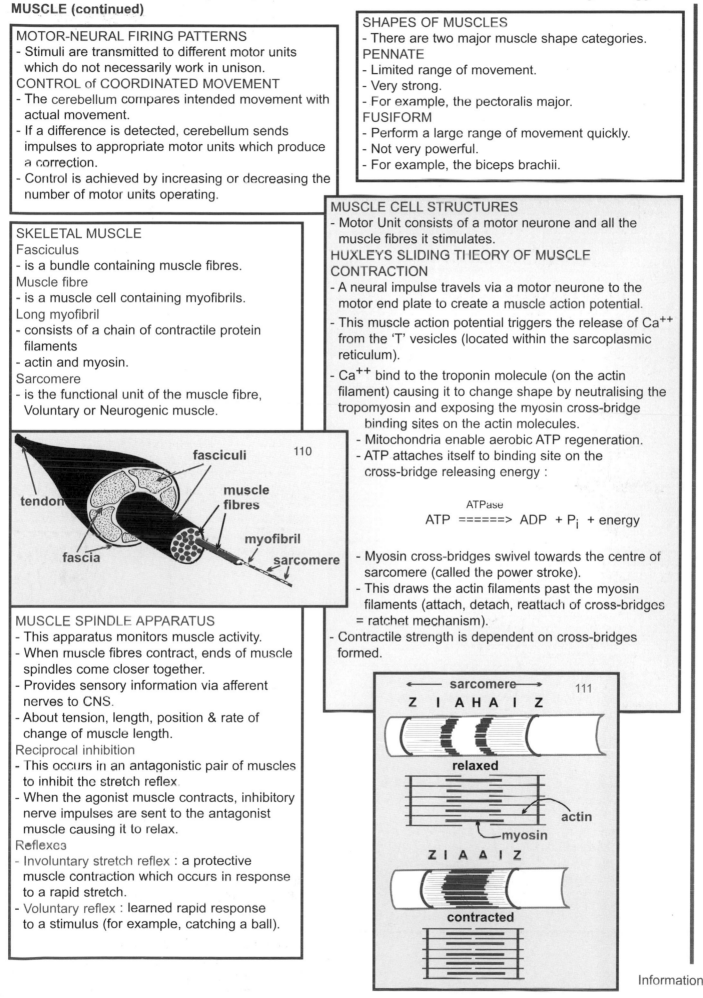

MUSCLE SPINDLE APPARATUS
- This apparatus monitors muscle activity.
- When muscle fibres contract, ends of muscle spindles come closer together.
- Provides sensory information via afferent nerves to CNS.
- About tension, length, position & rate of change of muscle length.

Reciprocal inhibition
- This occurs in an antagonistic pair of muscles to inhibit the stretch reflex.
- When the agonist muscle contracts, inhibitory nerve impulses are sent to the antagonist muscle causing it to relax.

Reflexes
- Involuntary stretch reflex : a protective muscle contraction which occurs in response to a rapid stretch.
- Voluntary reflex : learned rapid response to a stimulus (for example, catching a ball).

Information

MUSCLE (continued)

FIBRE TYPES - Responses to Training

- Endurance training results in type 11b being converted to type11a.
- Could explain why long steady work can result in loss of speed.

- High intensity anaerobic training causes increase in size and number of FT fibres (hypertrophy, hyperplasia respectively).
- Lack of training causes atrophy.

Recruitment
- Based on intensity of exercise.

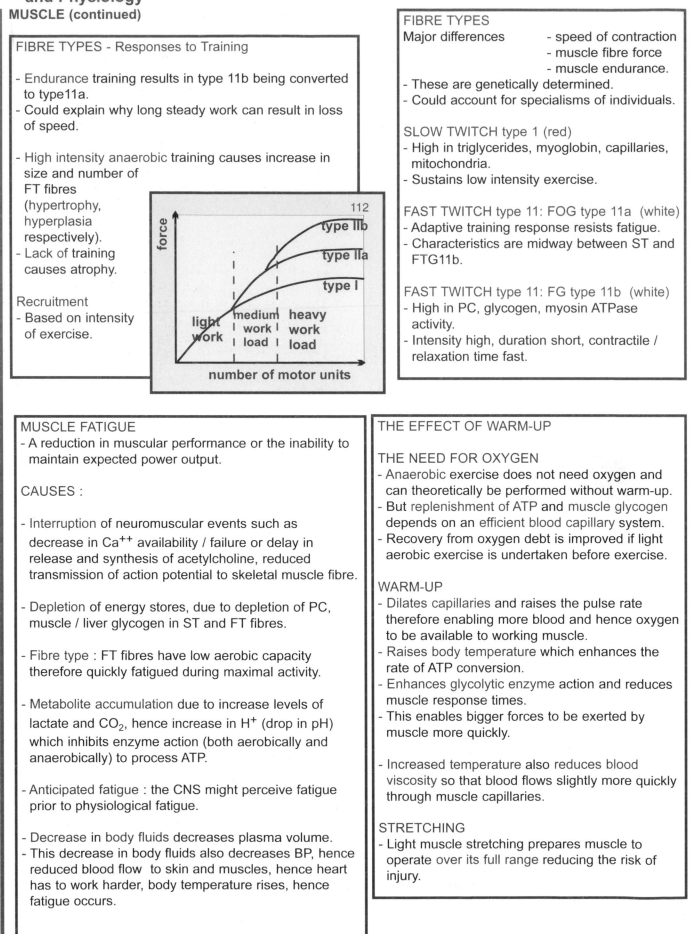

FIBRE TYPES

Major differences	- speed of contraction
	- muscle fibre force
	- muscle endurance.

- These are genetically determined.
- Could account for specialisms of individuals.

SLOW TWITCH type 1 (red)
- High in triglycerides, myoglobin, capillaries, mitochondria.
- Sustains low intensity exercise.

FAST TWITCH type 11: FOG type 11a (white)
- Adaptive training response resists fatigue.
- Characteristics are midway between ST and FTG11b.

FAST TWITCH type 11: FG type 11b (white)
- High in PC, glycogen, myosin ATPase activity.
- Intensity high, duration short, contractile / relaxation time fast.

MUSCLE FATIGUE
- A reduction in muscular performance or the inability to maintain expected power output.

CAUSES :

- Interruption of neuromuscular events such as decrease in Ca^{++} availability / failure or delay in release and synthesis of acetylcholine, reduced transmission of action potential to skeletal muscle fibre.

- Depletion of energy stores, due to depletion of PC, muscle / liver glycogen in ST and FT fibres.

- Fibre type : FT fibres have low aerobic capacity therefore quickly fatigued during maximal activity.

- Metabolite accumulation due to increase levels of lactate and CO_2, hence increase in H^+ (drop in pH) which inhibits enzyme action (both aerobically and anaerobically) to process ATP.

- Anticipated fatigue : the CNS might perceive fatigue prior to physiological fatigue.

- Decrease in body fluids decreases plasma volume.
- This decrease in body fluids also decreases BP, hence reduced blood flow to skin and muscles, hence heart has to work harder, body temperature rises, hence fatigue occurs.

THE EFFECT OF WARM-UP

THE NEED FOR OXYGEN
- Anaerobic exercise does not need oxygen and can theoretically be performed without warm-up.
- But replenishment of ATP and muscle glycogen depends on an efficient blood capillary system.
- Recovery from oxygen debt is improved if light aerobic exercise is undertaken before exercise.

WARM-UP
- Dilates capillaries and raises the pulse rate therefore enabling more blood and hence oxygen to be available to working muscle.
- Raises body temperature which enhances the rate of ATP conversion.
- Enhances glycolytic enzyme action and reduces muscle response times.
- This enables bigger forces to be exerted by muscle more quickly.

- Increased temperature also reduces blood viscosity so that blood flows slightly more quickly through muscle capillaries.

STRETCHING
- Light muscle stretching prepares muscle to operate over its full range reducing the risk of injury.

THE HEART

CARDIAC ANATOMY - GROSS STRUCTURE
- The heart consists of three layers :
Pericardium
- Double layer bag surrounding the heart, reduces friction.
Myocardium
- This is striped cardiac muscle tissue consisting of united fibres joined by intercalated discs.
- Activated by 'all-or-none law' and myogenic in nature.
Endocardium
- The endocardium is an inner glistening membrane, prevents friction between heart muscle & flowing blood.

HEART VALVES
Cuspid
- Mitral / bicuspid sited between left atria and left ventricle.
- Tricuspid sited between right atria and right ventricle.
Semi-lunar
- Semi-lunar valves guard the pulmonary artery and aorta.
- And control direction of blood flow.

HEART CHAMBERS :
Top
- The right and left atria have thin walls.
Bottom
- Right and left ventricles have thicker walls.
- The left ventricle wall is the thickest.
- Since this ventricle pumps blood to the main body mass.
Septum
- Consists of myocardial tissue (muscle) and divides the heart into a dual action pump.

BLOOD VESSELS attached to the heart :
Right side - vena cavae, pulmonary artery.
Left side - pulmonary vein, aorta.
Coronary BLOOD SUPPLY :
Arteries - supply glucose and O_2 to myocardial tissue.
Coronary veins - transport CO_2 and other wastes from heart muscle.

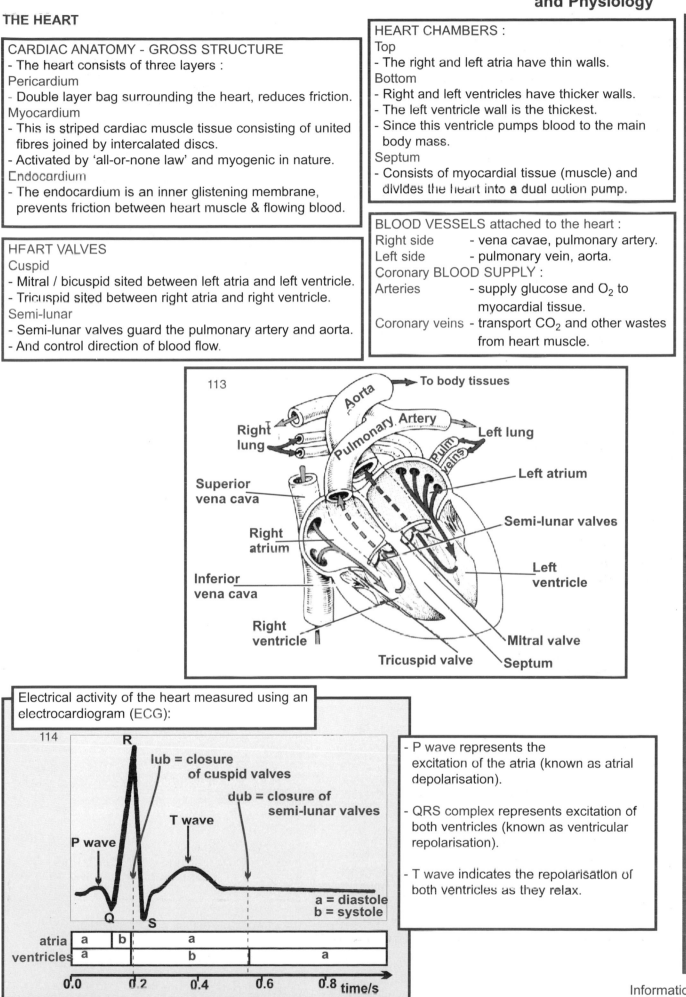

113

- P wave represents the excitation of the atria (known as atrial depolarisation).

- QRS complex represents excitation of both ventricles (known as ventricular repolarisation).

- T wave indicates the repolarisation of both ventricles as they relax.

Electrical activity of the heart measured using an electrocardiogram (ECG):

114

lub = closure of cuspid valves
dub = closure of semi-lunar valves
a = diastole
b = systole

THE HEART (continued)

HEART RATE (HR)
- HR is the number of beats per minute (bpm).
- Average resting HR
     - males 70 bpm, females 72 bpm.
- HR $_{trained}$ = 60 bpm (less = bradycardia).
- HR $_{untrained}$ = 70-90 bpm.
- HR $_{max}$ = 220 - age.

Stroke volume (SV)
- SV is the volume of blood pumped by the left ventricle of the heart per beat.
- SV trained = 110 ml.
- SV untrained = 70 ml.

Cardiac output ($\dot{Q}$)
- This is the volume of blood pumped by the left ventricle of the heart in one minute.
- The product of stroke volume and heart rate :
- $\dot{Q}$ = SV x HR

untrained person at rest :
- $\dot{Q}$ = 80 x 70 = 5.60 l/min (or dm^3 min^{-1}).

untrained person during maximal exercise :
- $\dot{Q}$ = 110 x 190 = 19.81 l/min (or dm^3 min^{-1}).

endurance athlete at rest :
- $\dot{Q}$ = 110 x 51 = 5.61 l/min.

endurance athlete during maximal exercise :
- $\dot{Q}$ = 190 x 200 = 38 l/min.

CARDIAC DYNAMICS

Cardiac impulse
- Is an electrical impulse which originates from the pacemaker in the sinoatrial (SA) node.
- It initiates contractions of the cardiac muscle.

CARDIAC CYCLE
Diastole (0.5 s)
- Relaxed heart muscle fills with blood.
- Cuspid valves open, semi-lunar valves close.

Systole (contracting heart muscle) 0.3 s
- Atrial systole, the SA node impulse causes a wave-like contraction over the atria forcing blood past cuspid valves into ventricles.
- Ventricular systole, the impulse reaches the AV node, cuspid values close, ventricular pressure rises as ventricles contract, semi-lunar valves open, blood is pushed out into pulmonary artery (lungs) and aorta (around body).

PULSE
- A wave of pressure produced by the contraction of the left ventricle.

115 **The CARDIAC IMPULSE**
myogenic — bundle ofHIS — Purkinje fibres — SA node — AV node

HEART RATE RESPONSE TO EXERCISE

116

HEART RATE RESPONSE to EXERCISE
- Interpretation of graphs.

a = Anticipatory rise due to hormonal action of adrenaline and norepinephrine.

b = Sharp rise - mainly anaerobic work :
 - due to proprioceptor / sensory stimulation,
 - also due to continued release of hormones and
 - action of the muscle pump.

c = Continued high HR due to maximal workloads which continue to stress anaerobic systems :
 - producing lactic acid + CO_2 + K^+
 - stimulating chemoreceptors
 - intrinsic factors also stimulated at maximal level.

d = Steady state and some recovery of O_2 debt (aerobic).

e = Rapid recovery due to cessation of proprioceptive stimuli / muscle pump / withdrawal of hormones.

f = Slow recovery, clearance of metabolites such as lactic acid, as systems return to normal resting values.

BLOOD AND THE VASCULAR SYSTEM

CONSTITUENTS OF BLOOD

55% Plasma — Transports dissolved nutrients and waste.

45% Corpuscles : Red — $Hb + O_2 \rightleftharpoons HbO_2$ (O_2 transport).

White — Produce antibodies & regulate immune system.

Platelets — Facilitate clotting.

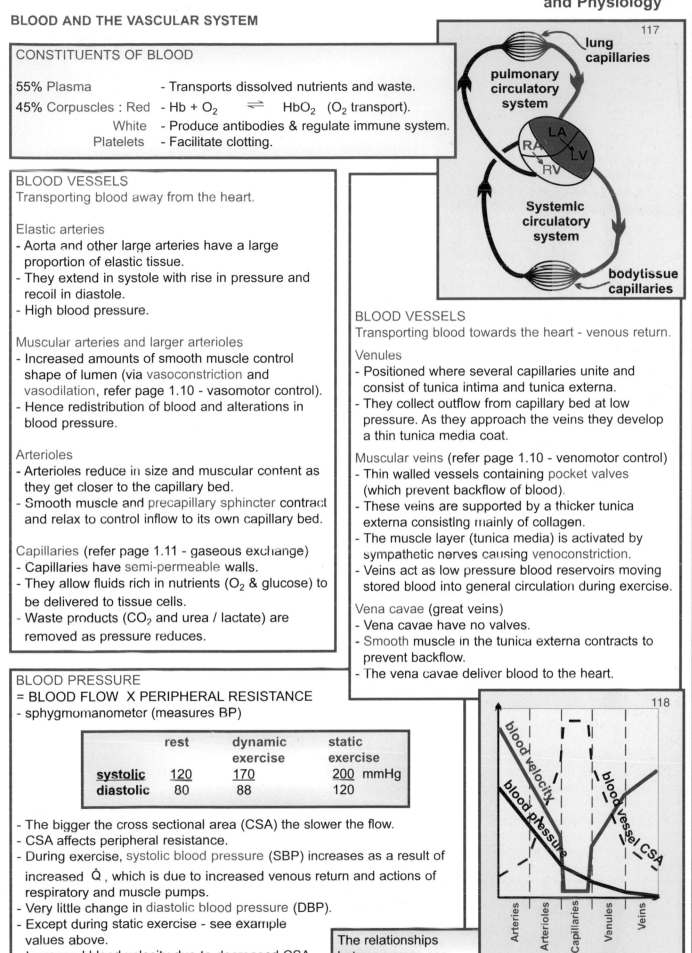

117

lung capillaries

pulmonary circulatory system

LA
RA LV
RV

Systemic circulatory system

bodytissue capillaries

BLOOD VESSELS
Transporting blood away from the heart.

Elastic arteries
- Aorta and other large arteries have a large proportion of elastic tissue.
- They extend in systole with rise in pressure and recoil in diastole.
- High blood pressure.

Muscular arteries and larger arterioles
- Increased amounts of smooth muscle control shape of lumen (via vasoconstriction and vasodilation, refer page 1.10 - vasomotor control).
- Hence redistribution of blood and alterations in blood pressure.

Arterioles
- Arterioles reduce in size and muscular content as they get closer to the capillary bed.
- Smooth muscle and precapillary sphincter contract and relax to control inflow to its own capillary bed.

Capillaries (refer page 1.11 - gaseous exchange)
- Capillaries have semi-permeable walls.
- They allow fluids rich in nutrients (O_2 & glucose) to be delivered to tissue cells.
- Waste products (CO_2 and urea / lactate) are removed as pressure reduces.

BLOOD VESSELS
Transporting blood towards the heart - venous return.

Venules
- Positioned where several capillaries unite and consist of tunica intima and tunica externa.
- They collect outflow from capillary bed at low pressure. As they approach the veins they develop a thin tunica media coat.

Muscular veins (refer page 1.10 - venomotor control)
- Thin walled vessels containing pocket valves (which prevent backflow of blood).
- These veins are supported by a thicker tunica externa consisting mainly of collagen.
- The muscle layer (tunica media) is activated by sympathetic nerves causing venoconstriction.
- Veins act as low pressure blood reservoirs moving stored blood into general circulation during exercise.

Vena cavae (great veins)
- Vena cavae have no valves.
- Smooth muscle in the tunica externa contracts to prevent backflow.
- The vena cavae deliver blood to the heart.

BLOOD PRESSURE
= BLOOD FLOW X PERIPHERAL RESISTANCE
- sphygmomanometer (measures BP)

	rest	dynamic exercise	static exercise
systolic	120	170	200 mmHg
diastolic	80	88	120

- The bigger the cross sectional area (CSA) the slower the flow.
- CSA affects peripheral resistance.
- During exercise, systolic blood pressure (SBP) increases as a result of increased $\dot{Q}$, which is due to increased venous return and actions of respiratory and muscle pumps.
- Very little change in diastolic blood pressure (DBP).
- Except during static exercise - see example values above.
- Increased blood velocity due to decreased CSA helps drive blood quickly through the venal system.

118

blood velocity

blood pressure

blood vessel CSA

Arteries | Arterioles | Capillaries | Venules | Veins

The relationships between cross sectional area, pressure and velocity of blood are shown in diagram 118.

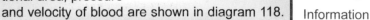

THE BLOOD and VASCULAR SYSTEM (continued)

VASOMOTOR CONTROL

- This is concerned with the ability of muscular arteries and arterioles to change their shape.
- During exercise sympathetic nerves carry impulses to smooth muscle walls of arteries and arterioles supplying non-active tissues.
- This causes vasoconstriction.
- In contrast, sympathetic stimulation in arteries and arterioles, supplying blood to active skeletal muscle, is reduced.
- Therefore these vessels dilate, vasodilation.
- And additional blood flows into active muscles.
- As a result of vasomotor control, blood flow is diverted to skeletal muscle where it is needed.
- Otherwise known as blood shunting or the vascular shunt.

VENOMOTOR CONTROL

- Regulation of blood flow by changes in shape in veins is limited due to thin tunica media.
- SNS (sympathetic nervous system) can alter lumen a little to affect changes in blood velocity.
- Called venoconstriction.

VENOUS RETURN MECHANISM depends on :

- Gravity, the actions of muscle, respiratory and cardiac pumps (Starling's law of the heart).
- The action of valves in the lower limb prevents backflow.
- Venoconstriction.

119 **The Vascular Shunt**

%blood flow — skeletal muscle / other organs — rest / exercise

THE EFFECTS of WARM-UP on the VASCULAR SYSTEM
- Due to vascular shunt mechanism, more blood flows through active muscle tissues as local vascular beds dilate, increasing metabolism and muscle temperature.
- Increased blood temperature reduces blood viscosity, so that blood flows slightly more quickly through active muscle tissues.

THE EFFECTS of COOL-DOWN on the VASCULAR SYSTEM
- Reduces 'blood pooling'.
- Maintains increased blood flow through the vascular system, flushing the capillary system with oxygenated blood and removing exercise metabolites such as CO_2 and lactic acid. Thus returning vascular system to pre-exercise state.

GASEOUS TRANSPORT

LUNG STRUCTURE

Trachea
- This consists of an incomplete ring of cartilage which keeps airway open and allows swallowing.
- Ciliated lining and mucous glands in nose, pharynx, larynx, trachea and bronchi provide a cleaning mechanism.

Pulmonary pleura
- This secretes pleural fluid which reduces friction between lung tissue and ribs, aids inspiration as pleural pressure reduces, and expiration as pleural pressure increases.

Lung tissue - alveolar structure
- Elastic, moist, permeable single layered epithelium surrounded by network of capillaries, adapted for gaseous exchange.

AIR PATHWAY Air route
- nasal cavity
    => pharynx
        => larynx
            => trachea
                => bronchi
                    => bronchioles
                        =>respiratory bronchioles
                            =>alveolar ducts
                                =>alveoli.

ASTHMA
- Recurrent attacks making breathing difficult, particularly during exhalation.
- Caused by increased constriction of smooth muscle of bronchioles to a variety of stimuli.
- And / or by increased mucous secretions and swelling of mucous membrane lining respiratory bronchioles.
- Exercise-induced asthma (EI A) :
    - Bronchioles dilate during exercise (for example during running).
    - And constrict at end of exercise making breathing difficult.

- Treatment : steroid-based inhalers, which need to be registered for competitions.

GASEOUS TRANSPORT (continued)

MECHANICS OF BREATHING
- Concerned with changes in lung volumes and associated changes in pulmonary air pressure.

Inspiration at rest
- External intercostal muscles and diaphragm contract, internal intercostals relax.
- Effect : volume of thoracic cavity increases, pleural and pulmonary pressures less than atmospheric pressure, so air rushes in.

Inspiration during exercise
- Additionally, scalenes, sternocleidomastoid, pectoralis minor muscles contract to create bigger volume, therefore more air rushes in.

Expiration at rest
- External intercostals and diaphragm relax.
- Effect : decrease in lung volume, increase in pleural and pulmonary pressure, therefore air is forced out.

Expiration during exercise
- Internal intercostal and abdominal muscles contract, air is forced out more rapidly.

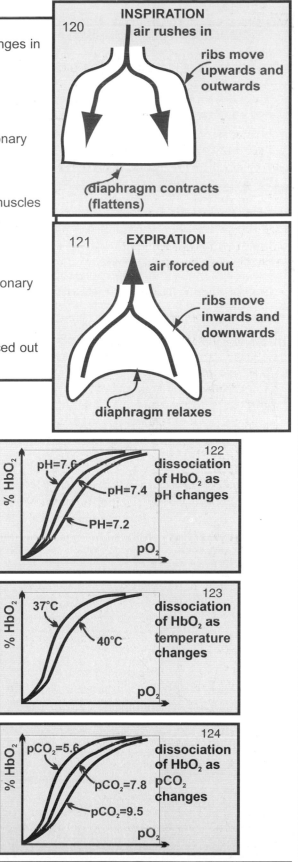

120 INSPIRATION air rushes in
ribs move upwards and outwards
diaphragm contracts (flattens)

121 EXPIRATION air forced out
ribs move inwards and downwards
diaphragm relaxes

GASEOUS EXCHANGE

GASEOUS EXCHANGE
- This depends on partial pressure of each gas, gas solubility and temperature.
- Partial pressure (p) : the pressure a gas exerts within a mixture of gases.
- Gases diffuse from high to low pressure.

In the alveoli :
- Maximum possible haemoglobin pO_2 = 13.3kPa, (as in alveolar air).
- In venous blood (arriving from tissues) pO_2 = 5.3kPa.
- Thus haemoglobin is forced to be saturated at 98% O_2.
- i.e. $Hb + O_2 ==> HbO_2$ (at 98%).
- pCO_2 in venous blood is higher in alveoli.
- Therefore CO_2 diffuses across alveolar membrane (from blood to air in lung) and is expired.

At tissue cell site :
- Arriving (arterial) blood pO_2 is greater than tissue pO_2.
- Myoglobin has a greater affinity for O_2 than Hb.
- Therefore O_2 is released into tissue cells.
- This O_2 is transported by myoglobin to the mitochondria.
- Where aerobic tissue cell respiration takes place.
- CO_2 diffuses across in opposite direction (from tissue to departing blood).

CO_2 transported in venous blood as :
- Carbonic acid (70%).
- Carbaminohaemoglobin (23%).
- Dissolved in plasma (7%).
- This CO_2 is excreted from the lungs during expiration.

122 dissociation of HbO_2 as pH changes
% HbO_2 pH=7.6 pH=7.4 PH=7.2 pO_2

123 dissociation of HbO_2 as temperature changes
% HbO_2 37°C 40°C pO_2

124 dissociation of HbO_2 as pCO_2 changes
% HbO_2 pCO_2=5.6 pCO_2=7.8 pCO_2=9.5 pO_2

Increased blood temperature / CO_2, or decreased pH cause a shift of the O_2 dissociation curve so that % of saturated haemoglobin with oxygen is reduced. This is called the 'Bohr effect', see graphs above. More O_2 is then available to active tissue.

RESPIRATION

EFFICIENCY OF GAS PROCESS

The efficiency of the gas process is due to :
- A thin alveolar membrane.
- Short distance between alveolar membrane and capillary network (less than 0.5μm) (the distance across which gas molecules have to travel is very small).
- A large surface area inside the alveoli (the surface across which molecules must be exchanged is very large).
- A moist lining which enables rapid solution of gas molecules.
- A constant blood supply into which gas can diffuse.
- Large amounts of red blood corpuscles (in blood), and myoglobin (in muscle cells).

PULMONARY RESPIRATION
- The process of supplying fresh air to alveoli.

TISSUE RESPIRATION
- The process by which cells use oxygen in order to release energy.

O_2 and CO_2 differences between inhaled and exhaled air

	inhaled(%)	exhaled (rest)(%)	exhaled (exercise)(%)
O_2	21	17	15
CO_2	0.003	3	6

LUNG VOLUMES and CAPACITIES

LUNG VOLUMES
- Of untrained and trained subjects at rest (see graph on right).

Lung capacities are made up of combinations of lung volumes :
- Inspiratory capacity = TV + IRV (3600 ml).
- Expiratory capacity = TV + ERV (1700 ml).
- Vital capacity (VC) = TV + IRV + ERV (4800 ml).
- Functional residual capacity = RV + ERV (2400 ml).
- Total lung capacity = VC + RV (6000 ml).

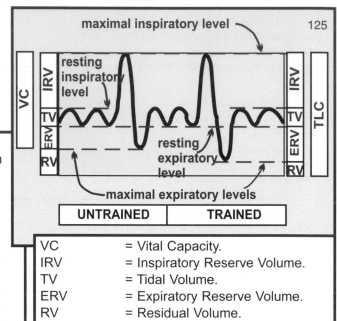

125

VC	= Vital Capacity.
IRV	= Inspiratory Reserve Volume.
TV	= Tidal Volume.
ERV	= Expiratory Reserve Volume.
RV	= Residual Volume.
TLC	= Total Lung Capacity.

CHANGES in MINUTE VENTILATION with EXERCISE

MINUTE VENTILATION

- (dm³) V̇E = TV x f
- at rest   6 = 0.5 x 12
- max   121 = 2.2 x 55
- submax 60 = 2.4 x 25.

- Refer to page 1.8 for interpretation of graph.

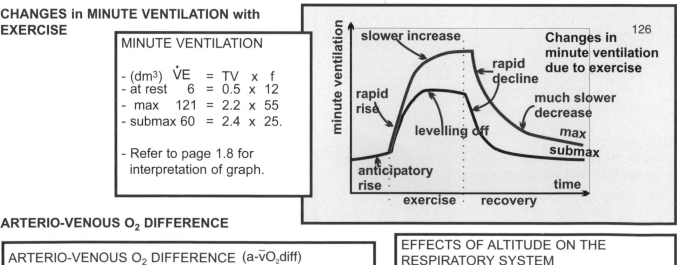

Changes in minute ventilation due to exercise

126

ARTERIO-VENOUS O_2 DIFFERENCE

ARTERIO-VENOUS O_2 DIFFERENCE (a-v̄O_2diff)
- This is the difference between the amount of O_2 leaving and returning to the heart.
- Examples :
at rest :   a-v̄O_2diff = 5 ml O_2 per 100 ml blood.
during exercise :   a-v̄O_2diff = 15 ml O_2 per 100 ml blood.

EFFECTS OF ALTITUDE ON THE RESPIRATORY SYSTEM

- Hypoxia (a decreased pressure of oxygen) stimulates central and peripheral chemoreceptors.
- Which cause increases in f and TV during the first week of residence.
- Decreased CO_2 makes urine more alkaline.

THE MECHANISMS OF REGULATION ON BODY SYSTEMS

CARDIAC REGULATION and RESPONSE to EXERCISE

Neural factors
- Heart beat is continually adjusted by nervous impulses travelling from the cardiac centre via sympathetic and parasympathetic nerves working antagonistically.
- Action of parasympathetic NS (stimulation via vagus nerve) :
    - slows HR
        - delays conduction at AV node
        - decreases force of contraction
        - decreases excitability.
- Action of sympathetic NS (stimulation via accelerator nerve) :
        - increases HR
        - increases conductivity
        - increases force of contraction
        - increases excitability.

Neural control
- Regulates feedback from important variables such as reflex actions of chemoreceptors via the PNS and SNS.

Reflex actions
- Stimulation of proprioceptors such as muscle spindles and golgi tendons increase HR via SNS.

- The baroreceptor reflexes detect changes in blood pressure and result in changes in HR and SV.

- Cerebral impulses also cause HR to rise in anticipation of exercise.

CARDIAC REGULATION and RESPONSE to EXERCISE

OTHER FACTORS
Intrinsic
- Changes in venous return results from changes in the actions of the muscle and respiratory pumps.
- Electrolyte balance (Na^+, K^+), and myocardial temperature.
- All alter HR and SV (Starling's Law of the Heart).
Gender differences
- Males have higher levels of testosterone which increases myocardial tissue & gives increased SV and reduced HR.
- Socio-cultural differences.
Age, Body position, Exercise are also regulatory factors.

127 **neural**   **others**

BODY SYSTEM REGULATORS

hormonal   **chemical**

CARDIAC REGULATION and RESPONSE to EXERCISE

Hormonal factors
- Noradrenaline and adrenaline act to accelerate heart rate (tachycardia).
- Acetylcholine slows the heart (bradycardia).
- Thyroid hormone and glucagon increase HR and SV.

CARDIAC REGULATION and RESPONSE to EXERCISE

Chemical factors
- Chemoreceptors (sensitive to increased CO_2 and H^+ concentrations, and decreased pH), increase HR and force of contraction (SV).

RESPIRATORY REGULATION and RESPONSE to EXERCISE
- Rhythmicity area.
- Pneumotaxic area (controls frequency - f).
- Apneustic area (controls tidal volume - TV).

Chemical Control
- Aim is to keep pCO_2 to below 5.3 kPa.
- Determines rate and depth of breathing.
- Central chemoreceptors (major regulator) respond to increased CO_2 and decreased pH.
- Peripheral chemoreceptors (aortic and carotid bodies) respond to increased CO_2 and decreased pH and O_2.
- Effect is to increase f of breaths and TV.
- Lack of O_2 (high altitude) stimulates respiration.

RESPIRATORY REGULATION and RESPONSE to EXERCISE

Nervous Control
- Respiratory centre regulates respiratory volumes and breathing frequency via phrenic and intercostal nerves.
- This stimulates the respiratory muscles.
- Proprioceptors (working muscle spindles) when stimulated cause increase in f and TV.
- Lung stretch receptors decrease inhalation and increases exhalation (Hering-Breuer reflex).

Hormonal Control
- Adrenaline and noradrenaline dilate bronchioles which increases f and TV.

Temperature Control
- Increase in body temperature increases f and TV via action of hypothalamus.

THE MECHANISMS OF REGULATION ON BODY SYSTEMS (continued)

CELLULAR RESPONSE to EXERCISE

Neural Cells
- Increased rate of firing of CNS, therefore increased stimulation of motor units.
- Therefore increased recruitment of FT and ST motor units.

Muscle Cells
- Increased rate of cellular respiration means increased O_2 consumption or $\dot{V}O_2$.
- Increased use of energy stores causes a decrease in PC, glycogen in ST and FT fibres, triglycerides, oxymyoglobin stores, and increase in ADP's , Mg^{++}, Ca^{++}.
- Reduced pH inhibits cellular enzymes.
- Resulting in a general increase in muscle fatigue as muscular performance reduces.

VASCULAR RESPONSE to EXERCISE

Neural Control
- Vasomotor control redistributes blood to meet metabolic requirements of working muscles.

Chemical Control
- Increased pCO_2, increased temperature and a fall in pH decreases the O_2 carrying capacity of RBC (Bohr effect), hence increased oxygen delivery to active tissues.

Hormonal Control
- Release of adrenaline brings about vasoconstriction of non-active arterioles.
- Vasodilation of arterioles to the heart and active skeletal muscle occurs.
- Then precapillary sphincters and blood capillaries open to increase muscle blood flow.
- Increased $\dot{Q}$ gives an increase in SBP.

Body fluid balance
- If body fluids reduce (hence plasma volume), this increases HR, BP and body temperature.

Jan Roscoe

Information

ENERGY CONCEPTS

EXERCISE PHYSIOLOGY

ENERGY
- Is the capacity to do work (measured in joules).
- Work = force x distance moved.

POWER = $\underline{\text{Energy (joules)}}$ = ?   Watts
                 time (sec)

INVESTIGATION   Margaria-Kalaman staircase test.

CHEMICAL ENERGY
- Is energy that is produced by a complex series
  of chemical reactions which can then be made
  available as mechanical energy.

KINETIC ENERGY
- Is energy due to movement which can be caused
  by muscular contraction.

POTENTIAL ENERGY
- Is stored energy due to gravity.

ATP
- Adenosine triphosphate, energy currency of the body.

EXOTHERMIC REACTIONS
- Give out energy (via enzyme ATPase).

$$\text{ATP} \overset{\text{ATPase}}{=====>} \text{ADP} + P_i + \text{Energy}$$

- This reaction releases energy which causes muscle
  to contract (and all other bodily functions).
- Only 2 secs supply during maximum work.
- Then ATP is created via the energy systems
  depending on intensity and duration of the exercise
  period.

ENDOTHERMIC REACTIONS
- Take in energy (i.e. restoration of ATP from ADP).

ATP/ PC (PHOSPHOCREATINE) SYSTEM
- Alactic anaerobic energy system.
- High intensity maximum work.
- Duration short (dominant system from 3-10 sec.).
- After 10 seconds of flat out work all the PC is used up.
- No oxygen needed therefore ANAEROBIC metabolism.
- Takes place in muscle sarcoplasm.

THE COUPLED REACTION
- Is the two stage process by which PC is used to
  recreate ATP once it has broken down into ADP + P_i

- Stage 1 $\overset{\text{creatine kinase}}{\text{PC} ===> P_i + C + \text{energy}}$
- Stage 2   energy + ADP + P_i ===> ATP
- Net effect   PC + ADP ===> ATP + C

TRAINING ADAPTATIONS
- Increase in ATP/ PC stores.
- Delayed alactic / lactic threshold.

RATE of ENERGY PRODUCTION — T = threshold point. Labels: ATP store, AT P/PC system, lactic acid system, overall performance, aerobic system, base rate, 201. Axis: % of maximum rate of energy production vs time (2 s, T, 10 s, T, 60 s, 2 hrs).

LACTIC ACID SYSTEM
- Occurs during glycolysis : i.e. anaerobic, in sarcoplasm.
- During high intensity exercise this system becomes
  dominant between 10 - 60 seconds.
- Glycolytic enzymes enable the breakdown of glucose to
  produce energy to recreate ATP from ADP and P_i :
  - glycogen phosphorylase (GPP),
  - phosphofructokinase (PFK),
  - lactate dehydrogenase (LDH).

TRAINING ADAPTATIONS
- Increased toleration to lactic acid.
- Increased glycogen stores.
- Delayed lactacid / aerobic threshold.

**EFFECTS OF CONTINUED HIGH
INTENSITY EXERCISE**
- Increased lactic acid (OBLA).
- Increased muscle fatigue and pain.
- Reduced pH inhibits glycolytic
  enzymes GPP, PFK and LDH.
- Reduction in physical performance.

EVENTS
- Lactic acid accumulates from 30 - 60 s.
- 400m sprint, 100m swim, 500m speedskate.

GLYCOLYSIS 202 — glucose $C_6H_{12}O_6$ → glycolytic enzymes → 2ATP; → pyruvic acid → LDH → lactic acid.

AEROBIC SYSTEM

Stage 1 = glycolysis in sarcoplasm (same as
  lactic acid system) - yields 2ATP.

Stage 2 = Kreb's cycle in cell mitochondria, in
  the presence of O_2.
- Yields 2ATP (per molecule of glucose) and
  CO_2 and releases H^+ and e^- into
  next stage.
- Fatty acids (acting enzyme
  lipoprotein lipase) and proteins (as
  keto acids) enter at this point.

Stage 3 = Electron transport chain
  in mitochondria creates 32 / 34
  ATPs per molecule of glucose.
- O_2 used to create ATP as H^+ and
  e^- meet with H_2O given off.

EXERCISE TYPES :
- Becomes the dominant energy
  system when activity is low
  intensity / long duration.
- Examples : hockey, jogging,
  cycle ride, swim.

MITOCHONDRIA

MITOCHONDRIA
- Located immediately beneath sarcolemma to provide energy for transport of ions and metabolites across sarcolemma.
- Located deep within muscle fibres to provide energy for muscle contraction (via ATP).
- Act as power plants of the cell.
- Where O_2 is consumed via the Electron Transport Chain in the creation of ATP.
- Slow twitch fibres have large numbers.

EFFICIENCY OF RESPIRATION
- Depends on food fuel biomechanical pathway :

Anaerobic route :
- 2 ATP from each molecule of glucose.
- Rapid fuel breakdown.

Aerobic route :
- 36-38 ATP from each molecule of glucose = 18-19 times more efficient than anaerobic route.

ENERGY CONTINUUM

ENERGY CONTINUUM
- This term prescribes the dominance of energy systems in relation to intensity and duration of workload.
- Factors affecting energy continuum :
    - Level of fitness : including training adaptations,
    - Diet : high CHO diet helps replenish glycogen stores, dietary supplements such as creatine and glutamine enhance anaerobic work.
    - Availability of O_2, for example reduced pO_2 at altitude.

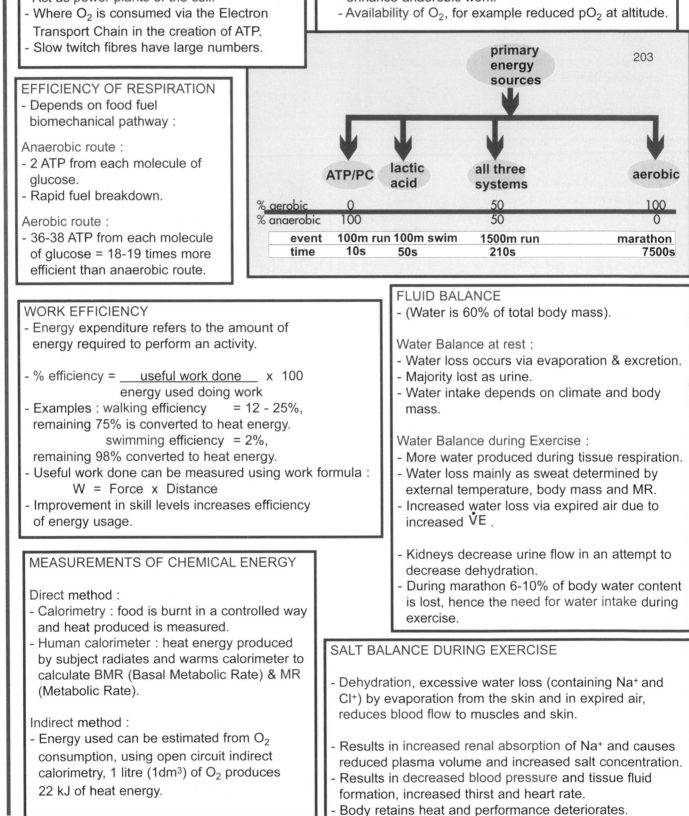

203

	primary energy sources		
	ATP/PC	lactic acid	all three systems	aerobic

	ATP/PC	lactic acid	all three systems	aerobic
% aerobic	0		50	100
% anaerobic	100		50	0
event	100m run	100m swim	1500m run	marathon
time	10s	50s	210s	7500s

WORK EFFICIENCY
- Energy expenditure refers to the amount of energy required to perform an activity.

- % efficiency = $\dfrac{\text{useful work done}}{\text{energy used doing work}}$ x 100
- Examples : walking efficiency = 12 - 25%, remaining 75% is converted to heat energy.
  swimming efficiency = 2%, remaining 98% converted to heat energy.
- Useful work done can be measured using work formula :
  W = Force x Distance
- Improvement in skill levels increases efficiency of energy usage.

MEASUREMENTS OF CHEMICAL ENERGY

Direct method :
- Calorimetry : food is burnt in a controlled way and heat produced is measured.
- Human calorimeter : heat energy produced by subject radiates and warms calorimeter to calculate BMR (Basal Metabolic Rate) & MR (Metabolic Rate).

Indirect method :
- Energy used can be estimated from O_2 consumption, using open circuit indirect calorimetry, 1 litre (1dm³) of O_2 produces 22 kJ of heat energy.

FLUID BALANCE
- (Water is 60% of total body mass).

Water Balance at rest :
- Water loss occurs via evaporation & excretion.
- Majority lost as urine.
- Water intake depends on climate and body mass.

Water Balance during Exercise :
- More water produced during tissue respiration.
- Water loss mainly as sweat determined by external temperature, body mass and MR.
- Increased water loss via expired air due to increased $\dot{V}E$.

- Kidneys decrease urine flow in an attempt to decrease dehydration.
- During marathon 6-10% of body water content is lost, hence the need for water intake during exercise.

SALT BALANCE DURING EXERCISE

- Dehydration, excessive water loss (containing Na^+ and Cl^+) by evaporation from the skin and in expired air, reduces blood flow to muscles and skin.

- Results in increased renal absorption of Na^+ and causes reduced plasma volume and increased salt concentration.
- Results in decreased blood pressure and tissue fluid formation, increased thirst and heart rate.
- Body retains heat and performance deteriorates.

ENERGY CONTINUUM (continued)

EFFICIENCY of HEAT PRODUCTION
- Body temperature is maintained by balancing heat input with heat loss :

TEMPERATURE REGULATION
- The thermoregulatory center is situated in the hypothalamus.
- Changes in body temperature are sensed by central and peripheral receptors.
- Body temperature is maintained by balancing heat input and heat loss.

HEAT INPUT
    metabolic heat
       exercise
          shivering
             Q_{10} effect

(This effect concerns the fact that the rate of chemical reactions double with each $10°C$ increase in temperature).

HEAT LOSS
    radiation
       conduction
          convection
             evaporation

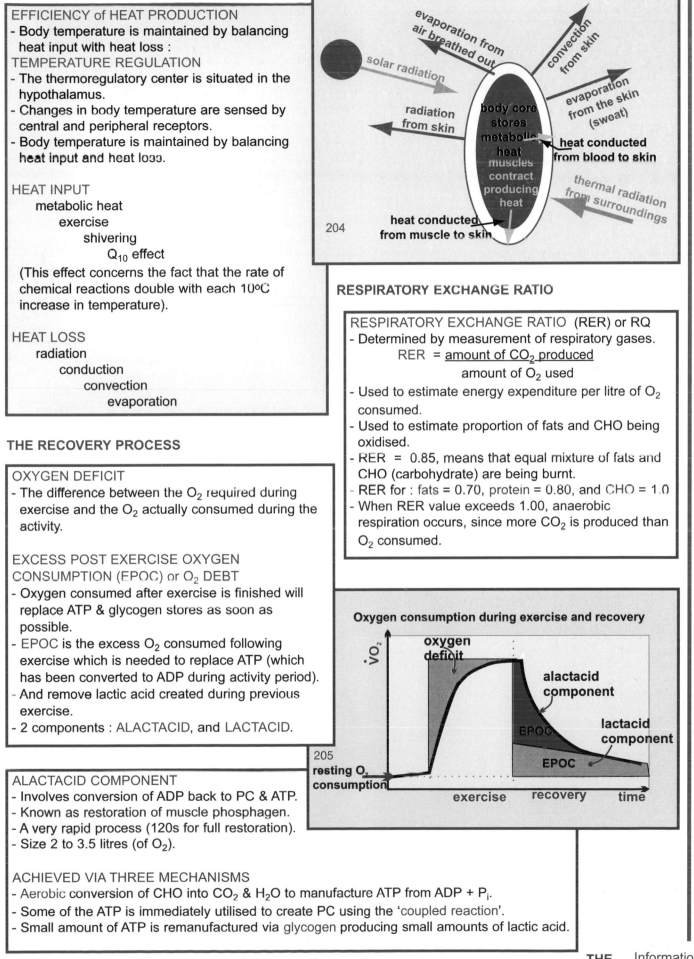

204

THE RECOVERY PROCESS

OXYGEN DEFICIT
- The difference between the O_2 required during exercise and the O_2 actually consumed during the activity.

EXCESS POST EXERCISE OXYGEN CONSUMPTION (EPOC) or O_2 DEBT
- Oxygen consumed after exercise is finished will replace ATP & glycogen stores as soon as possible.
- EPOC is the excess O_2 consumed following exercise which is needed to replace ATP (which has been converted to ADP during activity period).
- And remove lactic acid created during previous exercise.
- 2 components : ALACTACID, and LACTACID.

RESPIRATORY EXCHANGE RATIO

RESPIRATORY EXCHANGE RATIO (RER) or RQ
- Determined by measurement of respiratory gases.

$$RER = \frac{\text{amount of } CO_2 \text{ produced}}{\text{amount of } O_2 \text{ used}}$$

- Used to estimate energy expenditure per litre of O_2 consumed.
- Used to estimate proportion of fats and CHO being oxidised.
- RER = 0.85, means that equal mixture of fats and CHO (carbohydrate) are being burnt.
- RER for : fats = 0.70, protein = 0.80, and CHO = 1.0
- When RER value exceeds 1.00, anaerobic respiration occurs, since more CO_2 is produced than O_2 consumed.

205
resting O_2 consumption

ALACTACID COMPONENT
- Involves conversion of ADP back to PC & ATP.
- Known as restoration of muscle phosphagen.
- A very rapid process (120s for full restoration).
- Size 2 to 3.5 litres (of O_2).

ACHIEVED VIA THREE MECHANISMS
- Aerobic conversion of CHO into CO_2 & H_2O to manufacture ATP from $ADP + P_i$.
- Some of the ATP is immediately utilised to create PC using the 'coupled reaction'.
- Small amount of ATP is remanufactured via glycogen producing small amounts of lactic acid.

RECOVERY PROCESS (continued)

EFFECTS of TRAINING on the ALACTACID COMPONENT
- Increase ATP and PC stores in muscle cells.
- Improved ability to provide O_2.
- Therefore increase in possible size of alactacid component.

IMPLICATIONS for INTERVAL TRAINING
- If there is only a short interval between bouts of exercise.
- Level of phosphagen stores gradually reduces.

RESTORATION OF MUSCLE GLYCOGEN STORES
- Short duration high intensity exercise, restoration takes up to 2 hours.
- Prolonged low intensity aerobic exercise, restoration can take days.

- High carbohydrate diet speeds up this process.
- Therefore there is a need for athlete to enable full restoration to take place as soon as possible after the activity.
- Sportspeople should take high CHO loaded drinks immediately following exercise.

INCREASED BODY TEMPERATURE and **HORMONAL RELEASE** increase EPOC.

LACTACID COMPONENT
- High intensity exercise up to 60 seconds creates lactic acid.
- Relatively large amounts of lactic acid (15 to 20 times the resting value of 1 to 2 mmol/ litre) are produced during high intensity exercise.
- O_2 is needed to remove this lactic acid.
- Which begins to restore muscle and liver glycogen.
- The recovery process is relatively slow i.e. up to 1 hr.

FATE OF LACTIC ACID
- Oxidation into $CO_2 + H_2O$	65%
- Conversion into glycogen then stored in muscle and liver (Cori Cycle)	20%
- Conversion into protein	10%
- Conversion into glucose	5%

RESTORATION of MYOGLOBIN
- Myoglobin is reoxygenated within 2 minutes.

IMPLICATIONS for INTERVAL TRAINING
- Recovery between bouts of exercise is dependent on heart rate values (as HR falls during recovery, its value is a measure of the state of lactacid recovery).
- Active recovery / cool-down speeds up removal of lactic acid.
- Variance in sessions doesn't always stress lactic acid system.

EXERCISE AND NUTRITION

METABOLISM
- Is the sum total of all the chemical reactions that take place in the human body to sustain life.
BASAL METABOLIC RATE (BMR)
- Is the least rate of energy usage needed to carry out basic body functions.
- Measured lying down after 8 hours sleep and 12 hours fasting.
TOTAL METABOLIC RATE
- Is the sum of BMR + energy requirements for ALL daily activities.

PROTEINS
(15% of balanced diet)

- Used for growth & repair required by all tissues.
- Absorbed as amino acids in the small intestine.

- Only used as an energy source when the body is depleted of CHO and fat sources.
- Excess protein is deaminated and used as an energy supply (enters at Kreb's cycle).

CHO (CARBOHYDRATE) (60% of balanced diet)

- Is the principal energy giver.
- Absorbed as glucose (monosaccharides) in small intestine.

- Circulates as blood glucose and acts as an immediate fuel food for high intensity anaerobic exercise.
  - Excess stored as muscle and liver glycogen.
  - Then excess converted to fat.
  - 1 gm of CHO yields 17kJ of energy.

FATS (20-25% of balanced diet)

- Act as storage of fuel, and then as secondary fuel food (enters at Kreb's cycle during aerobic respiration).
- Absorbed as fatty acids and glycerol in small intestine.
- Stored as a triglyceride in adipose tissue.
- Recalled from fat deposits to liver.
- Converted to glucose, but a slow process i.e. it takes 20 mins.
- Therefore relevant as a fuel food for aerobic exercise.
- 1 gm of fat yields 39kJ of energy.

function of the liver
carbohydrate CHO
carboloading
fats
FUEL FOR EXERCISE
206
protein
glucagon
insulin

EXERCISE AND NUTRITION (continued)

CARBO / GLYCOGEN LOADING
- For endurance events.
- Principles : depletion / repletion.

FUEL FOR EXERCISE
- A balanced diet contains the correct proportions of CHO, fats, proteins minerals,vitamins, water and roughage needed to maintain good health.
- The liver acts as the food fuel exchange organ.

CARBO LOADING Classic method : (Bergstrom 1967)

- 7 day programme, starting with hard training which depletes glycogen stores in muscle and liver.
- Next 3 days moderate training, diet a mixture of fats / proteins which stimulates increased glycogen synthase activity.
- Remaining 4 days moderate training with high CHO + increased fluid intake.
- This increases muscle glycogen storage (repletion).

Problems with the classic method :
- Decreased energy levels, increased fatigue and water retention (needed for glycogen storage).

CARBO LOADING : (Sherman 1981)

- Low CHO intake for a single day, followed by 3-4 days high CHO intake and tapering of exercise during final week.
- Or normal mixed diet, followed by 3-4 days decreased training intensity and increased CHO intake.

EFFECTS of hormones INSULIN and GLUCAGON
- Affect levels of blood glucose.
- INSULIN converts excess blood glucose to glycogen.
- GLUCAGON raises blood glucose levels.
- Outputs based on negative feedback linked to concentration of blood glucose.

FUEL FOOD USAGE

- Depends on intensity and duration of exercise period.
- High intensity, short duration CHO only.
- Low intensity, long duration : mixture of CHO and fats.
- The longer the exercise the greater the utilisation of fats.

TRAINING ADAPTATION
- Glycogen sparing i.e. fats are used earlier on in exercise period, thus conserving glycogen stores.

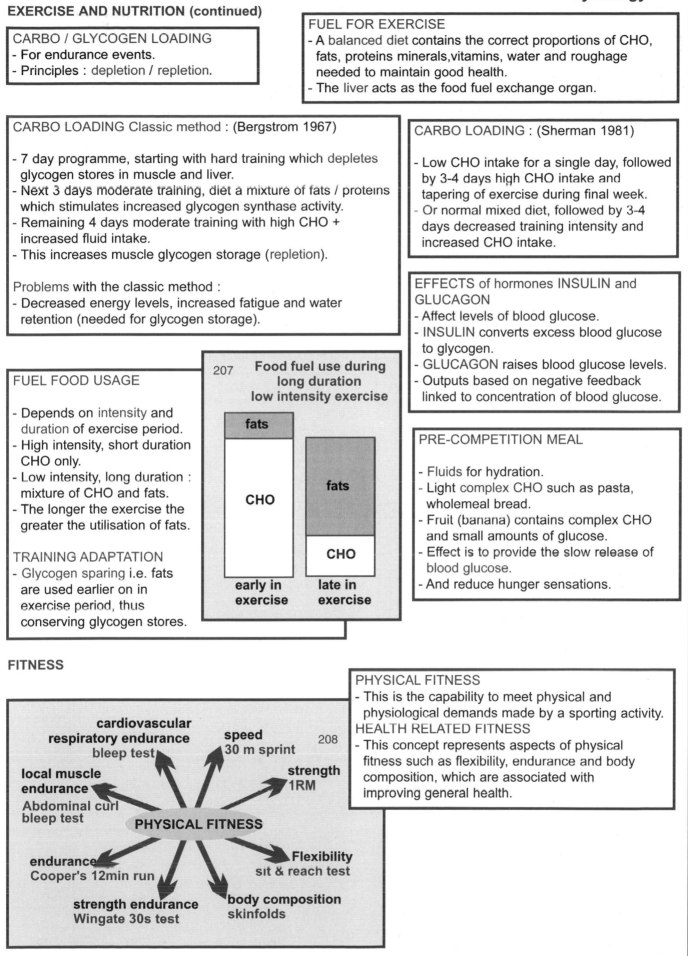

207   **Food fuel use during long duration low intensity exercise**

fats

CHO

fats

CHO

early in exercise   **late in exercise**

PRE-COMPETITION MEAL

- Fluids for hydration.
- Light complex CHO such as pasta, wholemeal bread.
- Fruit (banana) contains complex CHO and small amounts of glucose.
- Effect is to provide the slow release of blood glucose.
- And reduce hunger sensations.

FITNESS

PHYSICAL FITNESS
- This is the capability to meet physical and physiological demands made by a sporting activity.
HEALTH RELATED FITNESS
- This concept represents aspects of physical fitness such as flexibility, endurance and body composition, which are associated with improving general health.

cardiovascular respiratory endurance
bleep test

speed
30 m sprint   208

strength
1RM

local muscle endurance
Abdominal curl
bleep test

PHYSICAL FITNESS

Flexibility
sit & reach test

endurance
Cooper's 12min run

strength endurance
Wingate 30s test

body composition
skinfolds

FITNESS (continued)

MOTOR FITNESS
- This is the capability to perform successfully at a particular game.

AEROBIC CAPACITY

AEROBIC CAPACITY
- The ability to do work which is dependent on the aerobic mechanism of energy supply.
- Expressed as O_2 uptake.

$\dot{V}O_{2max}$
- Maximum amount of O_2 that a person can consume per minute during a progressive exercise test to exhaustion.
- Stresses Slow Twitch fibres.
- Relevant to activities / games lasting longer than a few minutes.

FACTORS AFFECTING $\dot{V}O_{2max}$
- Ability of the muscular cellular tissue system to extract O_2 (peripheral factors).
- Combined ability of cardiovascular / respiratory systems to transport O_2 (central factors).

USEFULNESS of $\dot{V}O_{2max}$ TESTING
- Gives maximal physiological capacity.
- Identifies weaknesses.
- Repeated tests give comparative profiles.

ONSET OF BLOOD LACTATE ACCUMULATION (OBLA)
- As work intensity increases lactic acid starts to accumulate above resting values.
- At a certain point this produces muscle fatigue and pain.
- The resultant low pH inhibits enzyme action and cross bridge formation.
- Hence muscle action is inhibited.
- And physical performance deteriorates.

209
agility
illinois run
speed
30m sprint
power
sergeant jump
MOTOR FITNESS
reaction time
stick drop test
static balance
beam balance
dynamic balance
cartwheel
coordination
juggling

TRAINING EFFECTS ON $\dot{V}O_{2max}$
- Large increases of $\dot{V}O_{2max}$ due to :
  - aerobic adaptation of heart & lungs (refer to page 2.11)
  - increased capillary density surrounding muscle tissue
  - increased enzyme activity within mitochondria
  - therefore increased a-$\bar{v}O_2$diff means more O_2 is available for tissue cell respiration.

AEROBIC TESTS

$\dot{V}O_{2max}$ by DIRECT MEASUREMENT
- Exhaled gas is passed through a GAS ANALYSER.
- Estimates CO_2 exhaled (per minute).
- Computer calculates $\dot{V}O_2$.
- For example, treadmill test / cycle ergometry.

PREDICTED $\dot{V}O_{2max}$ by INDIRECT MEASUREMENT
- Based on linear relationships between $\dot{V}O_2$ and heart rate.
- Measure HR, predict $\dot{V}O_2$ from tables linking HR with $\dot{V}O_2$.
- Examples, Queen's College Step Test, Harvard or Fitech Step Test, PWC170 Test.
- Or based on the relationship between distance run and $\dot{V}O_{2max}$.
- Examples, NCF Multistage Shuttle Run Test (bleep test), Cooper's 12 min Running Test.

210

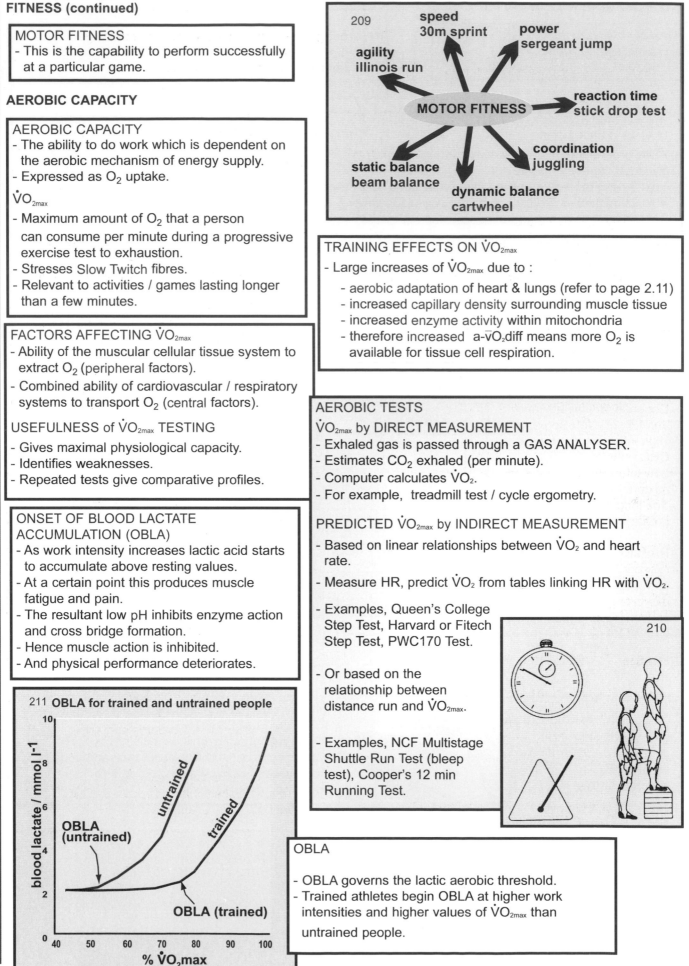

211 **OBLA for trained and untrained people**

blood lactate / mmol l⁻¹ (y-axis: 10, 8, 6, 4, 2, 0)

OBLA (untrained)
untrained
trained
OBLA (trained)

% $\dot{V}O_2$max (x-axis: 40, 50, 60, 70, 80, 90, 100)

OBLA
- OBLA governs the lactic aerobic threshold.
- Trained athletes begin OBLA at higher work intensities and higher values of $\dot{V}O_{2max}$ than untrained people.

AEROBIC CAPACITY (continued)

SPORTS SPECIFIC TESTS
- Recognise specificity of event.
- Example sprinting on a non-motorised treadmill.
- Use of flume pools for swimmers, paddle ergometers for canoeists, ski walking and rowing machines.

RELIABILITY of TESTS
- A test that gives consistent tests following retesting.

VALIDITY of TESTS
- A test measures what is claims to measure.

LIMITATIONS of TESTING
- Some tests are less reliable because there are so many variables which can vary between individuals taking a test.
- Examples would include the motivation of the individual to complete a test, or the skill level or technique of the subject.

PRINCIPLES OF MAXIMAL AND SUB-MAXIMAL TESTS

MAXIMAL FITNESS TESTS
- Maximal means that the subject makes 'all-out' effort or a test to exhaustion.
- In anaerobic work 1RM represents one repetition maximum.

- Examples of maximal anaerobic tests :
  30 metre sprint.
  Wingate 30 second cycle ergometer test.
- Examples of maximal aerobic tests :
  NCF multi-stage shuttle run test.
  Cooper's 12 minute run test.

SUBMAXIMAL FITNESS TESTS
- Submaximal means that the subject exercises below maximum effort.
- In sub-maximal work, extrapolation is used to estimate maximum capacities.

- Examples of submaximal aerobic tests are :
  PWC-170 test.
  Queen's College step test.
  Fitech step test (depends on heart rate recovery as a fitness indicator).

ANAEROBIC CAPACITY

ANAEROBIC CAPACITY
- This is the maximum amount of energy that can be created by anaerobic glycolysis.

- Measured by high intensity tests lasting up to 60s.
- Highest power output is represented as peak power (this is the alactacid capacity, produced by ATP-PC system).
- Lower output represented by lactacid capacity (lactic acid system).

- Stresses FG (Fast Twitch Glycolytic) fibres.

- Relevant to high intensity sports such as sprints.

- The Wingate 30 s cycling test has high reliability for mean and peak power, although alactacid and lactacid capacities cannot be clearly separated.

TRAINING APPLICATION
- Anaerobic Power only increased when training loads exceed 85 % of 1RM, low repetitions and sets (refer to page 2.12).

ANAEROBIC POWER TESTS

- Anaerobic Power is the maximum rate at which energy can be produced by the ATP/PC system.

- Sargeant (Vertical) Jump : high reliability, does not take into account length of levers.

- Standing long jump : less reliable because it is a more difficult skill.

- Margaria-Kalaman staircase climb estimates peak power:
$$P = \frac{m \times 9.8 \times D}{t}$$
high reliability, biased towards subject's body mass (m in kg).

- Isokinetic lido testing gives a high correlation between lean body mass and strength of knee extensors.

TRAINING PRINCIPLES AND PRACTICES

212

TRAINING PRINCIPLES
- overload
- duration
- repetition
- warm-up
- cool-down
- moderation
- variance
- specificity
- intensity
- reversibility

213

TRAINING PRACTICES
- mobility
  - active
  - passive
  - PNF
  - ballistic
- continuous
  - aerobic
- intensity variation
- periodisation
  - macro cycles
  - meso cycles
  - micro cycles
- interval
  - repetitions
  - sets
  - rest relief
  - aerobic
  - anaerobic
  - circuits
  - stage
  - weights

CARDIOVASCULAR ENDURANCE TRAINING

- Target heart rate (a specific HR to be achieved and maintained during exercise).

- Aerobic training zone (on graph) indicates range of HR at which training could take place.
- Actual HR used will depend on fitness of athlete.

- Karvonen formula :
- Maximum HR (HR_{max}) = 220 - age.
- Aerobic threshold HR calculated using :
  $HR = HR_{rest} + 0.6(HR_{max} - HR_{rest})$.

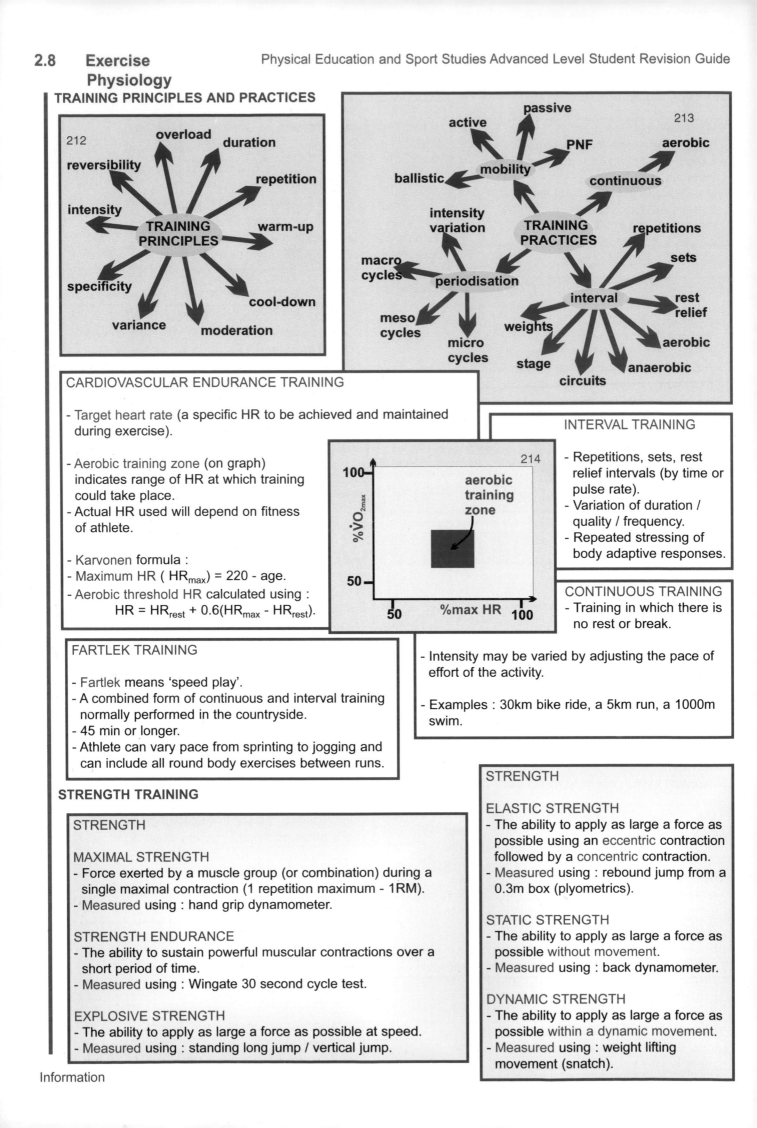

214

%$\dot{V}O_{2max}$ vs %max HR — aerobic training zone (graph ranging from 50 to 100 on both axes).

INTERVAL TRAINING

- Repetitions, sets, rest relief intervals (by time or pulse rate).
- Variation of duration / quality / frequency.
- Repeated stressing of body adaptive responses.

CONTINUOUS TRAINING
- Training in which there is no rest or break.

- Intensity may be varied by adjusting the pace of effort of the activity.

- Examples : 30km bike ride, a 5km run, a 1000m swim.

FARTLEK TRAINING

- Fartlek means 'speed play'.
- A combined form of continuous and interval training normally performed in the countryside.
- 45 min or longer.
- Athlete can vary pace from sprinting to jogging and can include all round body exercises between runs.

STRENGTH TRAINING

STRENGTH

MAXIMAL STRENGTH
- Force exerted by a muscle group (or combination) during a single maximal contraction (1 repetition maximum - 1RM).
- Measured using : hand grip dynamometer.

STRENGTH ENDURANCE
- The ability to sustain powerful muscular contractions over a short period of time.
- Measured using : Wingate 30 second cycle test.

EXPLOSIVE STRENGTH
- The ability to apply as large a force as possible at speed.
- Measured using : standing long jump / vertical jump.

STRENGTH

ELASTIC STRENGTH
- The ability to apply as large a force as possible using an eccentric contraction followed by a concentric contraction.
- Measured using : rebound jump from a 0.3m box (plyometrics).

STATIC STRENGTH
- The ability to apply as large a force as possible without movement.
- Measured using : back dynamometer.

DYNAMIC STRENGTH
- The ability to apply as large a force as possible within a dynamic movement.
- Measured using : weight lifting movement (snatch).

STRENGTH TRAINING (continued)

FACTORS AFFECTING STRENGTH

MUSCLE FIBRE TYPE
- Inherited.
- Affected by fibre type distribution.
- Examples : sprinters tend to have a majority of fast twitch type II.
- Endurance athletes tend to have a majority of slow twitch type I.

TYPE OF MUSCLE CONTRACTION
- Eccentric work exceeds the isometric maximum by about 30%.

- This is due to ability to mobilise a greater number of motor units.
- This large force acts to brake and control the movement.
- Diagram 216.

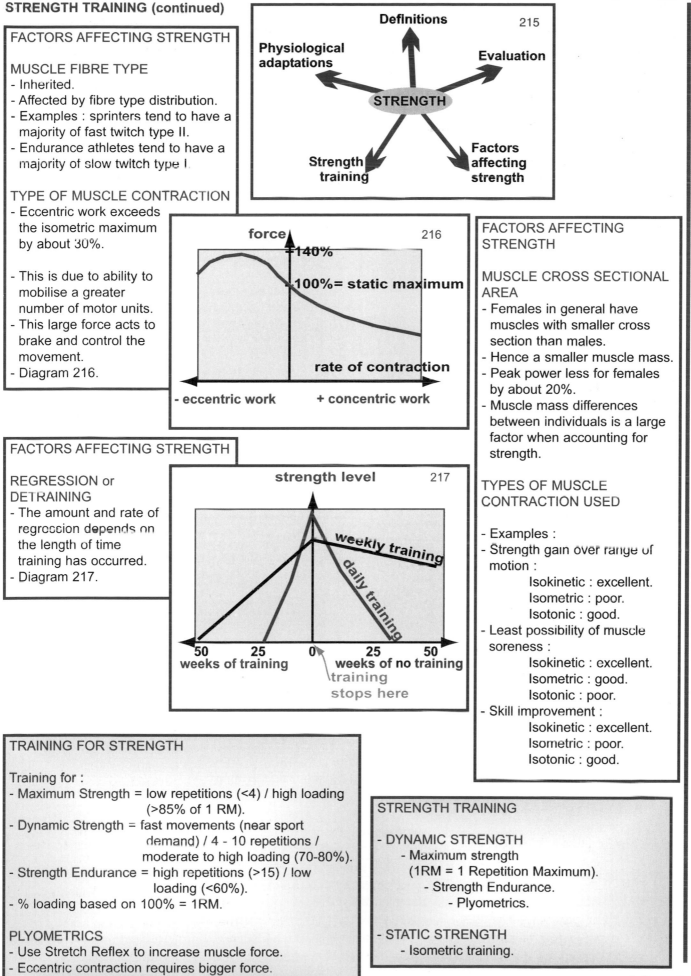

FACTORS AFFECTING STRENGTH

REGRESSION or DETRAINING
- The amount and rate of regression depends on the length of time training has occurred.
- Diagram 217.

FACTORS AFFECTING STRENGTH

MUSCLE CROSS SECTIONAL AREA
- Females in general have muscles with smaller cross section than males.
- Hence a smaller muscle mass.
- Peak power less for females by about 20%.
- Muscle mass differences between individuals is a large factor when accounting for strength.

TYPES OF MUSCLE CONTRACTION USED

- Examples :
- Strength gain over range of motion :
  - Isokinetic : excellent.
  - Isometric : poor.
  - Isotonic : good.
- Least possibility of muscle soreness :
  - Isokinetic : excellent.
  - Isometric : good.
  - Isotonic : poor.
- Skill improvement :
  - Isokinetic : excellent.
  - Isometric : poor.
  - Isotonic : good.

TRAINING FOR STRENGTH

Training for :
- Maximum Strength = low repetitions (<4) / high loading (>85% of 1 RM).
- Dynamic Strength = fast movements (near sport demand) / 4 - 10 repetitions / moderate to high loading (70-80%).
- Strength Endurance = high repetitions (>15) / low loading (<60%).
- % loading based on 100% = 1RM.

PLYOMETRICS
- Use Stretch Reflex to increase muscle force.
- Eccentric contraction requires bigger force.

STRENGTH TRAINING

- DYNAMIC STRENGTH
  - Maximum strength (1RM = 1 Repetition Maximum).
    - Strength Endurance.
      - Plyometrics.

- STATIC STRENGTH
  - Isometric training.

2.10 Exercise Physiology

LONG-TERM ANAEROBIC ADAPTIVE RESPONSES TO TRAINING

CONNECTIVE TISSUE RESPONSE
- Increase in thickness and strength of tendons.
- Increased flexibility of ligaments.
- Thickening and improved elasticity of cartilage.
- Strengthening of bone tissue due to increased depositing of calcium.
- Therefore reduced risk of injury.

MUSCLE CELL RESPONSE (fast twitch fibres)
- Muscle hypertrophy (of fast twitch fibres) increases cross sectional area of existing fibres by increasing :
    - number of myofibrils within each muscle cell
    - sarcoplasmic volume
    - contractile proteins : actin and myosin
    - mass of fast twitch fibres
    - number of fast twitch fibres (hyperplasia).
- Increase in muscle cell stores such as ATP, PC, and glycogen.
- Increase in anaerobic enzymes such as creatine kinase (CK), PFK, GPP, and LDH.
- Increase toleration of lactate in fast twitch fibres.
- Improved ability to remove lactate from muscle cell into blood.
- Therefore enhancement of alactic / lactate and lactate / aerobic thresholds. Delay in OBLA.
- Hence improved ability to maintain power output for longer.
- Decrease in DOMS (Delayed Onset Muscle Soreness), particularly following eccentric training.

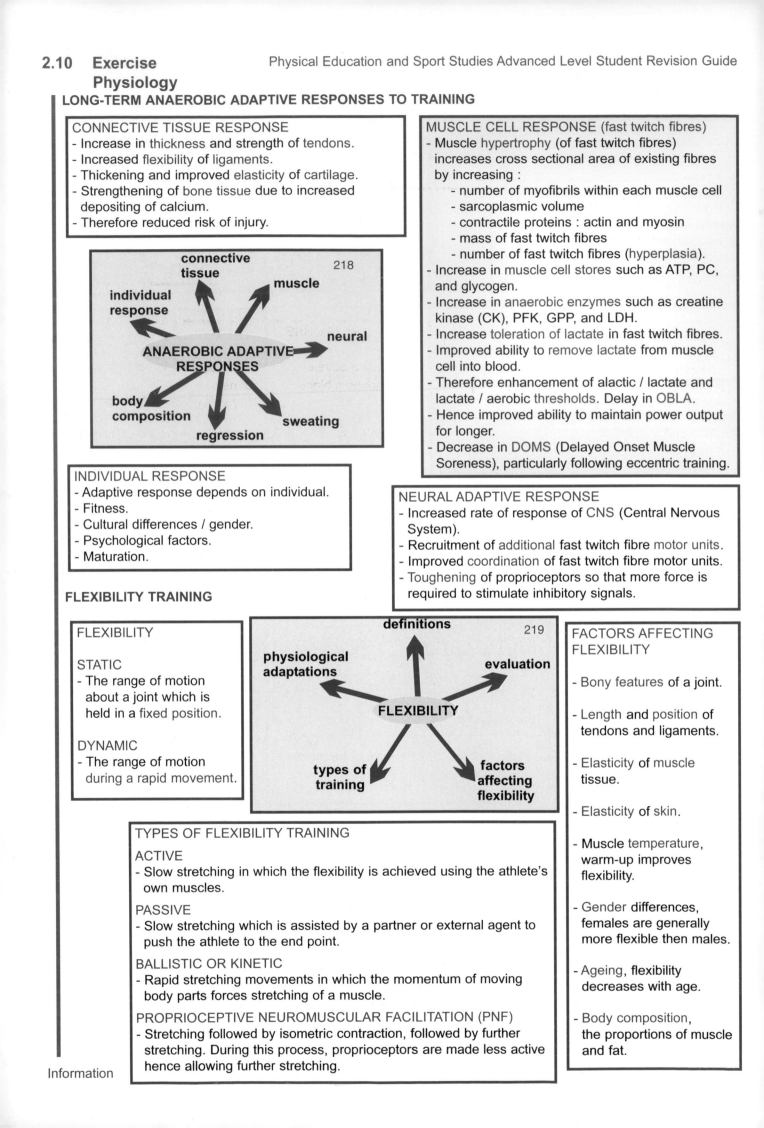

ANAEROBIC ADAPTIVE RESPONSES — connective tissue, muscle, neural, sweating, regression, body composition, individual response — 218

INDIVIDUAL RESPONSE
- Adaptive response depends on individual.
- Fitness.
- Cultural differences / gender.
- Psychological factors.
- Maturation.

NEURAL ADAPTIVE RESPONSE
- Increased rate of response of CNS (Central Nervous System).
- Recruitment of additional fast twitch fibre motor units.
- Improved coordination of fast twitch fibre motor units.
- Toughening of proprioceptors so that more force is required to stimulate inhibitory signals.

FLEXIBILITY TRAINING

FLEXIBILITY

STATIC
- The range of motion about a joint which is held in a fixed position.

DYNAMIC
- The range of motion during a rapid movement.

FLEXIBILITY — definitions, physiological adaptations, evaluation, types of training, factors affecting flexibility — 219

FACTORS AFFECTING FLEXIBILITY
- Bony features of a joint.
- Length and position of tendons and ligaments.
- Elasticity of muscle tissue.
- Elasticity of skin.
- Muscle temperature, warm-up improves flexibility.
- Gender differences, females are generally more flexible then males.
- Ageing, flexibility decreases with age.
- Body composition, the proportions of muscle and fat.

TYPES OF FLEXIBILITY TRAINING

ACTIVE
- Slow stretching in which the flexibility is achieved using the athlete's own muscles.

PASSIVE
- Slow stretching which is assisted by a partner or external agent to push the athlete to the end point.

BALLISTIC OR KINETIC
- Rapid stretching movements in which the momentum of moving body parts forces stretching of a muscle.

PROPRIOCEPTIVE NEUROMUSCULAR FACILITATION (PNF)
- Stretching followed by isometric contraction, followed by further stretching. During this process, proprioceptors are made less active hence allowing further stretching.

FLEXIBILITY TRAINING (continued)

EVALUATING FLEXIBILITY
- Use goniometer.
- Use flexibility tests, for example, the sit and reach test.

220

sit and reach test

PHYSIOLOGICAL ADAPTATIONS CAUSED BY FLEXIBILITY TRAINING
- Limited stretching of soft tissues : ligaments, tendons.
- Increase in resting / residual length of skeletal muscle tissue.

- Inhibition of stretch reflex as muscle spindles lengthen.
- The stretch reflex limits flexibility, therefore this inhibition would improve flexibility.

LONG-TERM AEROBIC ADAPTIVE RESPONSES TO TRAINING

RECOVERY
- Improved Oxygen recovery.
- Efficient cool-down improves lactic acid removal hence reduction in muscle soreness after exercise.

CARDIAC RESPONSE
- Bradycardia, which is a reduction of resting HR (HR_{rest}).
- Endurance athletes have HR_{rest} = 35 - 40 bpm.
- This means a bigger stronger heart.
- Mainly of left ventricle, hence greater ability of myocardial muscle tissue to contract.
- Up to 20% increase in SV means bigger volume of blood pumped per stroke.
- Greater rate of oxygen transport available.

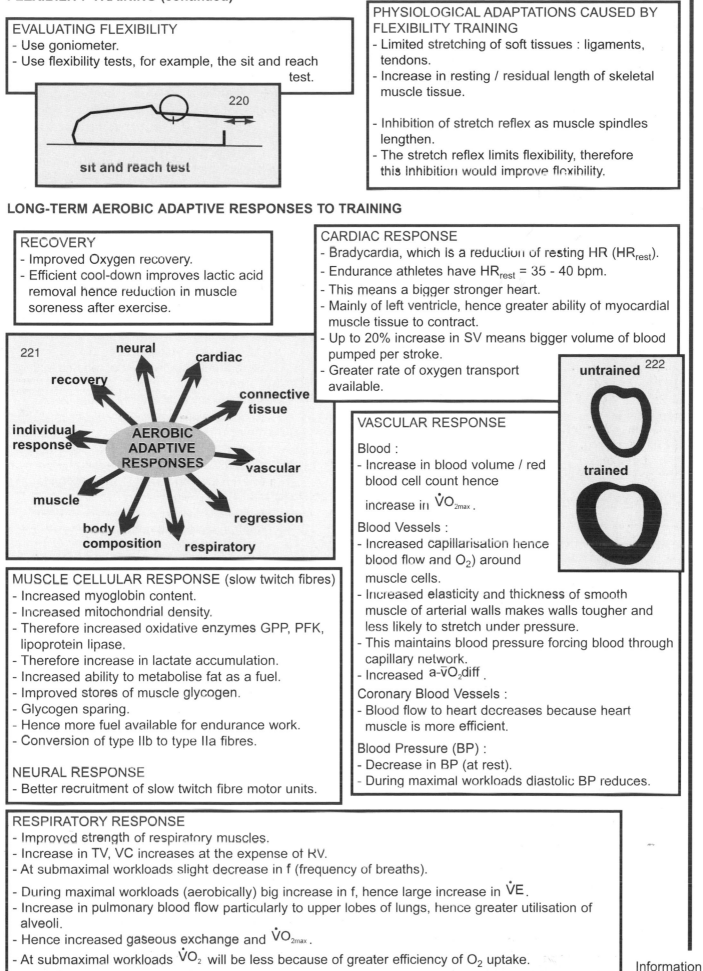

221

neural
recovery
cardiac
connective tissue
individual response
AEROBIC ADAPTIVE RESPONSES
vascular
muscle
regression
body composition
respiratory

untrained 222

trained

VASCULAR RESPONSE

Blood :
- Increase in blood volume / red blood cell count hence increase in $\dot{V}O_{2max}$.

Blood Vessels :
- Increased capillarisation hence blood flow and O_2) around muscle cells.
- Increased elasticity and thickness of smooth muscle of arterial walls makes walls tougher and less likely to stretch under pressure.
- This maintains blood pressure forcing blood through capillary network.
- Increased a-$\bar{v}O_2$diff .

Coronary Blood Vessels :
- Blood flow to heart decreases because heart muscle is more efficient.

Blood Pressure (BP) :
- Decrease in BP (at rest).
- During maximal workloads diastolic BP reduces.

MUSCLE CELLULAR RESPONSE (slow twitch fibres)
- Increased myoglobin content.
- Increased mitochondrial density.
- Therefore increased oxidative enzymes GPP, PFK, lipoprotein lipase.
- Therefore increase in lactate accumulation.
- Increased ability to metabolise fat as a fuel.
- Improved stores of muscle glycogen.
- Glycogen sparing.
- Hence more fuel available for endurance work.
- Conversion of type IIb to type IIa fibres.

NEURAL RESPONSE
- Better recruitment of slow twitch fibre motor units.

RESPIRATORY RESPONSE
- Improved strength of respiratory muscles.
- Increase in TV, VC increases at the expense of RV.
- At submaximal workloads slight decrease in f (frequency of breaths).
- During maximal workloads (aerobically) big increase in f, hence large increase in $\dot{V}E$.
- Increase in pulmonary blood flow particularly to upper lobes of lungs, hence greater utilisation of alveoli.
- Hence increased gaseous exchange and $\dot{V}O_{2max}$.
- At submaximal workloads $\dot{V}O_2$ will be less because of greater efficiency of O_2 uptake.

LONG-TERM AEROBIC ADAPTIVE RESPONSES TO TRAINING (continued)

BODY COMPOSITION
- Moderate intensity, long duration, exercise.
- Maximises energy expenditure.
- To promote negative energy balance.

Benefits of aerobic training :
- Modest gain in lean body mass (LBM).
- Loss of body fat.

TRAINING PROGRAMME GUIDELINES
- Alactic Anaerobic :
  - 3-5 sets of <6 repetitions
  - heavy work loads (80-100% of 1RM).
- Lactic Anaerobic :
  - 3-5 sets of 6-10 repetitions
  - work load (60-80% of 1RM).
- Aerobic :
  - sets of 10-20 repetitions
  - work load (at <50% 1RM).

TRAINING SCHEDULES

EXAMPLES OF TRAINING METHODS
A MICROCYCLE FOR AN ELITE MALE 800M RUNNER

day 1	a.m.	30 min medium paced run	continuous
	p.m.	strength maintenance weights power clean, full squat, bench press 4 sets of 5 repetitions @ 70% of 1RM	interval
	eve.	30 min medium paced run	continuous
day 2	a.m.	30 min easy paced run	continuous
	p.m.	3 sets of (2 x 400m (55s) 2 x 200m (26s)) 20 min recovery between sets	interval
day 3	a.m.	45 min medium paced run	continuous
day 4	a.m.	30 min easy paced run	continuous
	p.m.	2 x 30m, 40m, 50m, 60m walk back rec. 2 sets of 3 x 200m (25s) 5min recovery, 15 min recovery between sets	interval
day 5		rest	
day 6		competition	
day 7	a.m.	long medium-paced run 45 min	continuous

PERSONAL TRAINING PROGRAMME
- General principles :
  - medical examination
  - warm-up
  - cool-down
  - variance
  - frequency = 2 / 3 times per week
  - intensity = aerobic, 60%+ effort, easy breathing
  - duration 20 - 60 minutes
  - dependent on age, gender, and fitness level
  - take into account energy demands of occupation.
- Examples of activities :
  - aerobics   - golf
    - swimming   - jogging
      - cycling   - walking.
- Activity programme :
  - time allocation
  - energy system demands
  - general training demands
  - specific training demands
  - allow warm-up and cool-down
  - relate to periodisation
  - loadings / intensity / frequency
  - variance.

GENDER DIFFERENCES

STRUCTURAL GENDER DIFFERENCES — respiratory, metabolic, vascular, body composition, hormonal, cardiac — 223

GENDER ISSUES
- Major differences in body size and composition between boys and girls do not appear until puberty.
- Major cardiovascular and respiratory adaptations that accompany aerobic training do not appear to be gender specific.

DIFFERENCES in FITNESS MEASURES (examples)

STRUCTURAL	PHYSIOLOGICAL	TRAINING EFFECTS
Oestrogen, more fat in females	Increased long-term energy store	Training reduces fat stores
Testosterone, more muscle males	Increased male muscle hypertrophy	Increased strength in males
Body composition	Extra insulating body fat in females	Basal metabolic rate higher males
Respiratory volumes - body size	Smaller people have smaller $\dot{V}E$	No gender differences (size only)
Smaller hearts in females	Smaller SV, faster HR_{rest} in females	Bradycardia similar M and F
Smaller blood volume in females	Smaller VO_{2max} in females	Aerobic capacity similar M and F

ERGOGENIC AIDS

ERGOGENIC AID
- Any means of improving the efficiency and enhancing the quality of sporting performance.

MECHANICAL AIDS
- Nasal strip enables easier breathing.
- Specialist equipment such as carbon fibre bike frames are lighter and more aerodynamically efficient.
- Lycra sports clothing reduces drag.

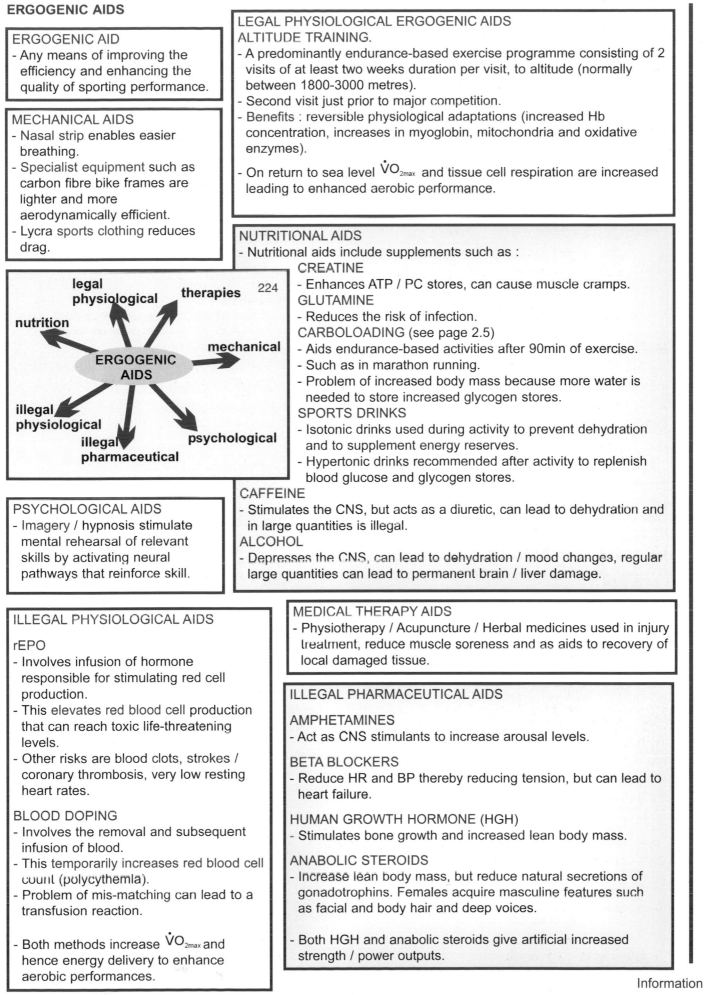

PSYCHOLOGICAL AIDS
- Imagery / hypnosis stimulate mental rehearsal of relevant skills by activating neural pathways that reinforce skill.

ILLEGAL PHYSIOLOGICAL AIDS

rEPO
- Involves infusion of hormone responsible for stimulating red cell production.
- This elevates red blood cell production that can reach toxic life-threatening levels.
- Other risks are blood clots, strokes / coronary thrombosis, very low resting heart rates.

BLOOD DOPING
- Involves the removal and subsequent infusion of blood.
- This temporarily increases red blood cell count (polycythemia).
- Problem of mis-matching can lead to a transfusion reaction.

- Both methods increase $\dot{V}O_{2max}$ and hence energy delivery to enhance aerobic performances.

LEGAL PHYSIOLOGICAL ERGOGENIC AIDS
ALTITUDE TRAINING.
- A predominantly endurance-based exercise programme consisting of 2 visits of at least two weeks duration per visit, to altitude (normally between 1800-3000 metres).
- Second visit just prior to major competition.
- Benefits : reversible physiological adaptations (increased Hb concentration, increases in myoglobin, mitochondria and oxidative enzymes).
- On return to sea level $\dot{V}O_{2max}$ and tissue cell respiration are increased leading to enhanced aerobic performance.

NUTRITIONAL AIDS
- Nutritional aids include supplements such as :
  #### CREATINE
  - Enhances ATP / PC stores, can cause muscle cramps.
  #### GLUTAMINE
  - Reduces the risk of infection.
  #### CARBOLOADING (see page 2.5)
  - Aids endurance-based activities after 90min of exercise.
  - Such as in marathon running.
  - Problem of increased body mass because more water is needed to store increased glycogen stores.
  #### SPORTS DRINKS
  - Isotonic drinks used during activity to prevent dehydration and to supplement energy reserves.
  - Hypertonic drinks recommended after activity to replenish blood glucose and glycogen stores.
CAFFEINE
- Stimulates the CNS, but acts as a diuretic, can lead to dehydration and in large quantities is illegal.
ALCOHOL
- Depresses the CNS, can lead to dehydration / mood changes, regular large quantities can lead to permanent brain / liver damage.

MEDICAL THERAPY AIDS
- Physiotherapy / Acupuncture / Herbal medicines used in injury treatment, reduce muscle soreness and as aids to recovery of local damaged tissue.

ILLEGAL PHARMACEUTICAL AIDS

AMPHETAMINES
- Act as CNS stimulants to increase arousal levels.

BETA BLOCKERS
- Reduce HR and BP thereby reducing tension, but can lead to heart failure.

HUMAN GROWTH HORMONE (HGH)
- Stimulates bone growth and increased lean body mass.

ANABOLIC STEROIDS
- Increase lean body mass, but reduce natural secretions of gonadotrophins. Females acquire masculine features such as facial and body hair and deep voices.

- Both HGH and anabolic steroids give artificial increased strength / power outputs.

DIFFERENCES WITH AGE

CHILDHOOD
- 3-8 yrs , boys & girls follow similar growth patterns.
- Hence similar amounts of muscle, bone mass and body proportion.
- 8 yrs onwards balance, agility, coordination improve as child's nervous system develops.

ADOLESCENTS
- Sexual hormones regulate growth & strength gains.
- Strength gains also associated with neural maturation.
- Because myelination of neurones increases neural conductivity.
- Hence improved motor firing patterns.

AEROBIC ASPECTS
Cardiovascular
- Small heart and vascular systems cause :
    - high HR (small SV and $\dot{Q}$)
    - low BP
    - lower Hb levels
    - low aerobic capacity increasing with age.

Respiratory
- Low minute ventilation ($\dot{V}E$) & high breathing rate.
- Low $\dot{V}O_{2max}$ value limits endurance performances.

Metabolic
- High resting metabolic rate (MR) because :
- Children have larger surface area to volume ratio than adults, therefore greater heat loss and MR.

Flexibility
- Natural flexibility that decreases during the growth spurt as muscle mass and bones increase in size.

ANAEROBIC ASPECTS
- Low ability to work anaerobically.
- Low O_2 debt due to a limited rate of anaerobic glycolysis, therefore quickly fatigued.
- Hence anaerobic mean and peak power outputs are lower in children than in adults.
- Gradual strength development as muscle mass increases, same for boys and girls.

TRAINING PROGRAMME
- 2 - 3 times per week for 20-30 min.
- Basic exercises with use of body weight as a resistance for strength gains.
- Variation of activity, example Pacesetters (a variety of runs / jumps / throws).
- Sport specific skill based activities.
- Gradual increase in training volume.

TRAINING EFFECTS
- Exercise essential for proper bone growth.
- Excessive training can injure growth plates, causing early termination of growth.
- Exercise improves strength, aerobic and anaerobic capabilities.
- Prepubescent strength gains due to :
    - improved motor skill coordination
    - increased motor unit activity
    - neurological adaptations.

AGEING
- Includes all the changes that occur in the body.
- Restricted joint flexibility, (osteoarthritis).
- Increased body fat.
- Osteoporosis, decreased bone mineral (oestrogen deficiency and lack of physical activity in females).
- Muscle atrophy and cardiovascular and respiratory.

AEROBIC DECLINE
Cardiovascular
- Decline in HR_{max} (HR_{max} = 220 - age).
- Increase in resting pulse rate due to decreased SV.
- Artery hardening increases resting systolic BP.
- Recovery takes longer after exercise.

Respiratory
- $\dot{V}O_{2max}$ declines about 10% per decade due to reduction in SV & HR_{max} & lack of aerobic exercise.
- VC & forced expiratory volume decrease with age.
- RV larger hence less air exchanged per breath.
- Less elasticity of alveoli walls & reduced strength of respiratory muscles decreases $\dot{V}O_{2max}$.
- Lower $a\text{-}\bar{v}O_2 diff$ since less O_2 extracted by muscles.

ANAEROBIC DECLINE
- Muscle and strength atrophy, shift towards ST fibres.
- Thinner myelinated sheath lengthens reaction times.
- Loss of neurones affects short-term memory and coordination.

TRAINING PROGRAMME
- Refer page 2.12 above.

TRAINING EFFECTS
Cardiovascular
- Exercise slows down degenerative diseases (CHD).
- Exercise increases High Density Lipoproteins (HDL), and decreases Low Density Lipoproteins (LDL) (responsible for depositing cholesterol and narrowing lumen of artery), hence BP stable.
- Thus preventing hypertension.

Respiratory
- Exercise slows down decline in $\dot{V}O_{2max}$.

Body Composition
- Exercise reduces obesity by burning off excess fat during and after activity when MR remains elevated.
- Cardiac workload less with lower body mass.
- Exercise relieves symptoms of osteoarthritis.
- Exercise prevents osteoporosis.

Neuromuscular
- Exercise sustains strength and coordination levels.
- Exercise enhances tensile strength & flexibility of tendons and ligaments.
- Thus allowing for a fuller range of joint movement.

Psychological
- Immediately following activity a person experiences a feeling of well being, reduction in anxiety.
- Long-term increase in work performance, hence a more positive attitude to work.
- Improved self-esteem and self-efficacy.
- Benefits of social interaction.

Information

HYPOKINETIC DISORDERS

HYPOKINETIC DISORDERS

- Definition : diseases that develop partly due to insufficient exercise.
- And result in a marked lack of physical mobility.

INACTIVITY

Leads to poor flexibility as muscles, tendons and ligaments become shorter and tighter.
- Often resulting in back pain.

OSTEOPOROSIS
- This is an age-related condition in which reduction of bone mass takes place.
- This is due to reabsorption of minerals that form part of bone structure.
- Making bones porous, brittle and liable to break.

SUGGESTED TRAINING REGIME
- Progressive interval weight training.
- Effects: Increase in bone density.
- Hence increase in body strength.

OSTEOARTHRITIS
- This is a condition where joints thicken with fluid-filled pockets, restricting joint flexibility.

SUGGESTED TRAINING REGIME
- Flexibility training.
- Effects: Increase of range of movement at joint sites.
- Reduction in pain.

OBESITY
- Overweight condition of the body.
- Exceeding 25% in males and 35% in females.
- Often caused by positive energy balance.
- Problem of heat dissipation due to fat insulation.
- Cardiovascular system has to work harder.
- Therefore obesity is often associated with CHD, hypertension, atherosclerosis and mechanical injury such as weakened joints.

SUGGESTED TRAINING REGIME
- Continuous aerobic training.
- Operating within the 'fat burning zone' (i.e. 50% of HRmax,) minimum 30minutes per session.
- Effects: Decrease in body fat.
- Increase in lean body mass (LBM)
- Therefore increase in muscle tone.
- Strengthening of joints.

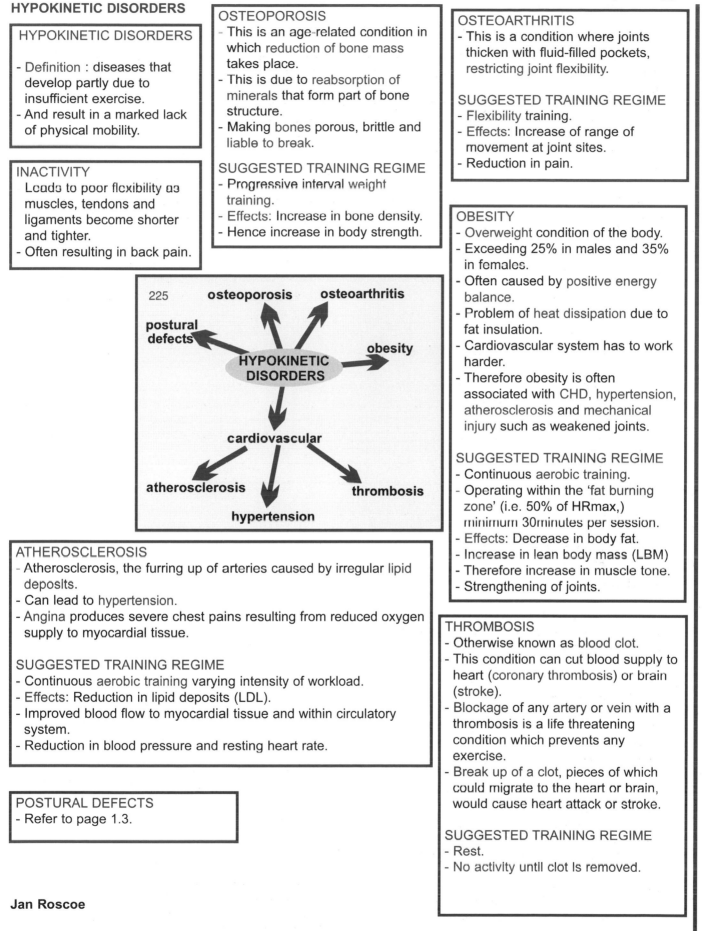

225 osteoporosis — osteoarthritis — postural defects — HYPOKINETIC DISORDERS — obesity — cardiovascular — atherosclerosis — thrombosis — hypertension

ATHEROSCLEROSIS
- Atherosclerosis, the furring up of arteries caused by irregular lipid deposits.
- Can lead to hypertension.
- Angina produces severe chest pains resulting from reduced oxygen supply to myocardial tissue.

SUGGESTED TRAINING REGIME
- Continuous aerobic training varying intensity of workload.
- Effects: Reduction in lipid deposits (LDL).
- Improved blood flow to myocardial tissue and within circulatory system.
- Reduction in blood pressure and resting heart rate.

THROMBOSIS
- Otherwise known as blood clot.
- This condition can cut blood supply to heart (coronary thrombosis) or brain (stroke).
- Blockage of any artery or vein with a thrombosis is a life threatening condition which prevents any exercise.
- Break up of a clot, pieces of which could migrate to the heart or brain, would cause heart attack or stroke.

SUGGESTED TRAINING REGIME
- Rest.
- No activity until clot is removed.

POSTURAL DEFECTS
- Refer to page 1.3.

Jan Roscoe

Information

MOTION

BIOMECHANICS

LINEAR MOTION

- Linear motion involves an object moving in a straight line.

- For example, a toboggan / bobsleigh / skier moving down a slope.

- No part of the sportsperson is turning twisting or rotating.

ANGULAR MOTION

- involves an object twisting or rotating or spinning.

- For example, a skater spinning, a gymnast performing a grand circle on the high bar.

- No part of the sportsperson is moving along in a straight line.

GENERAL MOTION

- This is motion which involves both linear movement and rotations or twisting movements.

- Almost all practical sports movements consist of a combination of rotating movements and moving in a straight line.

- For example, a sprinter moves his body linearly down the track, but his arms and legs rotate about shoulders and hips during the movement.

- A tumbling gymnast moves linearly through the air, but rotates her body as it twists and turns.

LINEAR MOTION

POSITION
- This is a way of explaining where a point is relative to some fixed point.

- Position is usually expressed in terms of coordinates (x and y) like a graph in maths.

- For example, the centre forward takes a shot from a position 20 m out from the goal line, and 10m to the left of the left hand post.

- The left hand post is the fixed point or origin of measurement.
- 20 m and 10 m are the coordinates of the position of the centre forward relative to that point.

DISTANCE means the total path length moved by a body. (measured in metres - m).
- Example, a 10,000 m race is run round and round the track, 25 times 400 m, starting and finishing POSITION are the same, but distance travelled is 10,000 m.

DISPLACEMENT
- This means the vector distance (measured in metres) from a fixed point (starting point or origin).

- This is the actual 'as the crow flies' distance between start and finish (with direction included).

- Example, the start and finish of a long distance race (Stage 5 of the Tours de France) may be 190 km apart due West, but the distance travelled may be 250 km!

SPEED $= \dfrac{\text{distance moved}}{\text{time taken}}$ $v = \dfrac{s}{t}$ unit ms^{-1}.
$= $ scalar (no direction)
VELOCITY $=$ speed in a given direction.
$=$ vector.

DISTANCE / TIME graph.
- Gradient of graph is velocity.

ACCELERATION / TIME graph

- Shows how acceleration changes with time.
- For the sprinter:
  - acceleration is highest at the start
  - falls rapidly to zero in the middle of the race
  - then becomes negative as the sprinter slows down (decelerates).
- Acceleration depends directly on the force applied.
- see Newton's 2nd Law.

ACCELERATION $= \dfrac{\text{change of velocity}}{\text{time taken to change}}$ $a = \dfrac{v - u}{t}$
- Unit ms^{-2}.

- An object changing direction is accelerating, since the velocity changes.
- Example, swerving rugby player.
- Direction of acceleration is along the radius of the curve (path of player).
- This is a radial acceleration.
- Deceleration is negative acceleration (slowing down).
- Acceleration in same direction as net force.
- Acceleration is a vector (has direction).

VELOCITY / TIME graph
- Gradient / slope of graph is acceleration.
- Area under graph is distance travelled.

Information

VECTORS

- A VECTOR has DIRECTION as well as SIZE (magnitude or value).

- A vector can be represented by a line on a piece of paper (graph paper).
- The length of the line represents the size (say the value of a force in newtons).
- The angle of the line to the horizontal represents the direction.

- Examples of vectors are force, acceleration, velocity, weight, momentum.

- A SCALAR has SIZE (value) only.

- Examples of scalars are mass, temperature, energy, speed, distance, volume, pressure, power.

ADDING VECTORS

- This is a process which involves finding the size and direction of a resultant (or net) of 2 or more vectors.
- Complete the parallelogram as shown in the example above.
- The resultant (net force or velocity) is the diagonal of the parallelogram.

- The resultant of two vectors at right angles found by completing the rectangle.

FORCE

FORCE is push or pull.

- Unit of force is the Newton (10 N is approximately the weight of 1 kg).

- Force changes the state of motion of an object.
- The link of force with acceleration (or deceleration).
- The more force exerted, the bigger the acceleration produced (Newton's Second law of motion).

RESULTANT / NET FORCE

- Net force is the result of all forces added together taking the direction into account (see VECTORS).

- Net force forwards produces acceleration - positive.
- Net force backwards produces deceleration - negative.
- Net force sideways produces change of direction, or swerving.

FORCE is a VECTOR

- Force has size (magnitude) and direction.
- Resultant of many forces acting in different directions.

- Example, a sprinter in the first 10m of a race.

- Note the point of action / direction of all the forces.

- And the resultant of several forces (black arrow).

FORCE

- When describing a force, it is important to indicate its point of action on a body as well as its size and direction.

PIN MEN DIAGRAMS

- Shape of the body should be represented approximately.

- Forces acting are represented by arrows in the direction of the force.

- The point of action of the force should be shown where the force acts :
  - at the foot
  - on the body
  - on the hand
  - the length of the arrow represents the size of the force.

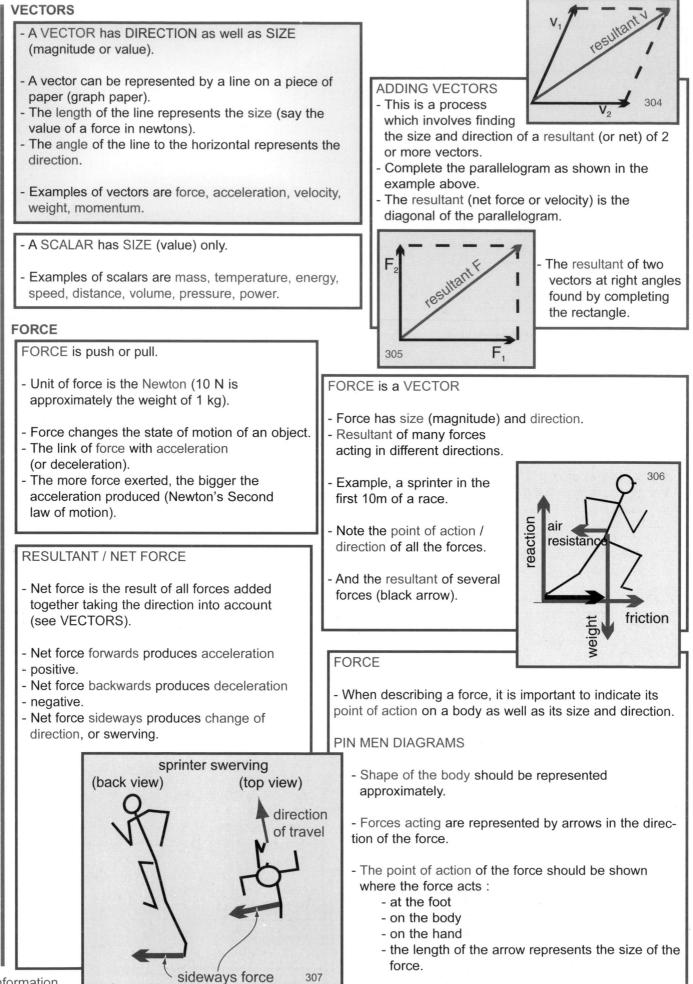

GRAVITY and WEIGHT

GRAVITY

- Gravity is a force field produced between any two objects which have mass.
- The two objects would attract each other, and for example a mutual force of attraction holds the moon in orbit around the Earth.
- In sport, the main effect of gravity is to pull your body downwards.
- The forces between two people due to gravity are very tiny and can be ignored!

WEIGHT and MASS are DIFFERENT

MASS

- Mass is the same everywhere and is related to amount of matter and inertia (inertia is the property of mass which means that it is hard to get a massive body moving, and also hard to stop it once it is moving).

- Measured in kilogrammes kg.

WEIGHT

- Weight is a FORCE produced by the gravitational force field acting on objects / bodies.
- It is a force which acts downwards towards the centre of the Earth.

- Weight is the predominant force experienced by objects moving freely through air.
- Flight of thrown object is a parabola if no air resistance.

- Your weight would be approximately the same everywhere on Earth (gravity field strength = 10 Newtons per kilogramme).

- W = m g (weight = mass x gravity field strength).

- Variations occur between poles and equator, and at altitude (less weight at altitude means slightly further jumps and throws).

WEIGHT

- Measured in newtons N.

NEWTON'S LAWS OF MOTION

NEWTON'S FIRST LAW

- What happens when zero net force acts?
- This means that all forces acting must cancel out (according to vector rules).

- When there is zero net force acting on an object :
  - The object is stationary.
  - Or the object moves at constant velocity.

- When a sprinter runs at constant speed, all forces must cancel out, the net force must be zero (diagram 308).

NEWTON'S SECOND LAW

- What happens when a net force acts on a body?
- This produces acceleration or deceleration of the body.
- Or changes the direction of the body (swerving).
- Force = mass x acceleration   F = m x a.

- In the motion of a sprinter the acceleration is produced by the net force applied
- Sort out directions and sizes of all forces acting.
- Compute resultant force.

- Sprinter decelerates, net force backwards (see diagram 309).

NEWTON'S THIRD LAW

- What happens when two bodies (or objects) exert forces on one another?
- Action and reaction are equal and opposite and always occur in pairs.

- At the sprint start - the athlete pushes back on the blocks as hard as possible.
- The blocks push forward - and provides forward acceleration - on the athlete.

- A swimmer drives backwards on water with hands and feet (force in black), the water thrusts the swimmer forward (force in red - diagram 310).

- For INTERNAL FORCES within the body when origin and insertion of a muscle pull in opposite directions to change the shape of the body (diagram 311).

water is driven backwards by swimmer

reaction : water thrusts forward on swimmer

Information

REACTION FORCES

REACTION FORCES

- Reaction forces are forces acting via Newton's Third Law.

- When one object pushes on another, the first object experiences a force equal but opposite in direction to the second.

- Jumper pushes down on the ground, ground pushes up on the jumper.

- Weight lifter pulls up on weight, weight pulls down on lifter.

reaction force upon jumper

jumper pushes downon ground

313

force upwards on weight

reaction force downwards on hands

314

INTERNAL FORCES

- Wirhed defined these forces as acting within the body caused by muscle action exerting force on a limb or body segment.

312

- Causes body to change shape.
- Internal forces are exerted on both origin and insertion of a muscle (see diagram 312 above).

- The force on the insertion (black) is a reaction to the force on the origin (red) (using Newton's Third Law).

- Force on origin pulls bone **H** to the right.
- Force on insertion pulls bone **U** to the left.
- The two forces are equal in size but opposite in direction.

REACTION FORCES

- In cycling, the tyre on the rear wheel pushes backward on the ground (action - black force).
- The ground pushes forward on the rear wheel (reaction - red force).

315

tyre pushes backwards on the ground

ground pushes forwards on the cycle wheel

- The sprinter pushes back and down on the ground (action - black force).
- The ground pushes upwards and forwards on the sprinter (reaction - red force).

316

sprinter pushes down and backwards on the ground

ground pushes up and forwards on the sprinter

FRICTION

FRICTION

- Friction is a force which acts sideways between two surfaces which tend to slide past one another.

- This force enables sportspeople to accelerate, slow down, swerve, walk, run.
- Grip of footwear on floor surface.
- Friction acts forwards on the feet of an accelerating runner.

FLUID FRICTION / AIR RESISTANCE

FLUID FRICTION (or DRAG)

- Fluid friction is a term applying to objects moving through fluids (gases or liquids).

- Force acts in the opposite direction to the direction of motion.

- Force depends on the shape and size of the moving object.

- Force depends on the speed of the moving object.

- Force also depends on the streamlining effect, hence body position and shape for swimmer, shape of helmets for cyclists, use of lycra clothing, shape of sports vehicles (cars / bikes).

Information

FLUID FRICTION (continued)

LOW VALUES OF FLUID FRICTION

- Low values compared with other forces.

- Any sprinter or game player.
- Air resistance is usually much less than friction effects and weight.
- Therefore streamlining is seen as less important.

- A shot or hammer in flight.
- Air resistance is much less than weight.
- Therefore angle of release for optimum distance should be around 45°, the flight path is almost a parabola.

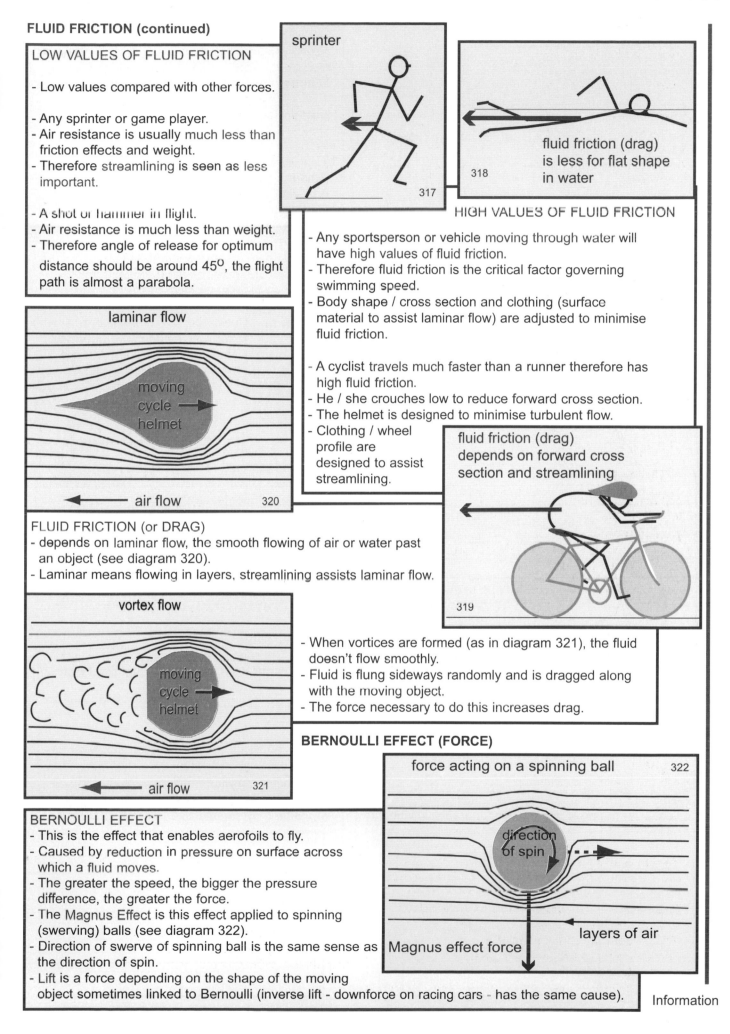

sprinter

317

318   fluid friction (drag) is less for flat shape in water

HIGH VALUES OF FLUID FRICTION

- Any sportsperson or vehicle moving through water will have high values of fluid friction.
- Therefore fluid friction is the critical factor governing swimming speed.
- Body shape / cross section and clothing (surface material to assist laminar flow) are adjusted to minimise fluid friction.

- A cyclist travels much faster than a runner therefore has high fluid friction.
- He / she crouches low to reduce forward cross section.
- The helmet is designed to minimise turbulent flow.
- Clothing / wheel profile are designed to assist streamlining.

laminar flow

moving cycle helmet

air flow   320

fluid friction (drag) depends on forward cross section and streamlining

319

FLUID FRICTION (or DRAG)
- depends on laminar flow, the smooth flowing of air or water past an object (see diagram 320).
- Laminar means flowing in layers, streamlining assists laminar flow.

vortex flow

moving cycle helmet

air flow   321

- When vortices are formed (as in diagram 321), the fluid doesn't flow smoothly.
- Fluid is flung sideways randomly and is dragged along with the moving object.
- The force necessary to do this increases drag.

BERNOULLI EFFECT (FORCE)

force acting on a spinning ball   322

direction of spin

Magnus effect force   layers of air

BERNOULLI EFFECT
- This is the effect that enables aerofoils to fly.
- Caused by reduction in pressure on surface across which a fluid moves.
- The greater the speed, the bigger the pressure difference, the greater the force.
- The Magnus Effect is this effect applied to spinning (swerving) balls (see diagram 322).
- Direction of swerve of spinning ball is the same sense as the direction of spin.
- Lift is a force depending on the shape of the moving object sometimes linked to Bernoulli (inverse lift - downforce on racing cars - has the same cause).

Information

MOMENTUM and IMPULSE

MOMENTUM is a concept derived from Newton's second law which says :

Force = rate of change of momentum.
- (Linear) momentum = mass x velocity.
- Linear means in a straight line.
- So an object which has a lot of momentum requires a lot of force to stop it.
- Which is a good argument for fast heavy rugby players or American footballers.
- Momentum is a vector (and therefore has direction).

CONSERVATION of MOMENTUM

- Again derived from Newton's laws.
- For a system in which no outside forces act momentum does not change.
- This is LINEAR momentum (in a straight line) (not to be confused with angular momentum whose law of conservation predicts the 'spinning skater' changes in rate of spin).

WHEN IS MOMENTUM CONSERVED?
- In collisions :
    - between balls in snooker / pool
    - between bowl and jack in bowls
    - between players (rugby)
    - between vehicles.
- Since momentum includes mass and velocity.
- The direction of the initial moving object (ball or person) must be taken into account.
- The mass of a moving person is significant.
- A massive rugby player is far more difficult to deflect or tackle.
- Since he / she would have a large momentum.
- Momentum would be continued by tackler and player after the tackle.
- It would be easy for the player to 'keep going' and keep most of his / her momentum.

TRANSFERENCE OF MOMENTUM
- During a collision or tackle, momentum carried by an incoming player can be transferred to a tackler (who is knocked over).

FLIGHT PATH OF PROJECTILES

- Affected by relative size of forces acting.
- The faster the projectile travels the greater will be air resistance, so at the start of flight air resistance will always be biggest, and will reduce as object slows down.

IMPULSE is another concept derived from Newton's second law.

- Impulse = total change of momentum
        = force x time.
- Useful when large forces are applied for short times.

Examples of use of impulse :
- Fielder catching a hard cricket ball.
- Bat, racquet, stick, golf club striking a ball.
- Footballer kicking a ball.
- Follow through when striking a ball :
    - Increases time of contact.
    - Therefore increases impulse.
    - Therefore increases final momentum of struck ball.

- Graph (323) of force against time for reaction force of ground on foot during a stride (running).
- Area under graph = impulse.

- Graph (324) of force v time for a ball being kicked.
- Area under graph
  = impulse
  = change of momentum of ball
  = mass of ball x change of speed.
- Enables you to calculate final speed of ball.

PROJECTILES

FACTORS AFFECTING RANGE of PROJECTILE

- Speed of release.
- Angle of release.
- Height of release (compared to landing height).

- The motion of most thrown or struck objects is affected by :
    - Air resistance.
    - Sometimes air flow (Bernoulli effect).
- Examples include badminton shuttle, table tennis ball, discus, javelin, american football, golf ball.
- Without air resistance (shot, hammer) flight path would be a symmetric curve called a parabola.

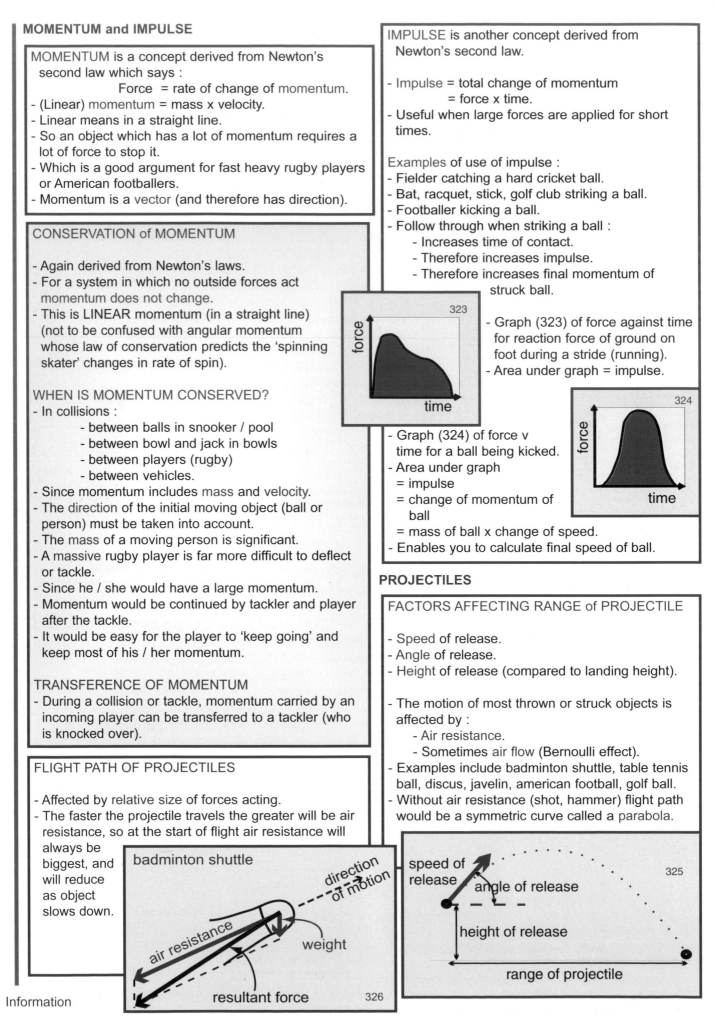

CENTRE of MASS (CENTRE of GRAVITY)

CENTRE OF GRAVITY
- Centre of mass is the better scientific term for this, since the idea works in gravity free conditions.

- Centre of Mass (CofM) is the single point (on a body) which represents all the spread out mass of the body.
- So, since gravity acts on mass to produce weight, the weight acts at the centre of mass of a body.
- Therefore CofM can also be defined as the point of balance of the body.

BALANCE
- The CofM must be over the base of support if a person is to be on balance.

WHAT HAPPENS to CofM of ATHLETE'S BODY IN FLIGHT?

- CofM must follow a parabola.
- Position of CofM depends on shape of body.
- Athlete's body can change shape.
- Example, a high jumper over a bar (his CofM passes under the bar, but he still could jump clear).

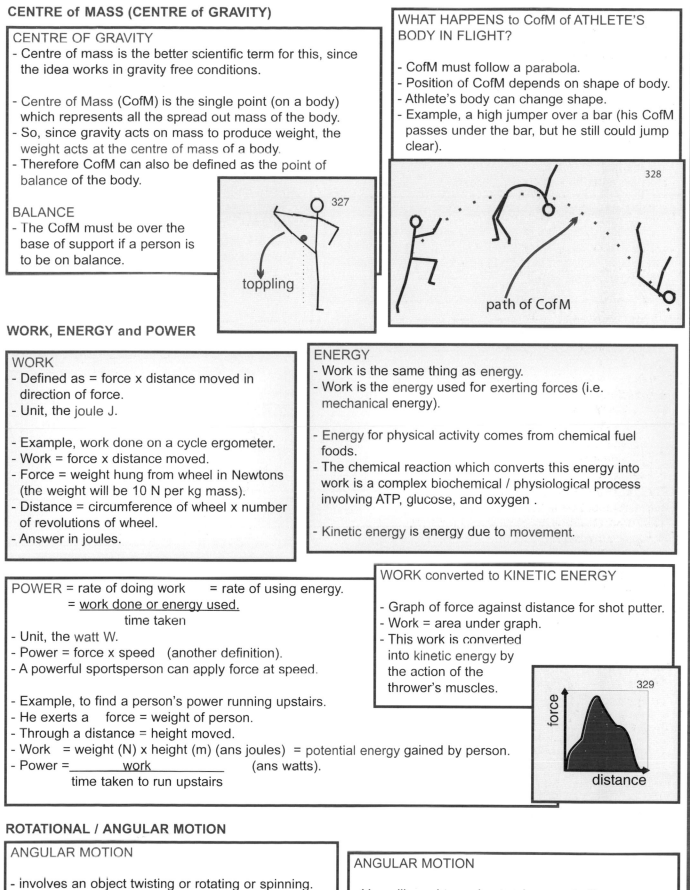

WORK, ENERGY and POWER

WORK
- Defined as = force x distance moved in direction of force.
- Unit, the joule J.

- Example, work done on a cycle ergometer.
- Work = force x distance moved.
- Force = weight hung from wheel in Newtons (the weight will be 10 N per kg mass).
- Distance = circumference of wheel x number of revolutions of wheel.
- Answer in joules.

ENERGY
- Work is the same thing as energy.
- Work is the energy used for exerting forces (i.e. mechanical energy).

- Energy for physical activity comes from chemical fuel foods.
- The chemical reaction which converts this energy into work is a complex biochemical / physiological process involving ATP, glucose, and oxygen .

- Kinetic energy is energy due to movement.

POWER = rate of doing work   = rate of using energy.
= work done or energy used.
time taken
- Unit, the watt W.
- Power = force x speed   (another definition).
- A powerful sportsperson can apply force at speed.

- Example, to find a person's power running upstairs.
- He exerts a   force = weight of person.
- Through a distance = height moved.
- Work   = weight (N) x height (m) (ans joules) = potential energy gained by person.
- Power = _____work_____   (ans watts).
time taken to run upstairs

WORK converted to KINETIC ENERGY

- Graph of force against distance for shot putter.
- Work = area under graph.
- This work is converted into kinetic energy by the action of the thrower's muscles.

ROTATIONAL / ANGULAR MOTION

ANGULAR MOTION

- involves an object twisting or rotating or spinning.

- For example, a skater spinning, a gymnast performing a grand circle on the high bar.

- No part of the sportsperson is moving along in a straight line.

ANGULAR MOTION

- You will need to understand concepts like:
  - angular velocity or rate of spinning.
  - moment of inertia (the equivalent of mass for rotating bodies).
  - as well as angle.

Information

ANGULAR MOTION (continued)

ANGULAR VELOCITY = angle turned through per second

$$\omega = \frac{\text{angle turned through}}{\text{time taken}} = \frac{\theta}{t}$$

ω = Greek letter omega.

- This is rate of spin, most easily understood as revolutions per second (revs per sec).
- Revs per sec would have to be converted to the unit radians per second for calculations.
1 rev per second = 2 x π = 6.28 rs^{-1}.

- Rates of spin apply to :
  - Tumbling gymnasts, trampolinists and divers (piked straight and tucked somersaults), discus and hammer throwers, spinning skaters, skiers turning and twisting between slalom gates.

ANGLE (angular displacement)

- To be scientifically correct angle should not be measured in degrees, but in RADIANS (r).
- Angle = $\frac{\text{arc length}}{\text{radius of arc}}$ = $\frac{l}{r}$
- 360 degrees = 2 x π radians = 6.28 radians
- 180° = π r = 3.14 r
- 90° = 1/2 π r = 1.57 r
- 30° = 1/6 π r = 0.52 r
- And so on (see maths text book for more).

ANGULAR ACCELERATION
- Rate of change of angular velocity.
- Angular acceleration

$$= \frac{\text{change of angular velocity}}{\text{time taken}}$$

$$A = \frac{\omega_2 - \omega_1}{t}$$

- (Note similarity of formula with linear motion).

- Used when rates of spin increase or decrease.
- Example, hammer thrower.

ACTION of FORCES in MUSCLES at JOINTS - LEVERS

LEVERS

- Levers have an effort, pivot (fulcrum) and load.
- And are a means of applying forces at a distance from the source of the force.

Resistance arm of lever:
- The structure of the lever between pivot and load (length d in diagram 330).

Effort arm of lever:
- The structure (part) of the lever between pivot and effort (length x in diagram 330).

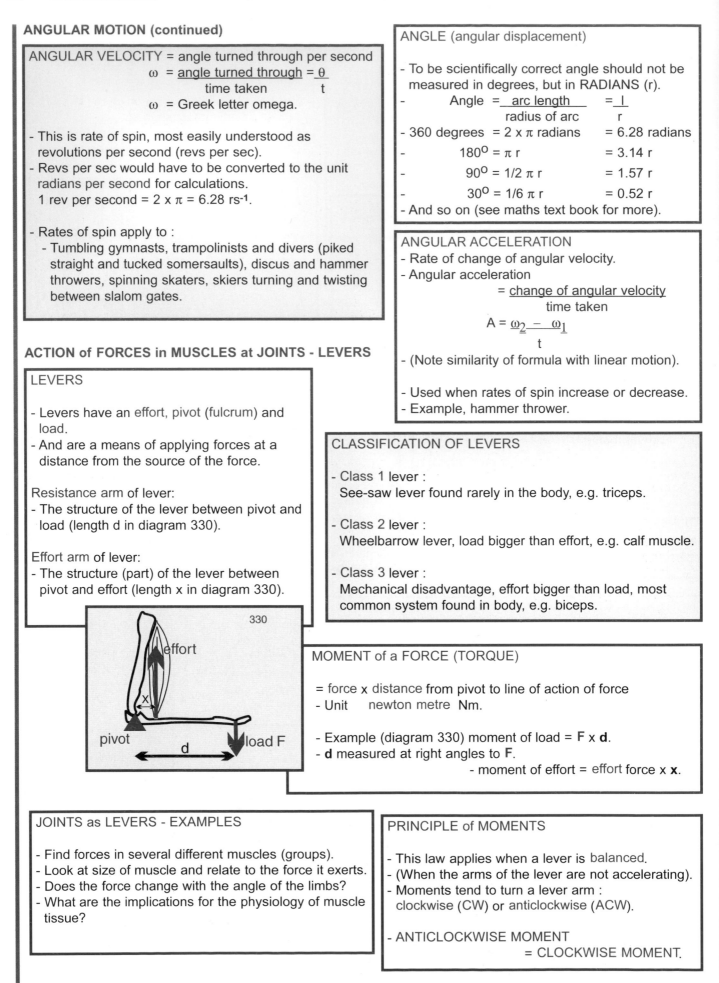

330

CLASSIFICATION OF LEVERS

- Class 1 lever :
  See-saw lever found rarely in the body, e.g. triceps.

- Class 2 lever :
  Wheelbarrow lever, load bigger than effort, e.g. calf muscle.

- Class 3 lever :
  Mechanical disadvantage, effort bigger than load, most common system found in body, e.g. biceps.

MOMENT of a FORCE (TORQUE)

= force x distance from pivot to line of action of force
- Unit   newton metre Nm.

- Example (diagram 330) moment of load = F x d.
- d measured at right angles to F.
  - moment of effort = effort force x x.

JOINTS as LEVERS - EXAMPLES

- Find forces in several different muscles (groups).
- Look at size of muscle and relate to the force it exerts.
- Does the force change with the angle of the limbs?
- What are the implications for the physiology of muscle tissue?

PRINCIPLE of MOMENTS

- This law applies when a lever is balanced.
- (When the arms of the lever are not accelerating).
- Moments tend to turn a lever arm :
  clockwise (CW) or anticlockwise (ACW).

- ANTICLOCKWISE MOMENT
              = CLOCKWISE MOMENT.

JOINTS AS LEVERS (continued)

FORCES in MUSCLES

- Examples from :
- Biceps muscle acting on elbow joint.

  class 3 lever.

- Triceps muscle acting on elbow joint.

  class 1 lever.

- Quadriceps acting on knee joint.

  class 3 lever.

- Gastrocnemius muscle acting on ankle joint via the achilles tendon.

  class 2 lever.

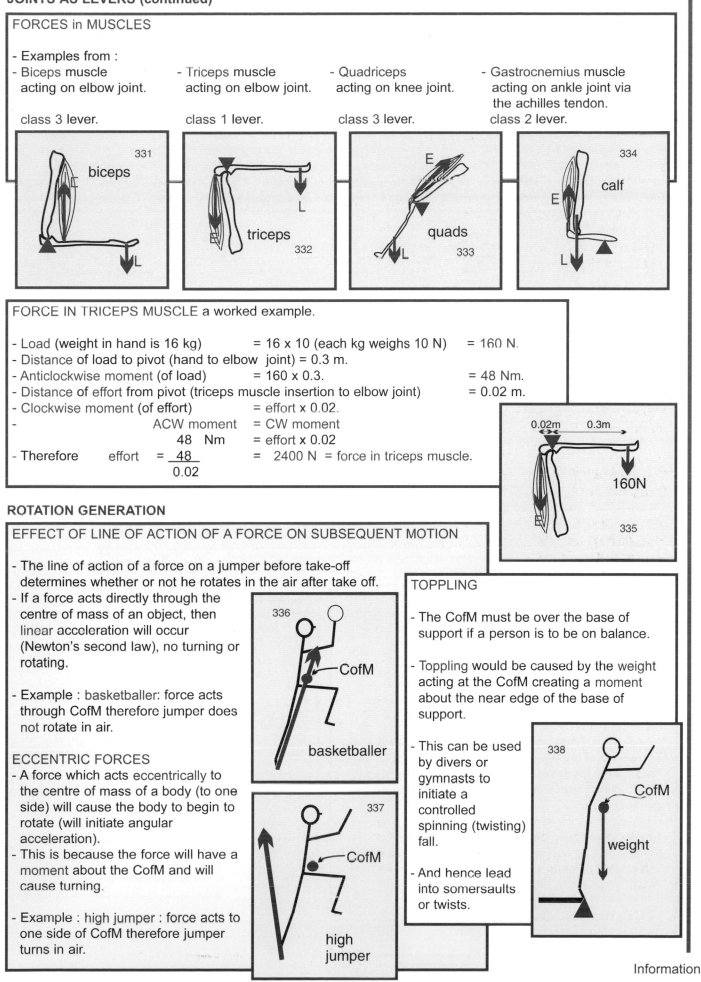

FORCE IN TRICEPS MUSCLE a worked example.

- Load (weight in hand is 16 kg)   = 16 x 10 (each kg weighs 10 N)   = 160 N.
- Distance of load to pivot (hand to elbow joint) = 0.3 m.
- Anticlockwise moment (of load)   = 160 x 0.3.   = 48 Nm.
- Distance of effort from pivot (triceps muscle insertion to elbow joint)   = 0.02 m.
- Clockwise moment (of effort)   = effort x 0.02.
-                          ACW moment   = CW moment
                           48   Nm   = effort x 0.02
- Therefore   effort = $\dfrac{48}{0.02}$ =   2400 N = force in triceps muscle.

ROTATION GENERATION

EFFECT OF LINE OF ACTION OF A FORCE ON SUBSEQUENT MOTION

- The line of action of a force on a jumper before take-off determines whether or not he rotates in the air after take off.
- If a force acts directly through the centre of mass of an object, then linear acceleration will occur (Newton's second law), no turning or rotating.

- Example : basketballer: force acts through CofM therefore jumper does not rotate in air.

ECCENTRIC FORCES

- A force which acts eccentrically to the centre of mass of a body (to one side) will cause the body to begin to rotate (will initiate angular acceleration).
- This is because the force will have a moment about the CofM and will cause turning.

- Example : high jumper : force acts to one side of CofM therefore jumper turns in air.

TOPPLING

- The CofM must be over the base of support if a person is to be on balance.

- Toppling would be caused by the weight acting at the CofM creating a moment about the near edge of the base of support.

- This can be used by divers or gymnasts to initiate a controlled spinning (twisting) fall.

- And hence lead into somersaults or twists.

MOMENT OF INERTIA

MOMENT OF INERTIA

- The equivalent of mass for rotating systems.
- Rotational inertia.
- Objects rotating with large MI require large moments of forces to change their angular velocity.
- Objects with small MI require small moments of force to change their angular velocity or ω.

MOMENT of INERTIA (MI) $= \Sigma\, Mr^2$

- MI depends on the spread of mass away from the axis of spin, hence body shape.
- The more spread out the mass, the bigger the MI.
- Unit kilogramme metre squared kgm^2.

- Bodies with arms held out wide have large MI.
- The further the mass is away from the axis of rotation increases the MI dramatically.
- Sportspeople use this to control all spinning or turning movements.
- Pikes and tucks are good examples of use of MI, both reduce MI.
- In diagram 339, I is the MI for the left most pin man, and I has a value of about 1 kgm^2 for an average person.

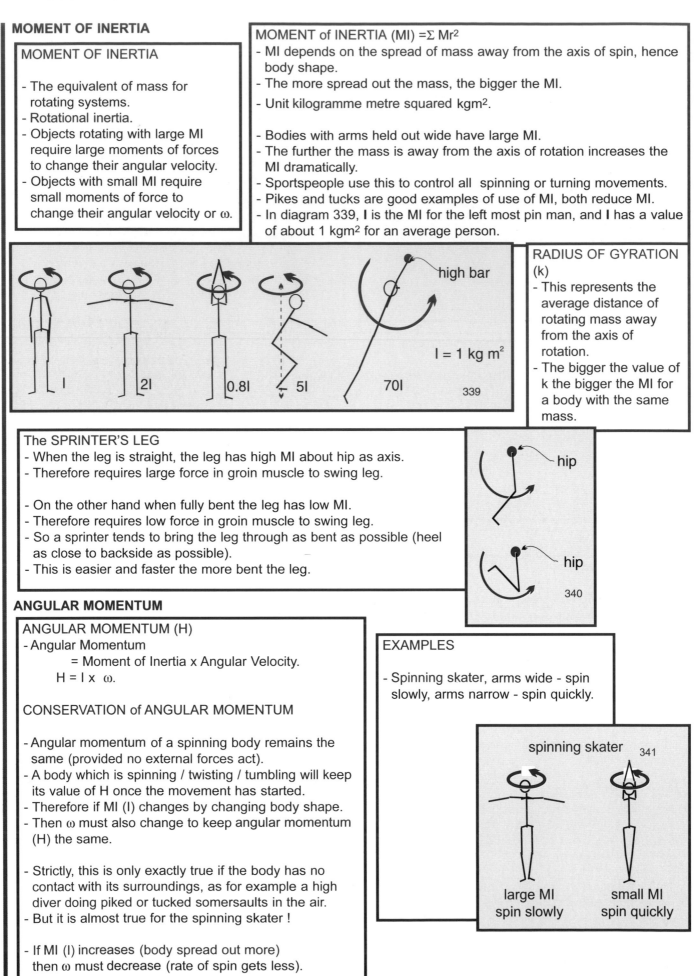

$I = 1\ kg\ m^2$

I   2I   0.8I   5I   70I   339

RADIUS OF GYRATION (k)

- This represents the average distance of rotating mass away from the axis of rotation.
- The bigger the value of k the bigger the MI for a body with the same mass.

The SPRINTER'S LEG

- When the leg is straight, the leg has high MI about hip as axis.
- Therefore requires large force in groin muscle to swing leg.

- On the other hand when fully bent the leg has low MI.
- Therefore requires low force in groin muscle to swing leg.
- So a sprinter tends to bring the leg through as bent as possible (heel as close to backside as possible).
- This is easier and faster the more bent the leg.

hip

hip

340

ANGULAR MOMENTUM

ANGULAR MOMENTUM (H)

- Angular Momentum
    = Moment of Inertia x Angular Velocity.
    $H = I \times \omega$.

CONSERVATION of ANGULAR MOMENTUM

- Angular momentum of a spinning body remains the same (provided no external forces act).
- A body which is spinning / twisting / tumbling will keep its value of H once the movement has started.
- Therefore if MI (I) changes by changing body shape.
- Then ω must also change to keep angular momentum (H) the same.

- Strictly, this is only exactly true if the body has no contact with its surroundings, as for example a high diver doing piked or tucked somersaults in the air.
- But it is almost true for the spinning skater !

- If MI (I) increases (body spread out more) then ω must decrease (rate of spin gets less).

EXAMPLES

- Spinning skater, arms wide - spin slowly, arms narrow - spin quickly.

spinning skater   341

large MI   small MI
spin slowly   spin quickly

ANGULAR MOMENTUM (continued)

EXAMPLES OF CONSERVATION OF ANGULAR MOMENTUM

- Tumbling gymnast, diver, or trampolinist,
  tuck - spin fast, straight body - spin slowly.

- Dancer executing spin jump,
  the movement is initiated with arms held wide
- highest possible MI.

- Once she has taken off, angular momentum is conserved.
- Flight shape has arms tucked across chest with lowest
  possible MI therefore highest possible rate of spin.

- Slalom skier crouches on approach to gate, as he / she passes
  the gate he / she stands straight up (reducing MI), so turns
  rapidly past the gate.

- Then crouches again (increasing MI) to resume slow turn
  between gates.

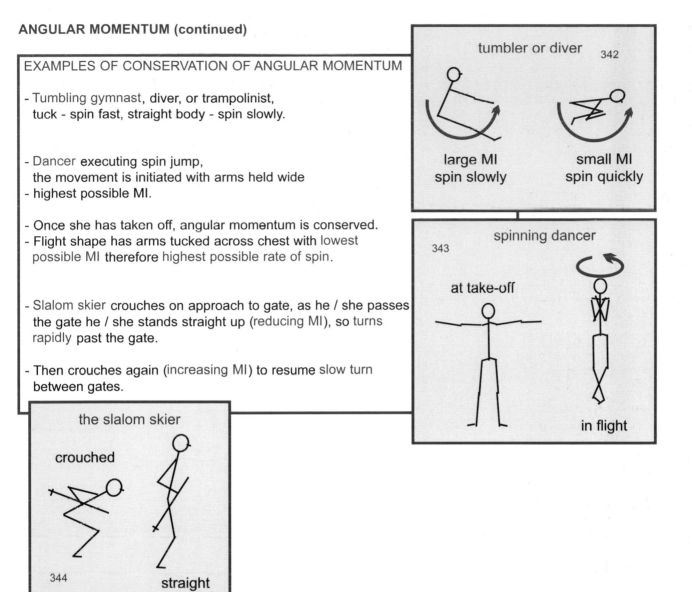

tumbler or diver   342

large MI
spin slowly

small MI
spin quickly

343   spinning dancer

at take-off

in flight

the slalom skier

crouched

344   straight

Dennis Roscoe

CHARACTERISTICS OF SKILL

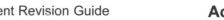

efficient   coordinated   401

predetermined   controlled

**CHARACTERISTICS
OF SKILL**

consistent   good
technique

learned   aesthetic

SKILL ACQUISITION

EFFICIENT
- No waste of energy.
- The movement seems effortless, example : gymnast
  performs handspring without unnecessary movements.
CO-ORDINATED
- Flowing and fluid movement, example : a trampolinist
  performs a smooth flowing routine.
CONTROLLED
- Performer has control over movement, example : soccer
  player has ball under control and is well balanced.
GOOD TECHNIQUE
- Movement follows acceptable pattern.
- Example : netball player has a good shooting technique.

SKILL IS : CONSISTENT
- The correct movement can be
  repeated, example : a shot putter can
  produce a good throwing technique
  over and over again.
LEARNED
- The skill is practised, example : a top
  class golfer is not born with specific
  golfing skills (although he / she may
  have been born with relevant
  underlying abilities).
PREDETERMINED
- Performer has a goal, example : a
  good tennis player will know where
  each shot should land in the opposing
  player's court.
AESTHETIC
- The movement looks good, example :
  a skilled rugby player who runs and
  passes the ball can be aesthetically
  pleasing.

TYPES OF SKILLS
MOTOR SKILL
- A voluntary body movement with a predetermined end result,
  example : hitting a ball with a bat.
FUNDAMENTAL MOTOR SKILL
- Basic skills that are learned when young. They form the basis
  of more complex movements, example : jumping.
PERCEPTUAL SKILL
- Being able to interpret information quickly at a given time and
  to make an appropriate decision, example : a goalkeeper in
  football assessing the movement of an opponent approaching.
COGNITIVE SKILL
- Being able to make sense of a problem and to solve it.
- These skills affect perception.
INDIVIDUAL SKILL
- Skill that is performed with no interaction with other performers,
  example : a discus thrower in athletics.
COACTIVE SKILL
- Skill that involves interacting with other performers,
  example : hockey player in a penalty corner drill.
INTERACTIVE SKILL
- A skill which involves the performer interacting with the
  environment, example : a rower.

CHARACTERISTICS OF ABILITY

FOUNDATION
- Ability is the foundation for skill learning.
- A successful sportsperson must be born with a number of relevant abilities.
GENETICALLY DETERMINED
- We are born with our abilities, example : some children
  can quickly pick up skills (such as catching a ball or
  riding a bike),
- Whereas others take much longer and are less
  successful at any given skill.
PSYCHOMOTOR ABILITY
- To process information about how and when we move.
  For example, reaction time, a rugby player must react
  quickly to an oncoming player who changes direction.
PERCEPTUAL ABILITY
- This is the ability to sense and interpret sensory inputs
  or information, example : awareness of a rugby player
  of the positions and actions of opponents.
ENDURING
- Ability is enduring, we largely hold on to our abilities
  throughout our lives, for example, riding a bike.

402   psychomotor
          gross motor   ability
          ability
                                    perceptual
    genetically   ability
    determined

                 **CHARACTERISTICS
                 OF ABILITY**   General

    enduring

    many groups   specific
    of abilities
                 the foundation
                 for skill learning

4.2 Acquisition of Skill

CHARACTERISTICS OF ABILITY (continued)

GROSS MOTOR ABILITY
- To be able to move using muscle movements, example : being able to run or ride a bike.

GENERAL ABILITY
- Does not really exist.
- We have specific abilities.

SPECIFIC ABILITIES
- Skills require different abilities.
- Example : gymnastics involves balance, strength and flexibility.

GROUPS OF ABILITIES
- A good sportsperson may have many different groups of abilities.
- Example : a good all round sportsman could have different specific abilities such as good hand eye coordination and balance which could be transferred to lots of different sports activities.

SKILL CLASSIFICATION

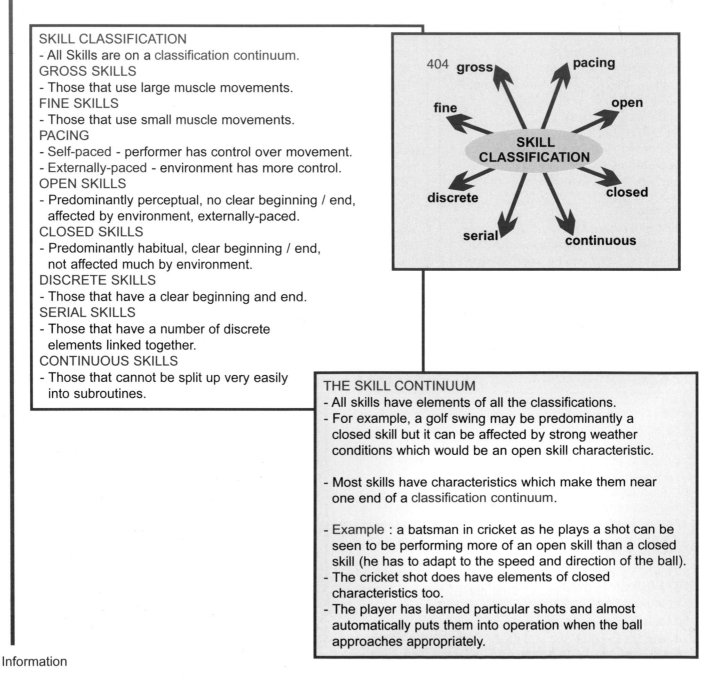

SKILL CLASSIFICATION
- All Skills are on a classification continuum.

GROSS SKILLS
- Those that use large muscle movements.

FINE SKILLS
- Those that use small muscle movements.

PACING
- Self-paced - performer has control over movement.
- Externally-paced - environment has more control.

OPEN SKILLS
- Predominantly perceptual, no clear beginning / end, affected by environment, externally-paced.

CLOSED SKILLS
- Predominantly habitual, clear beginning / end, not affected much by environment.

DISCRETE SKILLS
- Those that have a clear beginning and end.

SERIAL SKILLS
- Those that have a number of discrete elements linked together.

CONTINUOUS SKILLS
- Those that cannot be split up very easily into subroutines.

THE SKILL CONTINUUM
- All skills have elements of all the classifications.
- For example, a golf swing may be predominantly a closed skill but it can be affected by strong weather conditions which would be an open skill characteristic.
- Most skills have characteristics which make them near one end of a classification continuum.
- Example : a batsman in cricket as he plays a shot can be seen to be performing more of an open skill than a closed skill (he has to adapt to the speed and direction of the ball).
- The cricket shot does have elements of closed characteristics too.
- The player has learned particular shots and almost automatically puts them into operation when the ball approaches appropriately.

Information

SKILL CLASSIFICATION (continued)

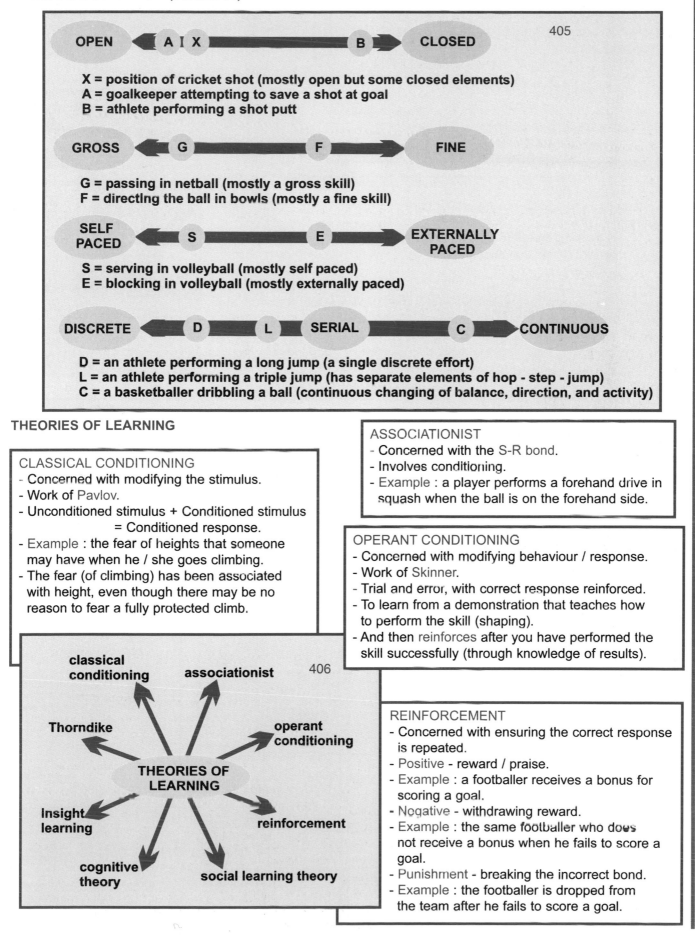

X = position of cricket shot (mostly open but some closed elements)
A = goalkeeper attempting to save a shot at goal
B = athlete performing a shot putt

G = passing in netball (mostly a gross skill)
F = directing the ball in bowls (mostly a fine skill)

S = serving in volleyball (mostly self paced)
E = blocking in volleyball (mostly externally paced)

D = an athlete performing a long jump (a single discrete effort)
L = an athlete performing a triple jump (has separate elements of hop - step - jump)
C = a basketballer dribbling a ball (continuous changing of balance, direction, and activity)

THEORIES OF LEARNING

ASSOCIATIONIST
- Concerned with the S-R bond.
- Involves conditioning.
- Example : a player performs a forehand drive in squash when the ball is on the forehand side.

CLASSICAL CONDITIONING
- Concerned with modifying the stimulus.
- Work of Pavlov.
- Unconditioned stimulus + Conditioned stimulus
        = Conditioned response.
- Example : the fear of heights that someone may have when he / she goes climbing.
- The fear (of climbing) has been associated with height, even though there may be no reason to fear a fully protected climb.

OPERANT CONDITIONING
- Concerned with modifying behaviour / response.
- Work of Skinner.
- Trial and error, with correct response reinforced.
- To learn from a demonstration that teaches how to perform the skill (shaping).
- And then reinforces after you have performed the skill successfully (through knowledge of results).

REINFORCEMENT
- Concerned with ensuring the correct response is repeated.
- Positive - reward / praise.
- Example : a footballer receives a bonus for scoring a goal.
- Negative - withdrawing reward.
- Example : the same footballer who does not receive a bonus when he fails to score a goal.
- Punishment - breaking the incorrect bond.
- Example : the footballer is dropped from the team after he fails to score a goal.

THEORIES OF LEARNING (continued)

INSIGHT LEARNING
- See learning as a problem to be solved by the performer.
- The more you understand why a movement is to be performed, the better the learning.
- Example : hockey players being encouraged to think about marking strategies against twin centre forwards.
- A problem to be solved which gives the players more insight and eventual understanding of the problem.

COGNITIVE THEORY
- Concerned with understanding and insight.
- Work of Gestaltists / German scientists who showed importance of perceiving a problem in its entirety.
- And the use of intervening variables.
- Example : a badminton player will understand the necessity of performing a 'clear' to wrong foot opponent.

THORNDIKE'S LAWS
- Concerned with strengthening the S-R bond.
- Law of exercise
    - Example : the more a basketballer practises shooting the more likely it is that that shooting technique will be repeated in the game situation.
- Law of effect
    - Example : if the basketballer feels that the movement is correct then he or she is more likely to repeat the movement.
- Law of readiness
    - Example : the more a basketballer is physically and mentally prepared to perform a shot then it is more likely to be performed well.

SOCIAL LEARNING THEORY
- Learning by copying others.
- More likely to copy 'significant others' - those who we see as high status role models.
- We copy because we wish to be accepted by others or to be held in high esteem.
- Skills are often copied :
    - to achieve the success that others enjoy.
    - and to be praised.

OBSERVATIONAL LEARNING
- Process of imitation after observation of motor skill activity.
- BANDURA - copying/modelling affected by 4 processes:
    - Observation
    >Attention >Retention >Motor Reproduction >Motivation
    - Performance.

OBSERVATION

↓

Attention

↓

Retention

↓

Motor reproduction

↓

Motivation

↓

PERFORMANCE

DEMONSTRATIONS
- These are important in the learning of skills for observational learning.
- The most successful demonstrations show :
    - Attention.
        - Retention.
            - Motor reproduction.
                - Motivation.
- High attention level of performer, (helped by cueing / success of model).
- High level of retention by performer, (helped by repetition by the model and effective mental rehearsal).
- The right level of physical performance, (to match the physical ability of the performer).
- The right level of motivation to copy the model's behaviour (there must be a high level of incentive to copy).

OBSERVATIONAL LEARNING
- This is at the heart of social learning theory.
- Learning takes place via watching and then imitating what is seen.
- Imitation is more likely if :
    - The model is seen as relevant.
    - The model complies with social norms.
    - The model is similar in age / ability.
    - The model's behaviour has been reinforced.
    - The model's performance is seen as successful e.g. a successful tennis player.

INFORMATION PROCESSING

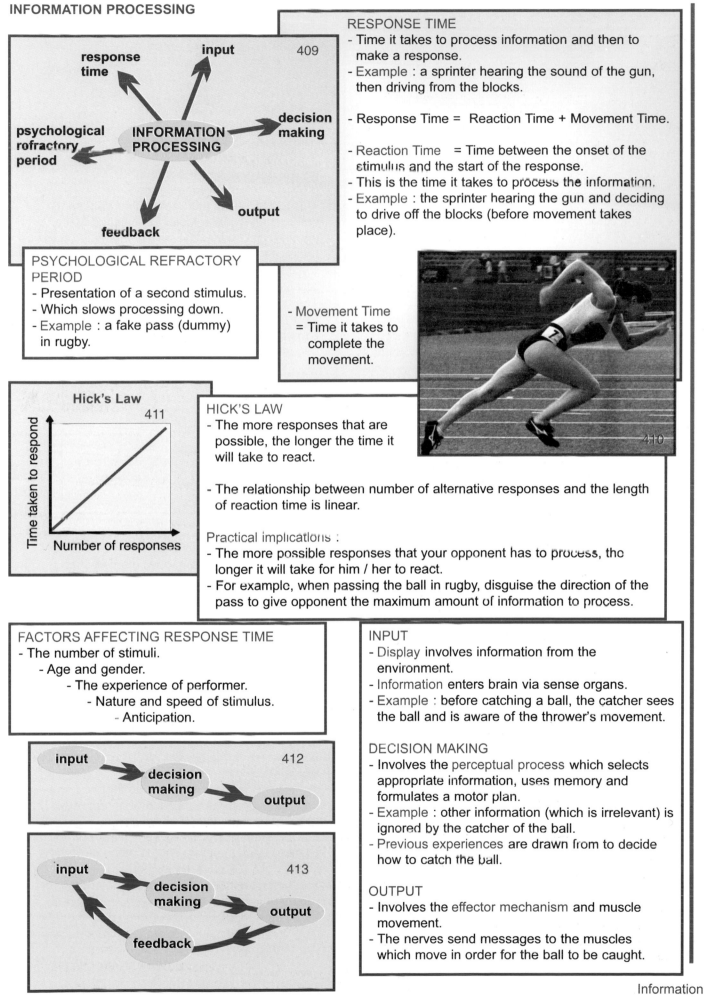

response
time

input   409

**INFORMATION
PROCESSING**

decision
making

psychological
refractory
period

output

feedback

RESPONSE TIME
- Time it takes to process information and then to
  make a response.
- Example : a sprinter hearing the sound of the gun,
  then driving from the blocks.

- Response Time = Reaction Time + Movement Time.

- Reaction Time = Time between the onset of the
  stimulus and the start of the response.
- This is the time it takes to process the information.
- Example : the sprinter hearing the gun and deciding
  to drive off the blocks (before movement takes
  place).

PSYCHOLOGICAL REFRACTORY
PERIOD
- Presentation of a second stimulus.
- Which slows processing down.
- Example : a fake pass (dummy)
  in rugby.

- Movement Time
  = Time it takes to
    complete the
    movement.

Hick's Law
                411

Time taken to respond

Number of responses

HICK'S LAW
- The more responses that are
  possible, the longer the time it
  will take to react.

- The relationship between number of alternative responses and the length
  of reaction time is linear.

Practical implications :
- The more possible responses that your opponent has to process, the
  longer it will take for him / her to react.
- For example, when passing the ball in rugby, disguise the direction of the
  pass to give opponent the maximum amount of information to process.

FACTORS AFFECTING RESPONSE TIME
- The number of stimuli.
  - Age and gender.
    - The experience of performer.
      - Nature and speed of stimulus.
        - Anticipation.

input   412
    decision
    making
              output

input   413
    decision
    making
              output
    feedback

INPUT
- Display involves information from the
  environment.
- Information enters brain via sense organs.
- Example : before catching a ball, the catcher sees
  the ball and is aware of the thrower's movement.

DECISION MAKING
- Involves the perceptual process which selects
  appropriate information, uses memory and
  formulates a motor plan.
- Example : other information (which is irrelevant) is
  ignored by the catcher of the ball.
- Previous experiences are drawn from to decide
  how to catch the ball.

OUTPUT
- Involves the effector mechanism and muscle
  movement.
- The nerves send messages to the muscles
  which move in order for the ball to be caught.

INFORMATION PROCESSING (continued)

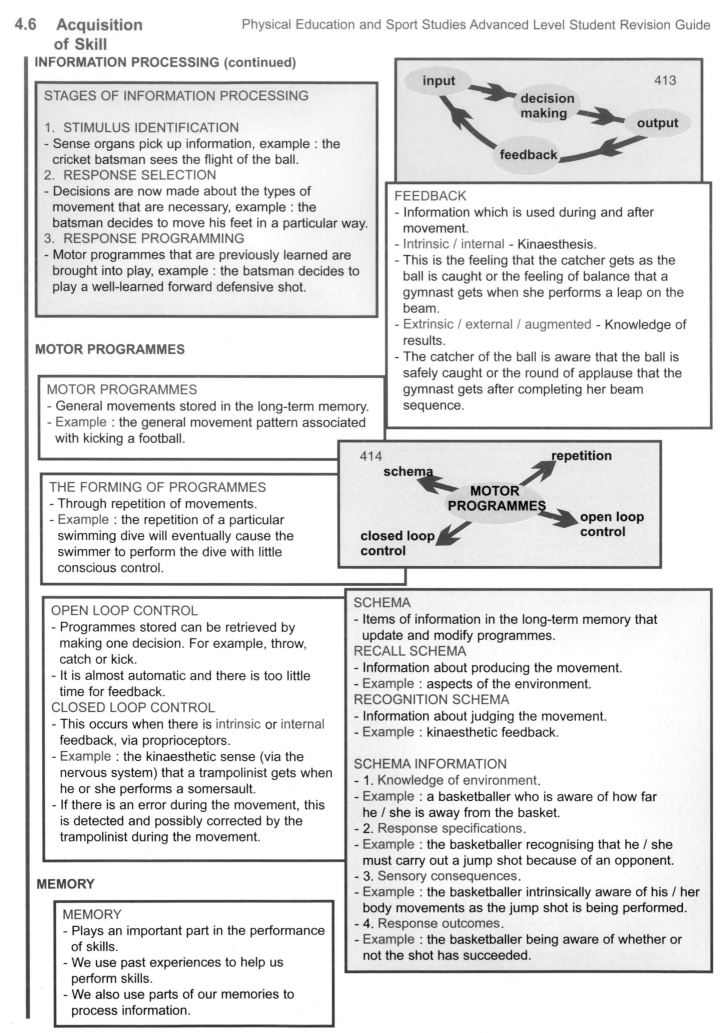

STAGES OF INFORMATION PROCESSING

1. STIMULUS IDENTIFICATION
- Sense organs pick up information, example : the cricket batsman sees the flight of the ball.
2. RESPONSE SELECTION
- Decisions are now made about the types of movement that are necessary, example : the batsman decides to move his feet in a particular way.
3. RESPONSE PROGRAMMING
- Motor programmes that are previously learned are brought into play, example : the batsman decides to play a well-learned forward defensive shot.

MOTOR PROGRAMMES

MOTOR PROGRAMMES
- General movements stored in the long-term memory.
- Example : the general movement pattern associated with kicking a football.

THE FORMING OF PROGRAMMES
- Through repetition of movements.
- Example : the repetition of a particular swimming dive will eventually cause the swimmer to perform the dive with little conscious control.

OPEN LOOP CONTROL
- Programmes stored can be retrieved by making one decision. For example, throw, catch or kick.
- It is almost automatic and there is too little time for feedback.

CLOSED LOOP CONTROL
- This occurs when there is intrinsic or internal feedback, via proprioceptors.
- Example : the kinaesthetic sense (via the nervous system) that a trampolinist gets when he or she performs a somersault.
- If there is an error during the movement, this is detected and possibly corrected by the trampolinist during the movement.

MEMORY

MEMORY
- Plays an important part in the performance of skills.
- We use past experiences to help us perform skills.
- We also use parts of our memories to process information.

FEEDBACK
- Information which is used during and after movement.
- Intrinsic / internal - Kinaesthesis.
- This is the feeling that the catcher gets as the ball is caught or the feeling of balance that a gymnast gets when she performs a leap on the beam.
- Extrinsic / external / augmented - Knowledge of results.
- The catcher of the ball is aware that the ball is safely caught or the round of applause that the gymnast gets after completing her beam sequence.

SCHEMA
- Items of information in the long-term memory that update and modify programmes.

RECALL SCHEMA
- Information about producing the movement.
- Example : aspects of the environment.

RECOGNITION SCHEMA
- Information about judging the movement.
- Example : kinaesthetic feedback.

SCHEMA INFORMATION
- 1. Knowledge of environment.
- Example : a basketballer who is aware of how far he / she is away from the basket.
- 2. Response specifications.
- Example : the basketballer recognising that he / she must carry out a jump shot because of an opponent.
- 3. Sensory consequences.
- Example : the basketballer intrinsically aware of his / her body movements as the jump shot is being performed.
- 4. Response outcomes.
- Example : the basketballer being aware of whether or not the shot has succeeded.

Information

MEMORY (continued)

SHORT-TERM SENSORY STORE (STSS)
- Information is passed through this store where it is filtered.
- This is where selective attention takes place.
- Example : a tennis player will select only the ball from the display which includes the other player, the crowd, and other movements behind the ball.

SHORT-TERM MEMORY (STM)
- The 'engine room', where all information that has been filtered passes through.
- Only stores small amounts of information (7 pieces +/- 2).
- Example : in table tennis, the player who is to receive a serve uses his / her STM to remember the position of the opposing player as the serve commences, his / her own position, and any other information that is less than one minute old.

- Amounts of information can be extended by 'chunking' (grouping / organising together information).
- Example : a rugby player may remember a set play at a lineout by memorising a number.

LONG-TERM MEMORY (LTM)
- Limitless capacity.
- Storing or remembering achieved through : repetition; association; novelty; meaningfulness.
- Motor programmes / schema stored here.
- Retrieved information from here is used in skill performance.

- Example : a hockey player who is experienced has information stored such as motor programmes related to stopping and hitting the ball, and strategies such as how to tackle effectively.

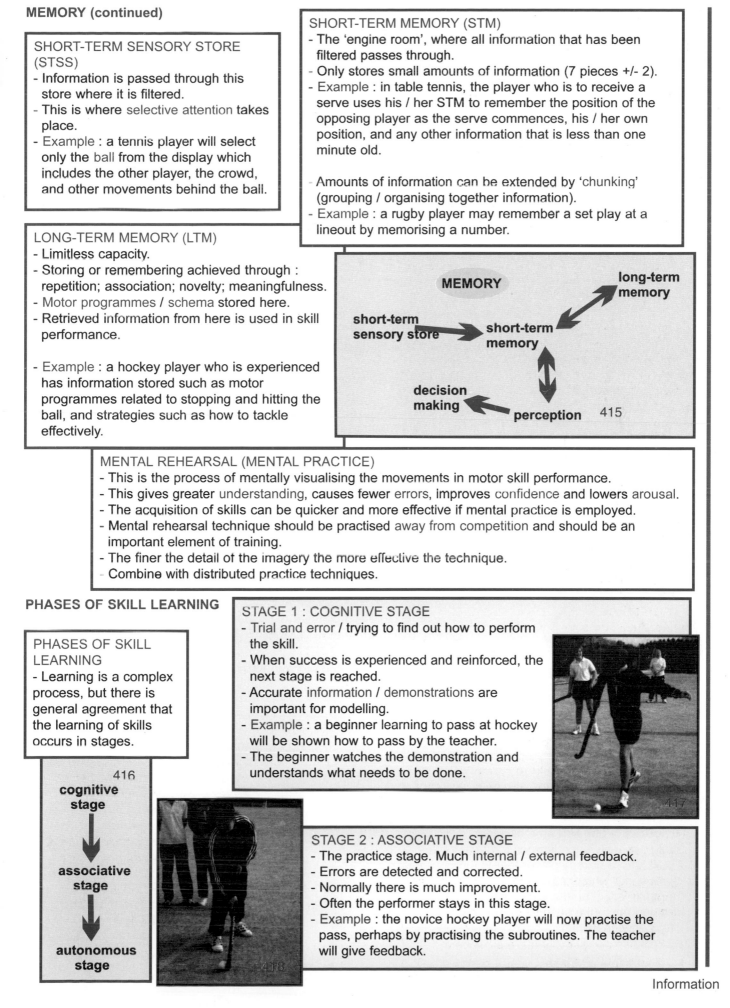

MEMORY

short-term sensory store → short-term memory ↔ long-term memory

decision making ← perception

415

MENTAL REHEARSAL (MENTAL PRACTICE)
- This is the process of mentally visualising the movements in motor skill performance.
- This gives greater understanding, causes fewer errors, improves confidence and lowers arousal.
- The acquisition of skills can be quicker and more effective if mental practice is employed.
- Mental rehearsal technique should be practised away from competition and should be an important element of training.
- The finer the detail of the imagery the more effective the technique.
- Combine with distributed practice techniques.

PHASES OF SKILL LEARNING

PHASES OF SKILL LEARNING
- Learning is a complex process, but there is general agreement that the learning of skills occurs in stages.

416

cognitive stage
↓
associative stage
↓
autonomous stage

STAGE 1 : COGNITIVE STAGE
- Trial and error / trying to find out how to perform the skill.
- When success is experienced and reinforced, the next stage is reached.
- Accurate information / demonstrations are important for modelling.
- Example : a beginner learning to pass at hockey will be shown how to pass by the teacher.
- The beginner watches the demonstration and understands what needs to be done.

417

STAGE 2 : ASSOCIATIVE STAGE
- The practice stage. Much internal / external feedback.
- Errors are detected and corrected.
- Normally there is much improvement.
- Often the performer stays in this stage.
- Example : the novice hockey player will now practise the pass, perhaps by practising the subroutines. The teacher will give feedback.

418

Information

PHASES OF SKILL LEARNING (continued)

STAGE 3 : AUTONOMOUS STAGE
- The skill is now performed without much conscious control.
- Motor programmes are run in this stage.
- This stage is only reached by the very skilful.
- Example : the hockey pass has been learnt, and the player can now pass with little conscious effort.

typical 420
performance / number of trials

linear 422
performance / number of trials

negative 423
performance / number of trials

positive acceleration 421
performance / number of trials

plateau 424
performance / number of trials

LEARNING CURVES
- These reflect the relationships which exist between trials of a skill and the success or performance rate.
- Learning curves show performances but can give a good indication of learning.
- Useful for goal setting and recognising the actual ability level of the performer.

- S shaped is a typical curve of learning of a gross motor skill.
- Positive acceleration
- Poor early performances but improves later.
- Linear
- Performance is directly proportional to the number of practice trials.
- Negative
- Good early performances but poorer performances in later trials.
- Plateau
- Not much change if at all in performances over a number of trials.

- To avoid a plateau:
    - Give new goals that can be reached.
    - Give praise that is deserved.
    - Ensure that there are regular rest intervals.
    - Maintain motivation and employ positive cognitive techniques.

TRANSFER

TRANSFER
- Influence of one skill on the performance of another.

RETROACTIVE TRANSFER
- Influence of one skill on a skill that has previously been learned.
- Example : a hockey player learns the flicking skill which may have a negative effect on the previously learned push (the push pass may be lifted unnecessarily).

POSITIVE TRANSFER
- One skill helping the learning / performance of another.
- Example : throwing a tennis ball over the net overarm may positively influence the player's arm action in the serve.

- Takes place if :
    - Skills are similar.
    - Skills performed in similar environment.
    - Information processing is similar.
    - Previous skill must be thoroughly learned.

425
retroactive   positive
proactive
TRANSFER
bilateral   zero   negative

Information

TRANSFER (continued)

PROACTIVE TRANSFER
- Influence of one skill on a skill yet to be learned.
- Example : having learned the forehand drive in tennis, the action is then modified to the forehand drive with top spin.

BILATERAL TRANSFER
- This is the transfer which takes place from one limb to another. Sometimes called lateralisation.
- Example : a soccer player learns to kick a ball with the non-preferred foot, the actions are learnt through reference by the brain to the preferred foot.

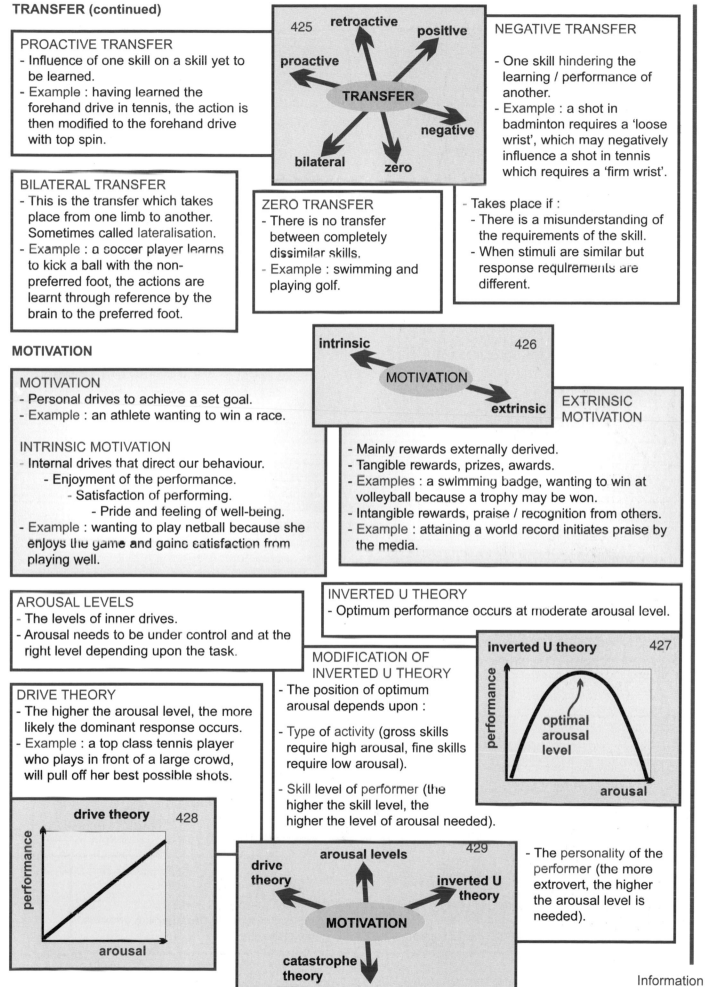

425
retroactive
positive
proactive
TRANSFER
negative
bilateral
zero

ZERO TRANSFER
- There is no transfer between completely dissimilar skills.
- Example : swimming and playing golf.

NEGATIVE TRANSFER
- One skill hindering the learning / performance of another.
- Example : a shot in badminton requires a 'loose wrist', which may negatively influence a shot in tennis which requires a 'firm wrist'.

- Takes place if :
  - There is a misunderstanding of the requirements of the skill.
  - When stimuli are similar but response requirements are different.

MOTIVATION

MOTIVATION
- Personal drives to achieve a set goal.
- Example : an athlete wanting to win a race.

INTRINSIC MOTIVATION
- Internal drives that direct our behaviour.
  - Enjoyment of the performance.
    - Satisfaction of performing.
      - Pride and feeling of well-being.
- Example : wanting to play netball because she enjoys the game and gains satisfaction from playing well.

intrinsic
426
MOTIVATION
extrinsic

EXTRINSIC MOTIVATION
- Mainly rewards externally derived.
- Tangible rewards, prizes, awards.
- Examples : a swimming badge, wanting to win at volleyball because a trophy may be won.
- Intangible rewards, praise / recognition from others.
- Example : attaining a world record initiates praise by the media.

AROUSAL LEVELS
- The levels of inner drives.
- Arousal needs to be under control and at the right level depending upon the task.

DRIVE THEORY
- The higher the arousal level, the more likely the dominant response occurs.
- Example : a top class tennis player who plays in front of a large crowd, will pull off her best possible shots.

INVERTED U THEORY
- Optimum performance occurs at moderate arousal level.

inverted U theory   427
performance
optimal arousal level
arousal

MODIFICATION OF INVERTED U THEORY
- The position of optimum arousal depends upon :
- Type of activity (gross skills require high arousal, fine skills require low arousal).
- Skill level of performer (the higher the skill level, the higher the level of arousal needed).
- The personality of the performer (the more extrovert, the higher the arousal level is needed).

drive theory   428
performance
arousal

429
arousal levels
drive theory
inverted U theory
MOTIVATION
catastrophe theory

MOTIVATION (continued)

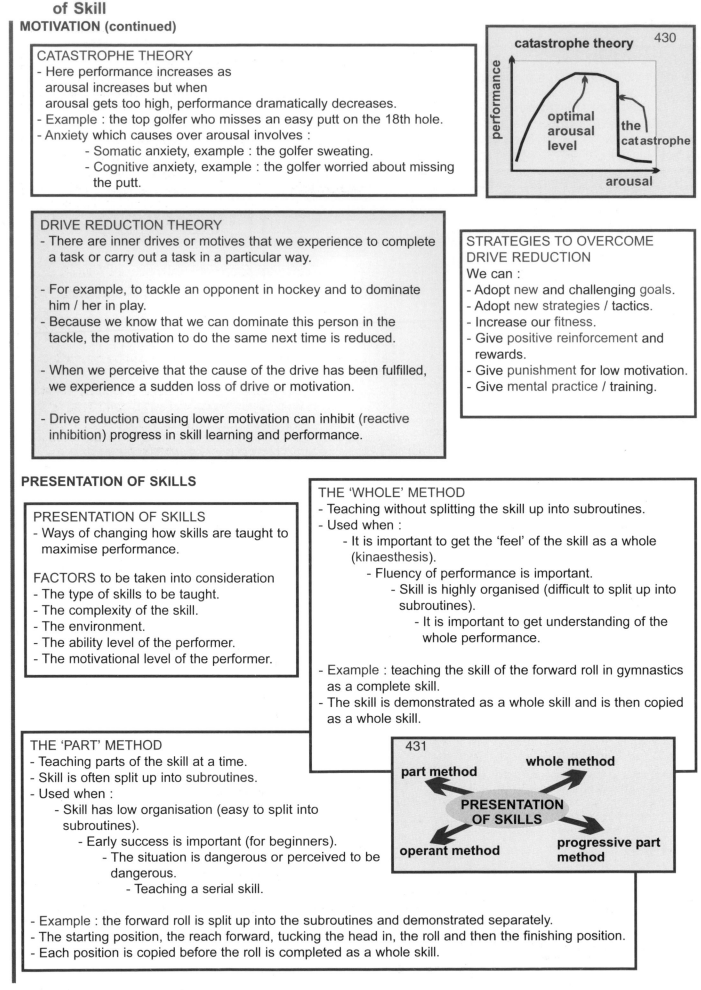

CATASTROPHE THEORY
- Here performance increases as
  arousal increases but when
  arousal gets too high, performance dramatically decreases.
- Example : the top golfer who misses an easy putt on the 18th hole.
- Anxiety which causes over arousal involves :
  - Somatic anxiety, example : the golfer sweating.
  - Cognitive anxiety, example : the golfer worried about missing the putt.

catastrophe theory   430
performance / optimal arousal level / the catastrophe / arousal

DRIVE REDUCTION THEORY
- There are inner drives or motives that we experience to complete a task or carry out a task in a particular way.

- For example, to tackle an opponent in hockey and to dominate him / her in play.
- Because we know that we can dominate this person in the tackle, the motivation to do the same next time is reduced.

- When we perceive that the cause of the drive has been fulfilled, we experience a sudden loss of drive or motivation.

- Drive reduction causing lower motivation can inhibit (reactive inhibition) progress in skill learning and performance.

STRATEGIES TO OVERCOME DRIVE REDUCTION
We can :
- Adopt new and challenging goals.
- Adopt new strategies / tactics.
- Increase our fitness.
- Give positive reinforcement and rewards.
- Give punishment for low motivation.
- Give mental practice / training.

PRESENTATION OF SKILLS

PRESENTATION OF SKILLS
- Ways of changing how skills are taught to maximise performance.

FACTORS to be taken into consideration
- The type of skills to be taught.
- The complexity of the skill.
- The environment.
- The ability level of the performer.
- The motivational level of the performer.

THE 'WHOLE' METHOD
- Teaching without splitting the skill up into subroutines.
- Used when :
  - It is important to get the 'feel' of the skill as a whole (kinaesthesis).
    - Fluency of performance is important.
      - Skill is highly organised (difficult to split up into subroutines).
        - It is important to get understanding of the whole performance.

- Example : teaching the skill of the forward roll in gymnastics as a complete skill.
- The skill is demonstrated as a whole skill and is then copied as a whole skill.

THE 'PART' METHOD
- Teaching parts of the skill at a time.
- Skill is often split up into subroutines.
- Used when :
  - Skill has low organisation (easy to split into subroutines).
    - Early success is important (for beginners).
      - The situation is dangerous or perceived to be dangerous.
        - Teaching a serial skill.

431
part method   whole method
PRESENTATION OF SKILLS
operant method   progressive part method

- Example : the forward roll is split up into the subroutines and demonstrated separately.
- The starting position, the reach forward, tucking the head in, the roll and then the finishing position.
- Each position is copied before the roll is completed as a whole skill.

Information

PRESENTATION OF SKILLS (continued)

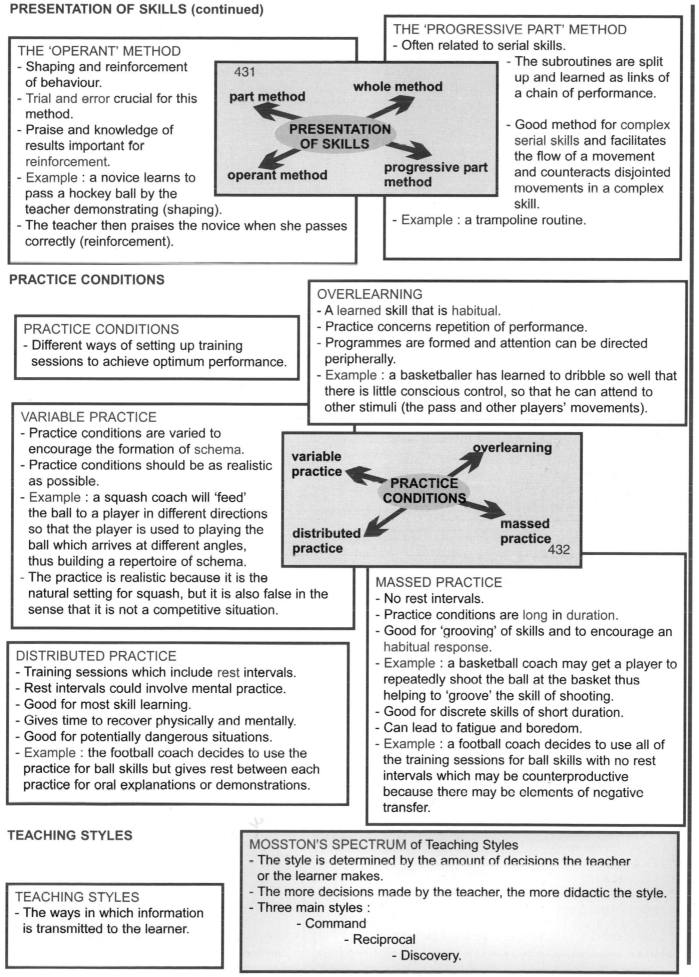

THE 'OPERANT' METHOD
- Shaping and reinforcement of behaviour.
- Trial and error crucial for this method.
- Praise and knowledge of results important for reinforcement.
- Example : a novice learns to pass a hockey ball by the teacher demonstrating (shaping).
- The teacher then praises the novice when she passes correctly (reinforcement).

THE 'PROGRESSIVE PART' METHOD
- Often related to serial skills.
- The subroutines are split up and learned as links of a chain of performance.
- Good method for complex serial skills and facilitates the flow of a movement and counteracts disjointed movements in a complex skill.
- Example : a trampoline routine.

431

part method — whole method
PRESENTATION OF SKILLS
operant method — progressive part method

PRACTICE CONDITIONS

PRACTICE CONDITIONS
- Different ways of setting up training sessions to achieve optimum performance.

OVERLEARNING
- A learned skill that is habitual.
- Practice concerns repetition of performance.
- Programmes are formed and attention can be directed peripherally.
- Example : a basketballer has learned to dribble so well that there is little conscious control, so that he can attend to other stimuli (the pass and other players' movements).

VARIABLE PRACTICE
- Practice conditions are varied to encourage the formation of schema.
- Practice conditions should be as realistic as possible.
- Example : a squash coach will 'feed' the ball to a player in different directions so that the player is used to playing the ball which arrives at different angles, thus building a repertoire of schema.
- The practice is realistic because it is the natural setting for squash, but it is also false in the sense that it is not a competitive situation.

variable practice — overlearning
PRACTICE CONDITIONS
distributed practice — massed practice
432

MASSED PRACTICE
- No rest intervals.
- Practice conditions are long in duration.
- Good for 'grooving' of skills and to encourage an habitual response.
- Example : a basketball coach may get a player to repeatedly shoot the ball at the basket thus helping to 'groove' the skill of shooting.
- Good for discrete skills of short duration.
- Can lead to fatigue and boredom.
- Example : a football coach decides to use all of the training sessions for ball skills with no rest intervals which may be counterproductive because there may be elements of negative transfer.

DISTRIBUTED PRACTICE
- Training sessions which include rest intervals.
- Rest intervals could involve mental practice.
- Good for most skill learning.
- Gives time to recover physically and mentally.
- Good for potentially dangerous situations.
- Example : the football coach decides to use the practice for ball skills but gives rest between each practice for oral explanations or demonstrations.

TEACHING STYLES

TEACHING STYLES
- The ways in which information is transmitted to the learner.

MOSSTON'S SPECTRUM of Teaching Styles
- The style is determined by the amount of decisions the teacher or the learner makes.
- The more decisions made by the teacher, the more didactic the style.
- Three main styles :
   - Command
     - Reciprocal
      - Discovery.

TEACHING STYLES (continued)

COMMAND
- Style which involves mostly the teacher making the decisions.
- Authoritarian and didactic.
- Example : in a hockey small game situation, the coach calls 'freeze' to preserve pitch position.

- Good for : novices, quick responses, dangerous situations, hostile groups, large groups.

- Not good for : high level performers, social interaction and creativity.

RECIPROCAL
- Style which involves learners becoming teachers of others.
- Example : the coach teaches the skill of a tumble turn to some of the swimmers, who in turn then teach others.
  - Good for :
    - social interaction
    - giving responsibility
    - personal development
    - feedback.
  - Not good for :
    - discipline
    - correct information delivered.
    - beginners
    - those who have poor communication skills.

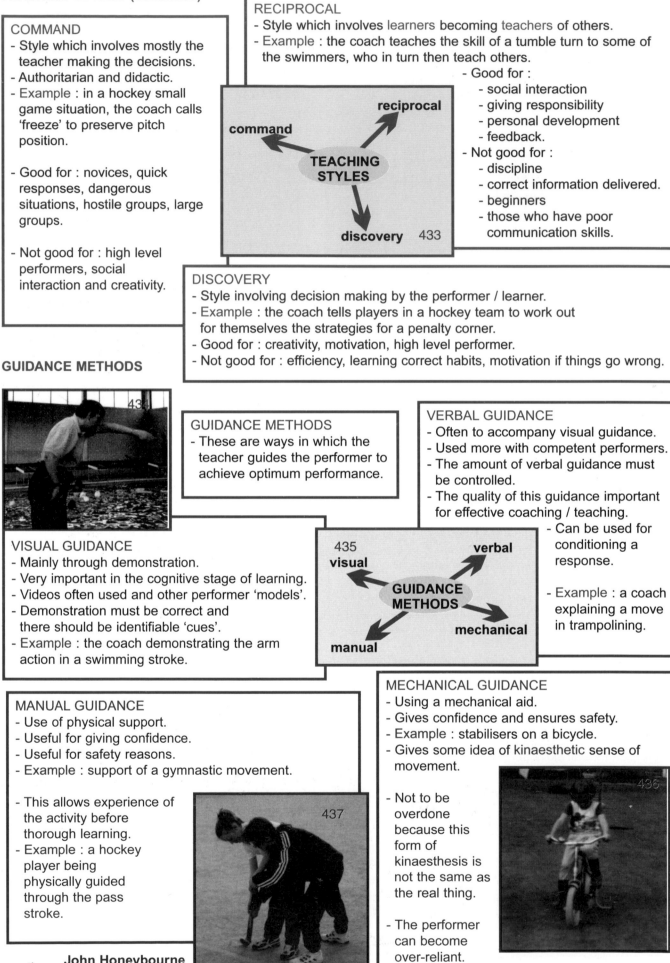

command ← **TEACHING STYLES** → reciprocal
↓
discovery 433

DISCOVERY
- Style involving decision making by the performer / learner.
- Example : the coach tells players in a hockey team to work out for themselves the strategies for a penalty corner.
- Good for : creativity, motivation, high level performer.
- Not good for : efficiency, learning correct habits, motivation if things go wrong.

GUIDANCE METHODS

434

GUIDANCE METHODS
- These are ways in which the teacher guides the performer to achieve optimum performance.

VERBAL GUIDANCE
- Often to accompany visual guidance.
- Used more with competent performers.
- The amount of verbal guidance must be controlled.
- The quality of this guidance important for effective coaching / teaching.
  - Can be used for conditioning a response.
  - Example : a coach explaining a move in trampolining.

VISUAL GUIDANCE
- Mainly through demonstration.
- Very important in the cognitive stage of learning.
- Videos often used and other performer 'models'.
- Demonstration must be correct and there should be identifiable 'cues'.
- Example : the coach demonstrating the arm action in a swimming stroke.

435
visual ← **GUIDANCE METHODS** → verbal
↓   ↓
manual   mechanical

MANUAL GUIDANCE
- Use of physical support.
- Useful for giving confidence.
- Useful for safety reasons.
- Example : support of a gymnastic movement.

- This allows experience of the activity before thorough learning.
- Example : a hockey player being physically guided through the pass stroke.

437

MECHANICAL GUIDANCE
- Using a mechanical aid.
- Gives confidence and ensures safety.
- Example : stabilisers on a bicycle.
- Gives some idea of kinaesthetic sense of movement.

- Not to be overdone because this form of kinaesthesis is not the same as the real thing.

- The performer can become over-reliant.

436

John Honeybourne

PSYCHOLOGY of SPORT

PERSONALITY

PERSONALITY
- The unique characteristics of an individual.
- No particular personality is suited for a particular sport.
- Knowledge about personality is important to ensure optimum performance.
- Example : a coach or teacher who knows what an individual is like in different situations, will know how to deal with that individual and to get the best out of him / her.

STABLE
- Behaviour is predictable.
- Example : a golfer who has an even temperament in most situations.

NEUROTIC
- Behaviour is unpredictable, often involving mood swings.
- Example : a soccer player who tends to fly off the handle if things are not going his way.

TRAIT APPROACH
- Innate characteristics.
- Enduring characteristics that individuals take to all situations.
- Example : the work of Eysenck.

SOCIAL LEARNING
- Behaviour is learned from others that are significant.
- Example : the work of Bandura.
- A soccer player might learn on the field behaviour (diving to obtain a penalty, or strutting and exhibitionism after scoring) from observing top players.

INTERACTIONIST
- A mixture of trait and social learning.
- B = f (p,e).
- (Behaviour is a result of the interaction of personality traits and the environment).
- Example : a soccer player may be an introvert after the game but reveals extrovert qualities during the game.

TYPE A
- Higher levels of stress, this person lacks tolerance and patience.
- Example : a gymnast who seems very anxious in most situations and does not suffer fools gladly.

TYPE B
- More relaxed, this person has low personal stress.
- Example : a volleyballer who tends to be calm in most situations and seems unflappable.

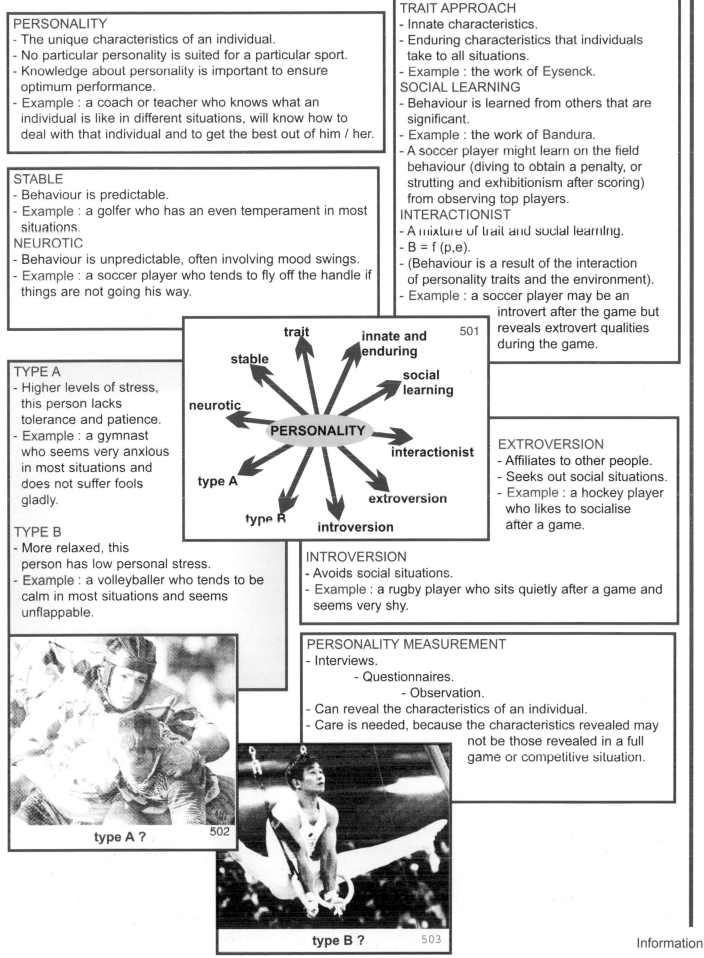

501

EXTROVERSION
- Affiliates to other people.
- Seeks out social situations.
- Example : a hockey player who likes to socialise after a game.

INTROVERSION
- Avoids social situations.
- Example : a rugby player who sits quietly after a game and seems very shy.

PERSONALITY MEASUREMENT
- Interviews.
   - Questionnaires.
      - Observation.
- Can reveal the characteristics of an individual.
- Care is needed, because the characteristics revealed may not be those revealed in a full game or competitive situation.

type A ? 502

type B ? 503

PERSONALITY (continued)

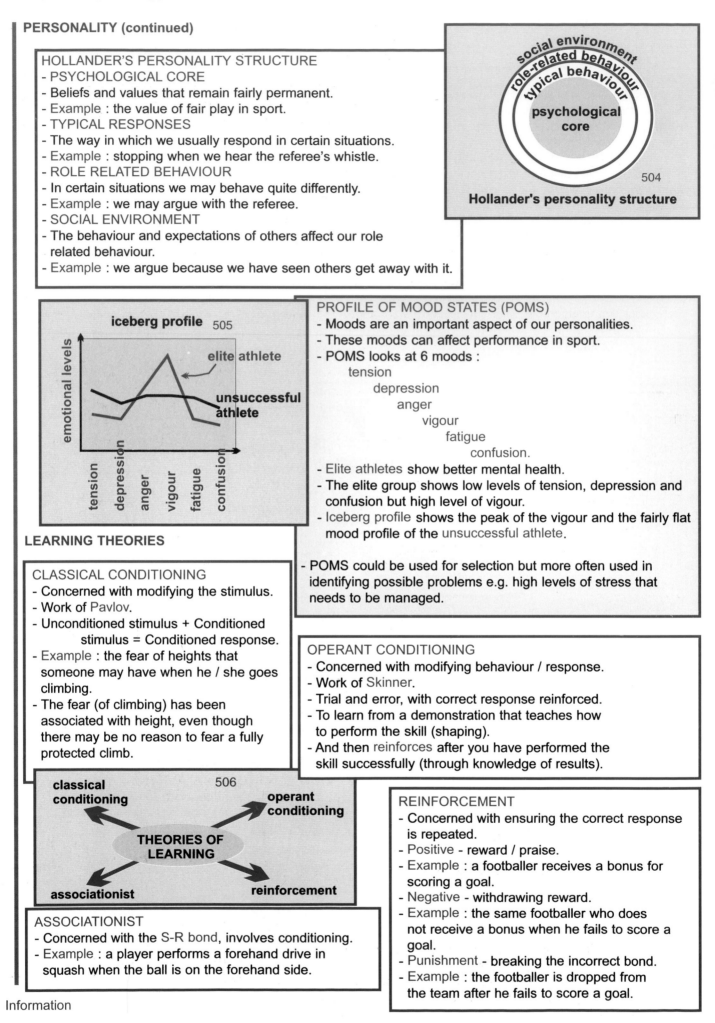

HOLLANDER'S PERSONALITY STRUCTURE
- PSYCHOLOGICAL CORE
- Beliefs and values that remain fairly permanent.
- Example : the value of fair play in sport.
- TYPICAL RESPONSES
- The way in which we usually respond in certain situations.
- Example : stopping when we hear the referee's whistle.
- ROLE RELATED BEHAVIOUR
- In certain situations we may behave quite differently.
- Example : we may argue with the referee.
- SOCIAL ENVIRONMENT
- The behaviour and expectations of others affect our role
  related behaviour.
- Example : we argue because we have seen others get away with it.

Hollander's personality structure 504

iceberg profile 505

PROFILE OF MOOD STATES (POMS)
- Moods are an important aspect of our personalities.
- These moods can affect performance in sport.
- POMS looks at 6 moods :
    tension
        depression
            anger
                vigour
                    fatigue
                        confusion.
- Elite athletes show better mental health.
- The elite group shows low levels of tension, depression and confusion but high level of vigour.
- Iceberg profile shows the peak of the vigour and the fairly flat mood profile of the unsuccessful athlete.

- POMS could be used for selection but more often used in identifying possible problems e.g. high levels of stress that needs to be managed.

LEARNING THEORIES

CLASSICAL CONDITIONING
- Concerned with modifying the stimulus.
- Work of Pavlov.
- Unconditioned stimulus + Conditioned
        stimulus = Conditioned response.
- Example : the fear of heights that someone may have when he / she goes climbing.
- The fear (of climbing) has been associated with height, even though there may be no reason to fear a fully protected climb.

OPERANT CONDITIONING
- Concerned with modifying behaviour / response.
- Work of Skinner.
- Trial and error, with correct response reinforced.
- To learn from a demonstration that teaches how to perform the skill (shaping).
- And then reinforces after you have performed the skill successfully (through knowledge of results).

506

THEORIES OF LEARNING

classical conditioning

operant conditioning

associationist

reinforcement

ASSOCIATIONIST
- Concerned with the S-R bond, involves conditioning.
- Example : a player performs a forehand drive in squash when the ball is on the forehand side.

REINFORCEMENT
- Concerned with ensuring the correct response is repeated.
- Positive - reward / praise.
- Example : a footballer receives a bonus for scoring a goal.
- Negative - withdrawing reward.
- Example : the same footballer who does not receive a bonus when he fails to score a goal.
- Punishment - breaking the incorrect bond.
- Example : the footballer is dropped from the team after he fails to score a goal.

ATTITUDES

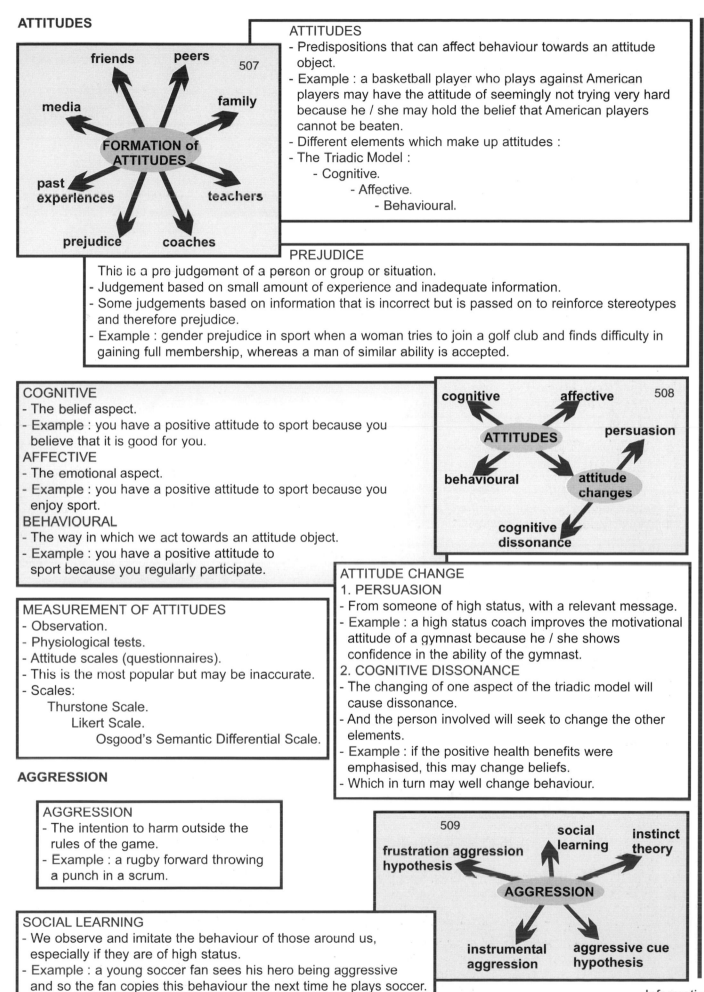

ATTITUDES
- Predispositions that can affect behaviour towards an attitude object.
- Example : a basketball player who plays against American players may have the attitude of seemingly not trying very hard because he / she may hold the belief that American players cannot be beaten.
- Different elements which make up attitudes :
- The Triadic Model :
    - Cognitive.
        - Affective.
            - Behavioural.

PREJUDICE
This is a pre judgement of a person or group or situation.
- Judgement based on small amount of experience and inadequate information.
- Some judgements based on information that is incorrect but is passed on to reinforce stereotypes and therefore prejudice.
- Example : gender prejudice in sport when a woman tries to join a golf club and finds difficulty in gaining full membership, whereas a man of similar ability is accepted.

COGNITIVE
- The belief aspect.
- Example : you have a positive attitude to sport because you believe that it is good for you.
AFFECTIVE
- The emotional aspect.
- Example : you have a positive attitude to sport because you enjoy sport.
BEHAVIOURAL
- The way in which we act towards an attitude object.
- Example : you have a positive attitude to sport because you regularly participate.

MEASUREMENT OF ATTITUDES
- Observation.
- Physiological tests.
- Attitude scales (questionnaires).
- This is the most popular but may be inaccurate.
- Scales:
    Thurstone Scale.
        Likert Scale.
            Osgood's Semantic Differential Scale.

ATTITUDE CHANGE
1. PERSUASION
- From someone of high status, with a relevant message.
- Example : a high status coach improves the motivational attitude of a gymnast because he / she shows confidence in the ability of the gymnast.
2. COGNITIVE DISSONANCE
- The changing of one aspect of the triadic model will cause dissonance.
- And the person involved will seek to change the other elements.
- Example : if the positive health benefits were emphasised, this may change beliefs.
- Which in turn may well change behaviour.

AGGRESSION

AGGRESSION
- The intention to harm outside the rules of the game.
- Example : a rugby forward throwing a punch in a scrum.

SOCIAL LEARNING
- We observe and imitate the behaviour of those around us, especially if they are of high status.
- Example : a young soccer fan sees his hero being aggressive and so the fan copies this behaviour the next time he plays soccer.

Information

AGGRESSION (continued)

FRUSTRATION - AGGRESSION HYPOTHESIS
- When goals are blocked, internal tension is created.
- To release the tension aggression takes place and catharsis is experienced.
- Frustration can occur due to :
    - Perceived unfairness.
    - Injury or poor personal play.
    - Spectator behaviour.
    - Provocation from opposition.
- Example : a netballer trips another player because her opponent is having a better game than her.

AGGRESSIVE CUE HYPOTHESIS
- Arousal level increases significantly because of increases in levels of frustration.
- Certain cues trigger off aggressive behaviour.
- Example : a football player may see an opponent push one of his fellow players.
- This is a cue for his own aggression and he joins in!

ACHIEVEMENT MOTIVATION

ACHIEVEMENT MOTIVATION
- Drive to succeed or persist with a task.

AROUSAL LEVELS
- The levels of inner drives.
- Arousal needs to be under control and at the right level depending upon the task.

DRIVE THEORY
- The higher the arousal level, the more likely the dominant response occurs.
- Example : a top class tennis player who plays in front of a large crowd, will pull off her best possible shots.

INSTINCT THEORY
- Says that aggression is innate.
- It has been retained throughout evolution, to defend territory and the species.
- Example : a boxer who bites ears could be said to be born with aggressive tendencies.

INSTRUMENTAL AGGRESSION
- This is channelled aggression.
- Forceful behaviour directed to achieve a goal within the rules of the game.
- Often referred to as assertion.
- Example : a hockey goalkeeper slides out and forcibly tackles a player and wins the ball.

INVERTED U THEORY
- Optimum performance occurs at moderate arousal level.

MODIFICATION OF INVERTED U THEORY
- The position of optimum arousal depends upon :

- Type of activity (gross skills require high arousal, fine skills require low arousal).
- Skill level of performer (the higher the skill level, the higher the level of arousal needed).

- The personality of the performer (the more extrovert, the higher the arousal level is needed).
                                          (Refer to 'RAS' page 5.5).

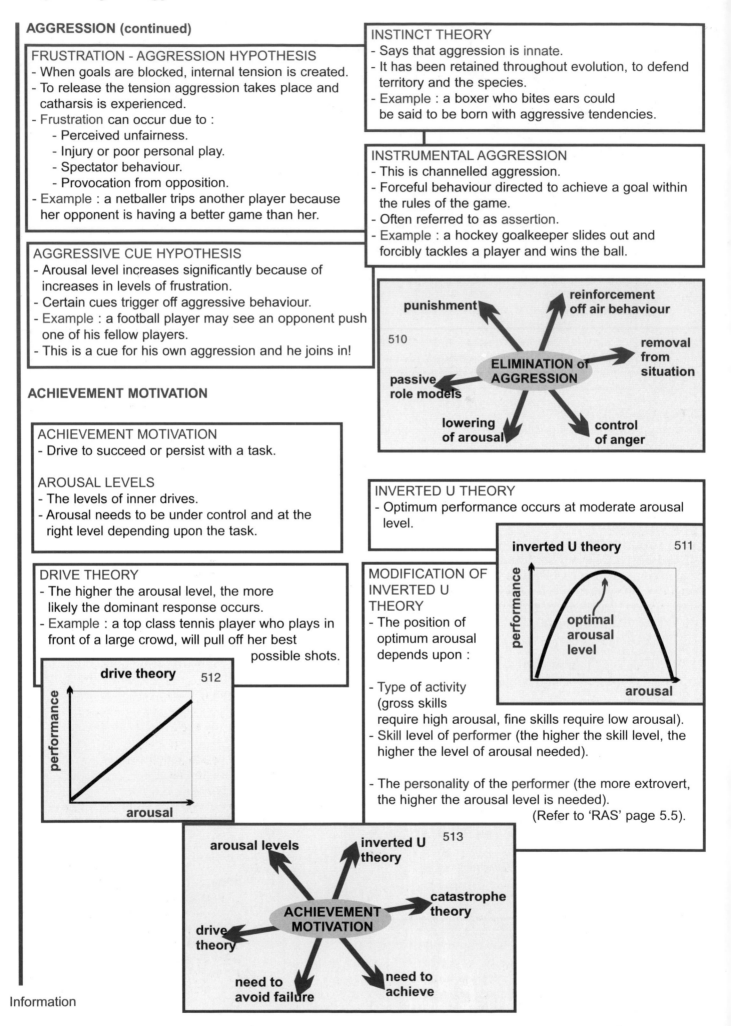

510 ELIMINATION of AGGRESSION — punishment, reinforcement off air behaviour, removal from situation, control of anger, lowering of arousal, passive role models

511 inverted U theory — optimal arousal level

512 drive theory

513 ACHIEVEMENT MOTIVATION — arousal levels, inverted U theory, catastrophe theory, need to achieve, need to avoid failure, drive theory

ACHIEVEMENT MOTIVATION (continued)

CATASTROPHE THEORY
- Here performance increases as arousal increases but when arousal gets too high, performance dramatically decreases.
- Example : the top golfer who misses an easy putt on the 18th hole.
- Anxiety which causes over arousal involves:
    - Somatic anxiety, example : the golfer sweating.
    - Cognitive anxiety, example : the golfer worried about missing the putt.

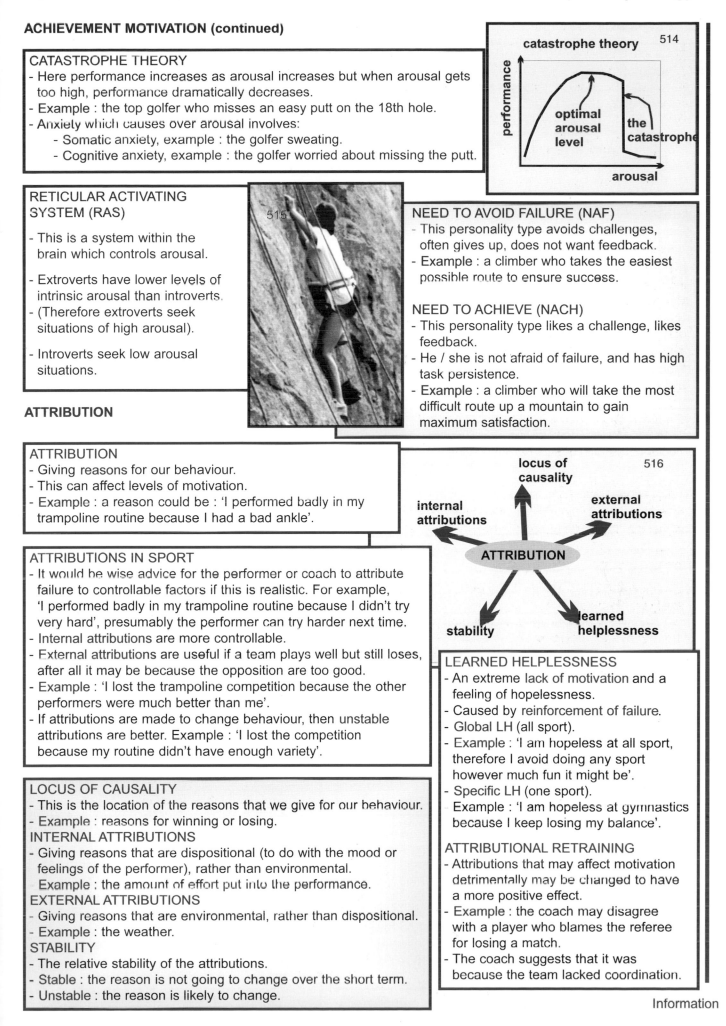

RETICULAR ACTIVATING SYSTEM (RAS)
- This is a system within the brain which controls arousal.
- Extroverts have lower levels of intrinsic arousal than introverts.
- (Therefore extroverts seek situations of high arousal).
- Introverts seek low arousal situations.

NEED TO AVOID FAILURE (NAF)
- This personality type avoids challenges, often gives up, does not want feedback.
- Example : a climber who takes the easiest possible route to ensure success.

NEED TO ACHIEVE (NACH)
- This personality type likes a challenge, likes feedback.
- He / she is not afraid of failure, and has high task persistence.
- Example : a climber who will take the most difficult route up a mountain to gain maximum satisfaction.

ATTRIBUTION

ATTRIBUTION
- Giving reasons for our behaviour.
- This can affect levels of motivation.
- Example : a reason could be : 'I performed badly in my trampoline routine because I had a bad ankle'.

ATTRIBUTIONS IN SPORT
- It would be wise advice for the performer or coach to attribute failure to controllable factors if this is realistic. For example, 'I performed badly in my trampoline routine because I didn't try very hard', presumably the performer can try harder next time.
- Internal attributions are more controllable.
- External attributions are useful if a team plays well but still loses, after all it may be because the opposition are too good.
- Example : 'I lost the trampoline competition because the other performers were much better than me'.
- If attributions are made to change behaviour, then unstable attributions are better. Example : 'I lost the competition because my routine didn't have enough variety'.

LOCUS OF CAUSALITY
- This is the location of the reasons that we give for our behaviour.
- Example : reasons for winning or losing.
INTERNAL ATTRIBUTIONS
- Giving reasons that are dispositional (to do with the mood or feelings of the performer), rather than environmental.
- Example : the amount of effort put into the performance.
EXTERNAL ATTRIBUTIONS
- Giving reasons that are environmental, rather than dispositional.
- Example : the weather.
STABILITY
- The relative stability of the attributions.
- Stable : the reason is not going to change over the short term.
- Unstable : the reason is likely to change.

LEARNED HELPLESSNESS
- An extreme lack of motivation and a feeling of hopelessness.
- Caused by reinforcement of failure.
- Global LH (all sport).
- Example : 'I am hopeless at all sport, therefore I avoid doing any sport however much fun it might be'.
- Specific LH (one sport).
- Example : 'I am hopeless at gymnastics because I keep losing my balance'.

ATTRIBUTIONAL RETRAINING
- Attributions that may affect motivation detrimentally may be changed to have a more positive effect.
- Example : the coach may disagree with a player who blames the referee for losing a match.
- The coach suggests that it was because the team lacked coordination.

SELF-EFFICACY

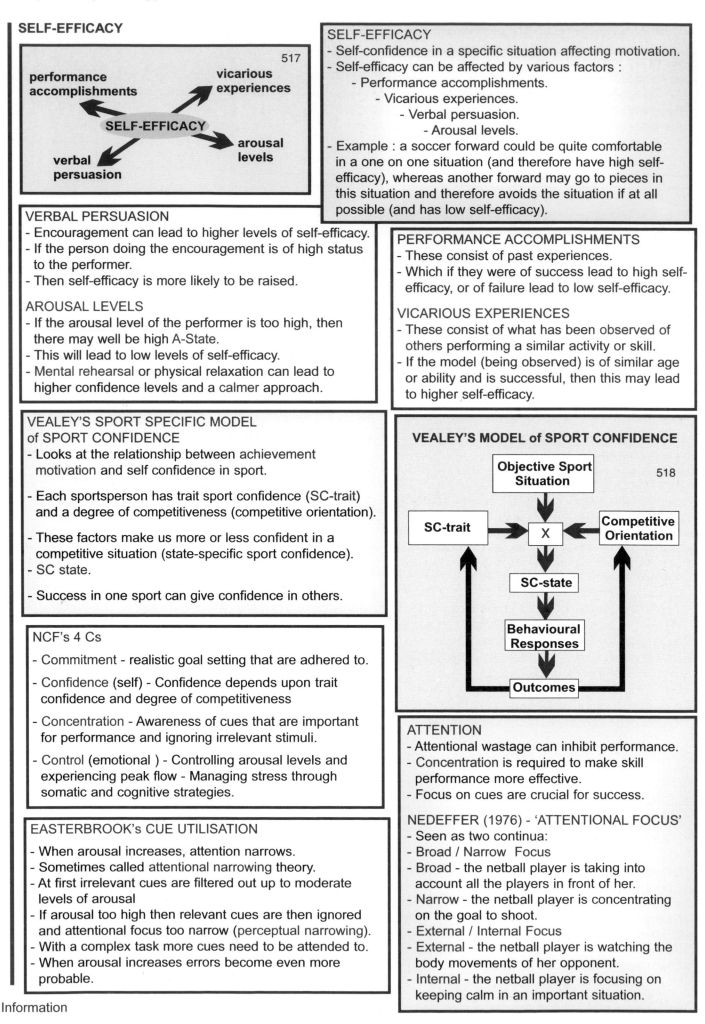

517

performance accomplishments

vicarious experiences

SELF-EFFICACY

verbal persuasion

arousal levels

SELF-EFFICACY
- Self-confidence in a specific situation affecting motivation.
- Self-efficacy can be affected by various factors :
    - Performance accomplishments.
        - Vicarious experiences.
            - Verbal persuasion.
                - Arousal levels.
- Example : a soccer forward could be quite comfortable in a one on one situation (and therefore have high self-efficacy), whereas another forward may go to pieces in this situation and therefore avoids the situation if at all possible (and has low self-efficacy).

VERBAL PERSUASION
- Encouragement can lead to higher levels of self-efficacy.
- If the person doing the encouragement is of high status to the performer.
- Then self-efficacy is more likely to be raised.

AROUSAL LEVELS
- If the arousal level of the performer is too high, then there may well be high A-State.
- This will lead to low levels of self-efficacy.
- Mental rehearsal or physical relaxation can lead to higher confidence levels and a calmer approach.

PERFORMANCE ACCOMPLISHMENTS
- These consist of past experiences.
- Which if they were of success lead to high self-efficacy, or of failure lead to low self-efficacy.

VICARIOUS EXPERIENCES
- These consist of what has been observed of others performing a similar activity or skill.
- If the model (being observed) is of similar age or ability and is successful, then this may lead to higher self-efficacy.

VEALEY'S SPORT SPECIFIC MODEL
of SPORT CONFIDENCE
- Looks at the relationship between achievement motivation and self confidence in sport.

- Each sportsperson has trait sport confidence (SC-trait) and a degree of competitiveness (competitive orientation).

- These factors make us more or less confident in a competitive situation (state-specific sport confidence).
- SC state.

- Success in one sport can give confidence in others.

VEALEY'S MODEL of SPORT CONFIDENCE

518

Objective Sport Situation

SC-trait → X ← Competitive Orientation

SC-state

Behavioural Responses

Outcomes

NCF's 4 Cs

- Commitment - realistic goal setting that are adhered to.

- Confidence (self) - Confidence depends upon trait confidence and degree of competitiveness

- Concentration - Awareness of cues that are important for performance and ignoring irrelevant stimuli.

- Control (emotional) - Controlling arousal levels and experiencing peak flow - Managing stress through somatic and cognitive strategies.

ATTENTION
- Attentional wastage can inhibit performance.
- Concentration is required to make skill performance more effective.
- Focus on cues are crucial for success.

NEDEFFER (1976) - 'ATTENTIONAL FOCUS'
- Seen as two continua:
- Broad / Narrow Focus
- Broad - the netball player is taking into account all the players in front of her.
- Narrow - the netball player is concentrating on the goal to shoot.
- External / Internal Focus
- External - the netball player is watching the body movements of her opponent.
- Internal - the netball player is focusing on keeping calm in an important situation.

EASTERBROOK's CUE UTILISATION

- When arousal increases, attention narrows.
- Sometimes called attentional narrowing theory.
- At first irrelevant cues are filtered out up to moderate levels of arousal
- If arousal too high then relevant cues are then ignored and attentional focus too narrow (perceptual narrowing).
- With a complex task more cues need to be attended to.
- When arousal increases errors become even more probable.

SOCIAL LEARNING

SOCIAL LEARNING
- Is important in the process of socialisation (adopting the norms and values of your culture).
- Example : a child will watch his / her mother's behaviour and copy it.
- Learning how to behave appropriately.
- Example : a player responding in a controlled way to an unfavourable refereeing decision.

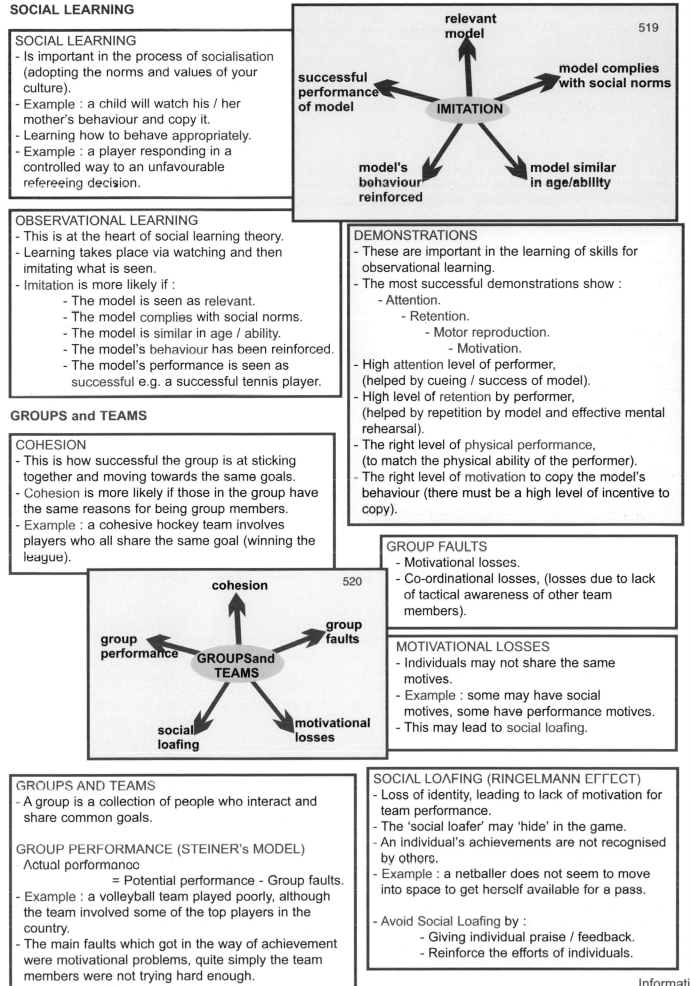

519

IMITATION
- relevant model
- model complies with social norms
- successful performance of model
- model's behaviour reinforced
- model similar in age/ability

OBSERVATIONAL LEARNING
- This is at the heart of social learning theory.
- Learning takes place via watching and then imitating what is seen.
- Imitation is more likely if :
  - The model is seen as relevant.
  - The model complies with social norms.
  - The model is similar in age / ability.
  - The model's behaviour has been reinforced.
  - The model's performance is seen as successful e.g. a successful tennis player.

DEMONSTRATIONS
- These are important in the learning of skills for observational learning.
- The most successful demonstrations show :
  - Attention.
    - Retention.
      - Motor reproduction.
        - Motivation.
- High attention level of performer, (helped by cueing / success of model).
- High level of retention by performer, (helped by repetition by model and effective mental rehearsal).
- The right level of physical performance, (to match the physical ability of the performer).
- The right level of motivation to copy the model's behaviour (there must be a high level of incentive to copy).

GROUPS and TEAMS

COHESION
- This is how successful the group is at sticking together and moving towards the same goals.
- Cohesion is more likely if those in the group have the same reasons for being group members.
- Example : a cohesive hockey team involves players who all share the same goal (winning the league).

520

GROUPS and TEAMS
- cohesion
- group faults
- group performance
- social loafing
- motivational losses

GROUP FAULTS
- Motivational losses.
- Co-ordinational losses, (losses due to lack of tactical awareness of other team members).

MOTIVATIONAL LOSSES
- Individuals may not share the same motives.
- Example : some may have social motives, some have performance motives.
- This may lead to social loafing.

GROUPS AND TEAMS
- A group is a collection of people who interact and share common goals.

GROUP PERFORMANCE (STEINER's MODEL)
Actual performance
= Potential performance - Group faults.
- Example : a volleyball team played poorly, although the team involved some of the top players in the country.
- The main faults which got in the way of achievement were motivational problems, quite simply the team members were not trying hard enough.

SOCIAL LOAFING (RINGELMANN EFFECT)
- Loss of identity, leading to lack of motivation for team performance.
- The 'social loafer' may 'hide' in the game.
- An individual's achievements are not recognised by others.
- Example : a netballer does not seem to move into space to get herself available for a pass.

- Avoid Social Loafing by :
  - Giving individual praise / feedback.
  - Reinforce the efforts of individuals.

GROUPS and TEAMS (continued)

CARRON's ANTECEDENTS
These are pre-requisites for group cohesion :

1. Motives for individuals to join a group (Individual Orientation).
> Interpersonal attraction > Group goals > Social interaction > Group activities
> Rewards for being part of a group.
2. Motives of the group (Group Orientation).
> Group as a separate identity.
> Individual behaves differently in a group because of reponses to different stimuli.
> Desire for group success > Desire to avoid group failure.

SOCIAL FACILITATION

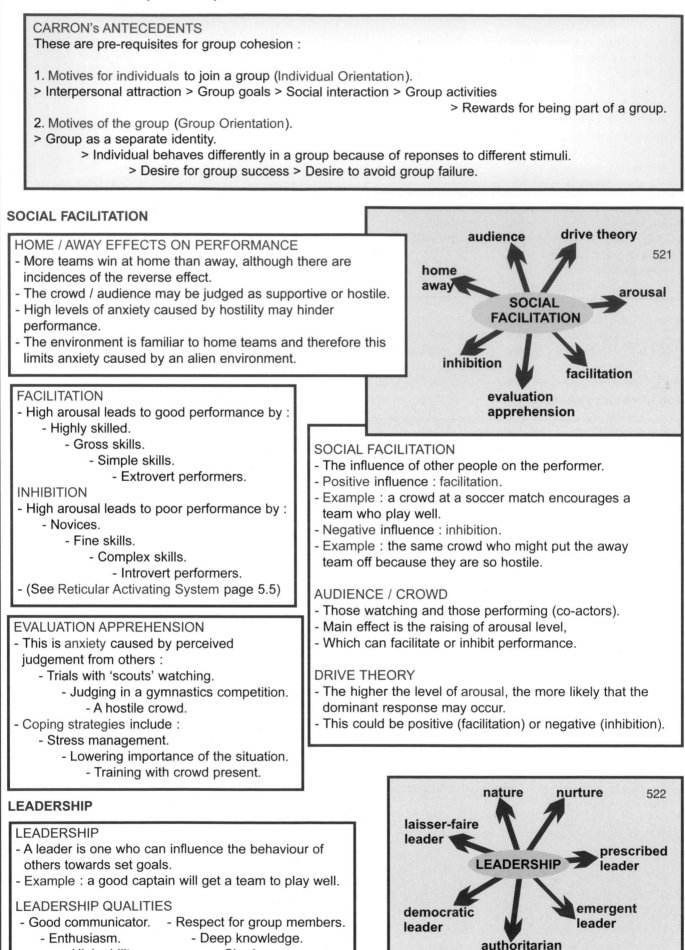

HOME / AWAY EFFECTS ON PERFORMANCE
- More teams win at home than away, although there are incidences of the reverse effect.
- The crowd / audience may be judged as supportive or hostile.
- High levels of anxiety caused by hostility may hinder performance.
- The environment is familiar to home teams and therefore this limits anxiety caused by an alien environment.

FACILITATION
- High arousal leads to good performance by :
    - Highly skilled.
        - Gross skills.
            - Simple skills.
                - Extrovert performers.
INHIBITION
- High arousal leads to poor performance by :
    - Novices.
        - Fine skills.
            - Complex skills.
                - Introvert performers.
- (See Reticular Activating System page 5.5)

EVALUATION APPREHENSION
- This is anxiety caused by perceived judgement from others :
    - Trials with 'scouts' watching.
        - Judging in a gymnastics competition.
            - A hostile crowd.
- Coping strategies include :
    - Stress management.
        - Lowering importance of the situation.
            - Training with crowd present.

SOCIAL FACILITATION
- The influence of other people on the performer.
- Positive influence : facilitation.
- Example : a crowd at a soccer match encourages a team who play well.
- Negative influence : inhibition.
- Example : the same crowd who might put the away team off because they are so hostile.

AUDIENCE / CROWD
- Those watching and those performing (co-actors).
- Main effect is the raising of arousal level,
- Which can facilitate or inhibit performance.

DRIVE THEORY
- The higher the level of arousal, the more likely that the dominant response may occur.
- This could be positive (facilitation) or negative (inhibition).

LEADERSHIP

LEADERSHIP
- A leader is one who can influence the behaviour of others towards set goals.
- Example : a good captain will get a team to play well.

LEADERSHIP QUALITIES
- Good communicator.   - Respect for group members.
    - Enthusiasm.   - Deep knowledge.
        - High ability.   - Charisma.

LEADERSHIP (continued)

NATURE
- This theory says that 'Leaders are born not made'.
- And leadership qualities are innate (for example, charisma).

NURTURE
- This notion says that leaders learn their skills through social learning, like for example watching and imitating models.

FIEDLER'S CONTINGENCY THEORY OF LEADERSHIP
- The effectiveness of a leader depends on the situation.
- If the situation is extremely favourable or extremely unfavourable, then task-oriented leaders are more effective.
- If the situation is moderately favourable then democratic leadership is more effective.
- Favourableness depends upon :
  - The power of the leader.
  - The complexity of the task.
  - Pressure of time.
  - Relationships with members of the group.

LEADERSHIP STYLES

AUTHORITARIAN
- This style is task-oriented, and is best for team motivation, large groups, hostile groups, dangerous situations and when time is short.
- Example : the coach who shouts instructions during a game.

DEMOCRATIC
- This style is person-oriented, and is best for individual performers, those who are highly skilled, and when problems need to be solved.
- Example : a team coach who asks the opinions of his team members so that collective decisions can be made.

LAISSEZ-FAIRE
- This is when no real leader position exists, and is best for highly motivated and skilled performers.
- Example : a coach who does not hold any type of meeting, and lets players play as they wish.

EMERGENT LEADERS
- Those that are chosen by the group from within the group.
- Example : a swimming team may vote for its captain.

PRESCRIBED LEADERS
- Those who are appointed by an external body to a group.
- Example : the team is told who their captain is by the management committee.

STYLES
- Depend on :
  - Situation.
    - Leader's personality.
      - Group members' personalities.

CHELLADURAI's MULTI-DIMENSIONAL MODEL

523

CHELLADURAI's MULTIDIMENSIONAL MODEL (LEADERSHIP)
- A sports specific model.
- The effectiveness of the style adopted by the leader depends on:
1. The situation.
2. Characteristics of the leader.
3. Demands of the group.
- To achieve high quality of performance & high levels of team satisfaction, a leader must be able to adapt.
- The more closely actual behaviour of leader matches the preferred behaviour of the group and the type of leadership demanded by the situation, then the greater chance of high performance and high levels of team satisfaction.

STRESS

524

STRESS
- Levels of stress depend upon our perception of demands and our abilities to cope with the demands.
POSITIVE ASPECTS
- Stress will drive us to achieve more.
- It is human nature to challenge the body / mind.
- Stress can help to avoid dangerous situations.
- Example : the athlete who runs faster if he is frightened of the consequences of losing.

STRESS (continued)

ANXIETY
- This is the negative aspect of stress response.

- A-Trait = Trait anxiety, which is enduring, and an innate part of the personality of the person involved.
- Example : a cross country runner who never appears to be anxious in any situation.

- A-State = State anxiety, which is only experienced in certain situations.
- Example : the cricket player who only gets anxious when it is time to bat.
- High A-trait leads to high A-State.
- Indicated through the SCAT test.

PEAK FLOW EXPERIENCE (PFE)
- Many elite athletes refer to the 'In zone'.
- This is when the athlete is fully focused on the task in hand and is not distracted by any other stimuli.

- The emotional state of the athlete during this 'super concentration' has been described as the peak flow experience.

- PFE is a state of euphoria and optimism when all the skills seem to flow.
- Example : a skier who feels that every movement he makes is perfect and flows into the next movement. He feels in control and knows that he will win.

GOAL SETTING

GOAL SETTING
- Can increase motivation and control stress / anxiety.
- Example : a golfer sets a target of shots to be played around a course, this may well motivate him to play well.

TYPES OF GOALS
- Outcome - this would be the end result of the activity.
- Example : a goal for a swimmer could be to win a race.
- Performance - judging against other performances.
- Example : a goal for a swimmer may be to beat his or her best time.
- Process - this would be related to techniques or the way in which the activity is undertaken.
- Example : the goal might be to improve the swimmer's leg kick action.

SHORT-TERM GOALS
- These are more process oriented and lead on to long-term aims.
- Example : a sprinter tries to improve her start technique.

LONG-TERM GOALS
- These are more product oriented and are to be achieved over a long period of time.
- They must be attainable to be motivating.
- Example : the sprinter aims to get into the British Olympic Team.

STRESS RESPONSE
- General Adaptation Syndrome (GAS) :
  - Alarm reaction.
    - Resistance.
      - Exhaustion.

MEASUREMENT OF STRESS
- Questionnaires are easy to administer but there is a response bias (people may give an answer which they think the coach would like rather than their own response).
- Observation of behaviour :
  - Real life / high ecological validity.
  - But high demand characteristics.
- Physiological measures :
  - Are objective.
  - But could interfere with anxiety response.
  - Difficult to administer.

STRESS MANAGEMENT
- Lowering of arousal levels :
  - Cognitive (positive thinking, imagery).
  - Somatic (relaxation of the body).

MULTIDIMENSIONAL ANXIETY THEORY
- In a competitive situation anxiety is made up of three components:
1. Cognitive state anxiety.
2. Somatic state anxiety.
3. Self confidence (affected by expectations of success or failure.
- Moderate level of somatic state anxiety increases optimum performance.
- Low level of cognitive state anxiety increases optimum performance.

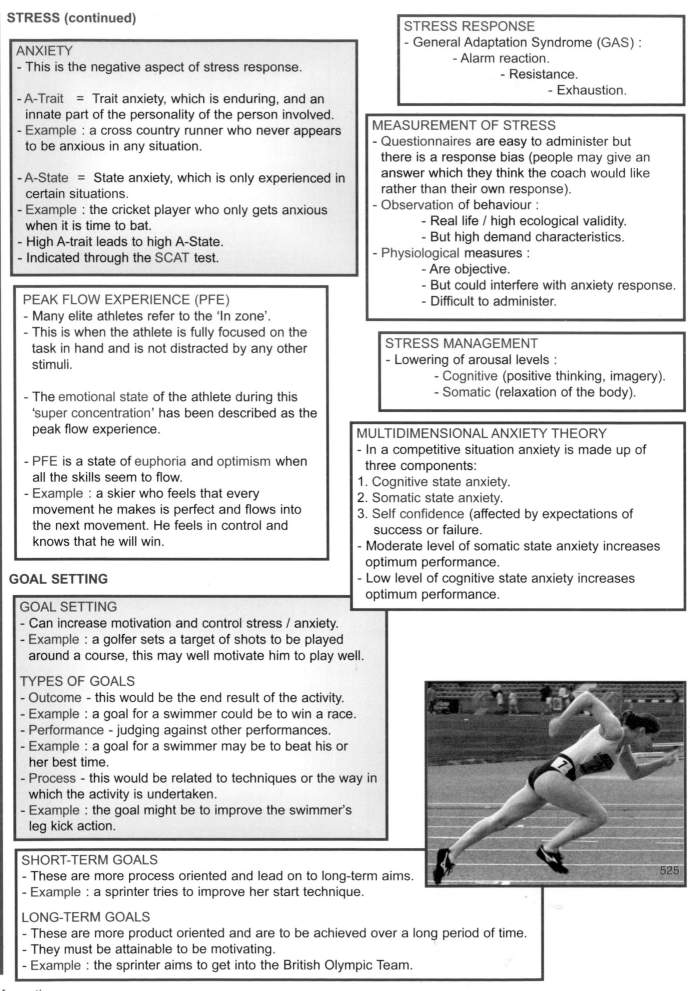

525

GOAL SETTING (continued)

SMARTER GOALS (NCF)

S - Specific - Clear and unambiguous.
M - Measurable - Important for monitoring.
A - Agreed - Sharing of goal setting between coach and performer.
R - Realistic - motivation will improve.
T - Timed - Short-term goals that are progressive.
E - Exciting - Stimulating activities.
R - Recorded - For monitoring and motivation.

John Honeybourne

FACTORS AFFECTING GOAL SETTING

- Set goals that are achievable but challenging.
- Goals must be clear and specific and relevant.
- They need to progress from short-term to long-term.
- They need to be measured as time goes on.
- They also need to be evaluated and modified if necessary.
- Goals that are shared between performer and the coach are more effective.

CONCEPTS

LEISURE

LEISURE
- Leisure is time in which there is opportunity for choice (Arnold).
- Leisure consists of relatively self-determining activity-experiences which fall into one's economically free-time roles (Kaplan).

LEISURE
- We can recognise it because it is an activity (apart from obligations).
- This involves :   free time
                    choice
                    opportunity.

LEISURE
- It functions as an activity (positive attempt to allow) :
        free development (personal choice)
        relaxation (recovery)
        re-creation (creative opportunity).

- Leisure is more than an activity, it is a valuable experience.

- Leisure is potentially : self-realising
                            socialising and
                            culturally civilising.

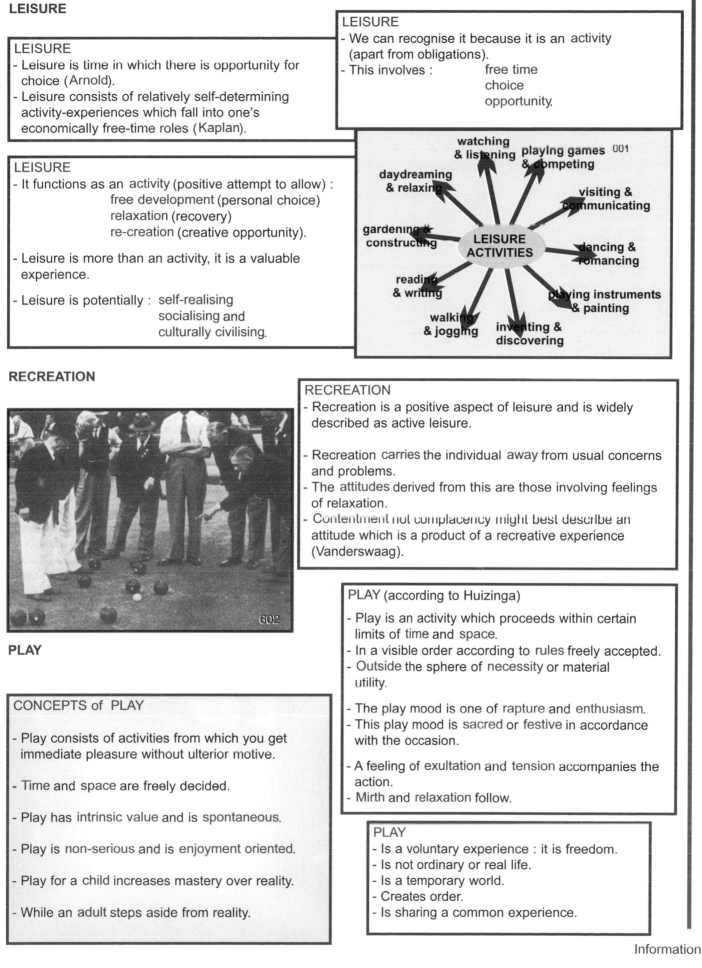

LEISURE ACTIVITIES
- watching & listening
- playing games & competing 001
- daydreaming & relaxing
- visiting & communicating
- gardening & constructing
- dancing & romancing
- reading & writing
- playing instruments & painting
- walking & jogging
- inventing & discovering

RECREATION

RECREATION
- Recreation is a positive aspect of leisure and is widely described as active leisure.

- Recreation carries the individual away from usual concerns and problems.
- The attitudes derived from this are those involving feelings of relaxation.
- Contentment not complacency might best describe an attitude which is a product of a recreative experience (Vanderswaag).

602

PLAY

CONCEPTS of PLAY

- Play consists of activities from which you get immediate pleasure without ulterior motive.

- Time and space are freely decided.

- Play has intrinsic value and is spontaneous.

- Play is non-serious and is enjoyment oriented.

- Play for a child increases mastery over reality.

- While an adult steps aside from reality.

PLAY (according to Huizinga)

- Play is an activity which proceeds within certain limits of time and space.
- In a visible order according to rules freely accepted.
- Outside the sphere of necessity or material utility.

- The play mood is one of rapture and enthusiasm.
- This play mood is sacred or festive in accordance with the occasion.

- A feeling of exultation and tension accompanies the action.
- Mirth and relaxation follow.

PLAY
- Is a voluntary experience : it is freedom.
- Is not ordinary or real life.
- Is a temporary world.
- Creates order.
- Is sharing a common experience.

PHYSICAL RECREATION

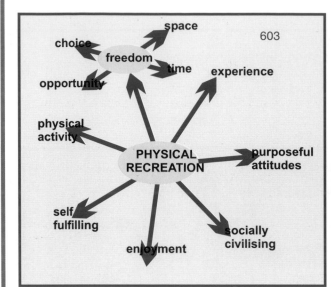

RECREATION
- Recreation is a concept closely related to play.
- It means literally to re-create or to refresh oneself in body and / or engagement.
- Recreational activity is also limited in time and space by the actor.
- It requires no preparation or training.

PHYSICAL RECREATION
- Recreation is also non-utilitarian in product (Edwards).
- Physical recreation identifies with recreative attitudes in a physical activity.
- Physically challenging without necessarily being competitive.

OUTDOOR RECREATION
- This is physical activity in the natural environment which includes the notion of adventure.

SPORT

SPORT
- Is an institutionalised competitive activity that involves vigorous physical exertion.
- Or the use of relatively complex physical skills.
- By individuals whose participation is motivated by a combination of :
    - Intrinsic satisfaction associated with the activity itself.
    - And external rewards earned through participation (Coakley).

CHARACTERISTICS of SPORT

- Any physical activity which has the character of play and which takes the form of a struggle with oneself or involves competition with others is a sport.

- If this activity involves competition, then it should always be performed with a spirit of sportsmanship. There can be no true sport without the idea of fair play.

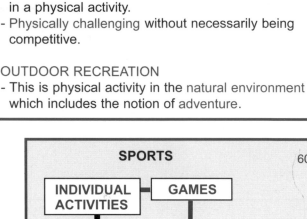

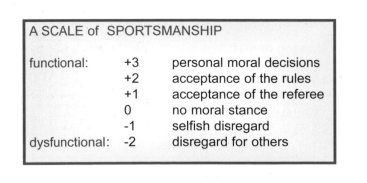

A SCALE of SPORTSMANSHIP

functional:	+3	personal moral decisions
	+2	acceptance of the rules
	+1	acceptance of the referee
	0	no moral stance
	-1	selfish disregard
dysfunctional:	-2	disregard for others

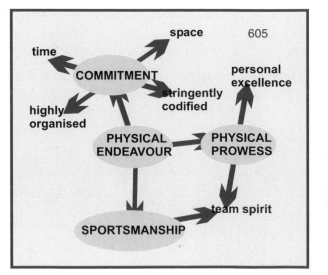

PHYSICAL EDUCATION

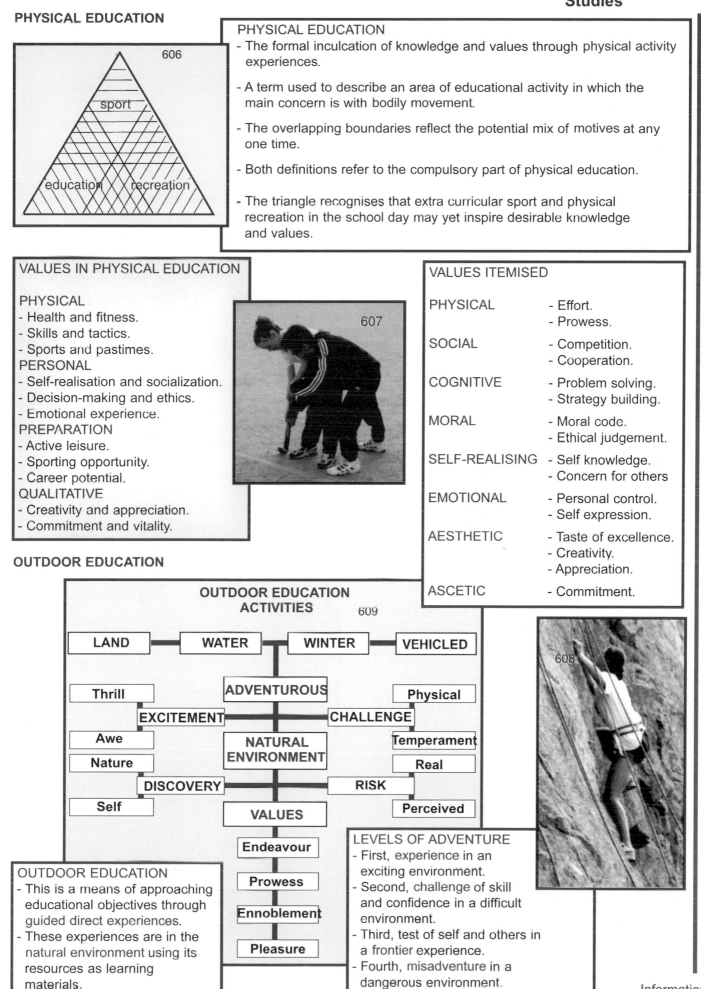

606

sport

education   recreation

PHYSICAL EDUCATION
- The formal inculcation of knowledge and values through physical activity experiences.

- A term used to describe an area of educational activity in which the main concern is with bodily movement.

- The overlapping boundaries reflect the potential mix of motives at any one time.

- Both definitions refer to the compulsory part of physical education.

- The triangle recognises that extra curricular sport and physical recreation in the school day may yet inspire desirable knowledge and values.

VALUES IN PHYSICAL EDUCATION

PHYSICAL
- Health and fitness.
- Skills and tactics.
- Sports and pastimes.
PERSONAL
- Self-realisation and socialization.
- Decision-making and ethics.
- Emotional experience.
PREPARATION
- Active leisure.
- Sporting opportunity.
- Career potential.
QUALITATIVE
- Creativity and appreciation.
- Commitment and vitality.

607

VALUES ITEMISED

PHYSICAL	- Effort. - Prowess.
SOCIAL	- Competition. - Cooperation.
COGNITIVE	- Problem solving. - Strategy building.
MORAL	- Moral code. - Ethical judgement.
SELF-REALISING	- Self knowledge. - Concern for others
EMOTIONAL	- Personal control. - Self expression.
AESTHETIC	- Taste of excellence. - Creativity. - Appreciation.
ASCETIC	- Commitment.

OUTDOOR EDUCATION

OUTDOOR EDUCATION ACTIVITIES
609

LAND	WATER	WINTER	VEHICLED

Thrill	ADVENTUROUS	Physical

EXCITEMENT CHALLENGE

Awe	NATURAL	Temperament

ENVIRONMENT

Nature		Real

DISCOVERY RISK

Self	VALUES	Perceived

Endeavour

Prowess

Ennoblement

Pleasure

608

LEVELS OF ADVENTURE
- First, experience in an exciting environment.
- Second, challenge of skill and confidence in a difficult environment.
- Third, test of self and others in a frontier experience.
- Fourth, misadventure in a dangerous environment.

OUTDOOR EDUCATION
- This is a means of approaching educational objectives through guided direct experiences.
- These experiences are in the natural environment using its resources as learning materials.

Information

SPORT AND CULTURE
TRIBAL CULTURE

SPORT AND TRIBAL CULTURE (example SAMOA)
- There are still many tribal communities such as the Polynesians, Eskimos and Aborigines, where the original tribal sports and pastimes can still be found.
- They reflect the needs of the community in terms of survival in the natural world.
- But also ritual and festival elements which bound the community together.
- The advent of Colonialism led to subjugation, ritual curtailment and social conditioning through colonial conquest, education and sports.
- Today we find a re-emergence of the old culture where games have gone through adaptation, reversion or adoption.

EMERGENT CULTURE

EMERGENT COUNTRIES
- Nation Building.
  Racial Integration.
    Improved Health.
      Increased Social Control.

DISPROPORTIONATE FUNDING
Elitism.
  Selectivity.
    Occupational.
      Excellence.
INTERNAL APPEASEMENT / EXTERNAL EXPOSURE
Role models.   World arena.
  Opportunity.   Fundings return.
    Provision.   Talent pay-back.

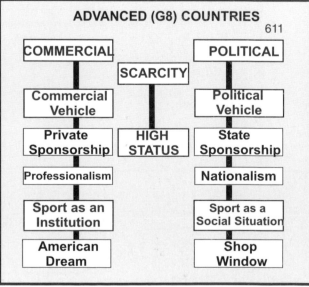

ADVANCED CULTURE

SPORT IN ADVANCED CULTURES
COMMERCIAL - POLITICAL
- In looking at advanced industrialised countries, identifiable as the G8.
- There is a political and socio-economic polarisation from the American extreme of a multi-party democracy and capitalism, identifiable as the 'American Dream'.
- To the old Soviet Union and countries like China (authoritarian single party control existing in a Marxist-socialist society), identifiable in the 'Shop Window'.
- Most West European countries lie between these two, as alternative conservative - socialist governments working within a mixed economy.
- In the US model, sport exists as a social institution, where a technical, managerial and corporate organisation is present.
- And as a social situation where sport occurs at a producer and consumer level.
- In the case of the capitalist model, commercialism and the professionalisation of sport is uppermost.
- Whereas the socialist model has a political agenda.
- In both cases mass participation & sporting excellence is endorsed at voluntary, public and private levels.
- But varying in terms of the domination of one of these.

ETHNIC SPORTS AND PASTIMES
Survival - related to warfare.
  Economic.
    Social - related to ritual.
COLONIAL CONQUEST AND IMPOSITION
Military (force).
  Diplomatic (social control).
    Economic (trade).
      Rational sports (school games).
        Missionary (Christianity).
POST-COLONIAL EMERGENCE
Adaptation - (Samoan Rugby).
  Reversion - (Trobriand Cricket).
    Adoption - (Bungee Jumping).

SPORT AND EMERGENT CULTURE (example KENYA)
- Many countries have progressed beyond their tribal origins and as 'Third World Countries' are striving to improve the quality of life.
- This is where sport is seen as a way of satisfying the needs of the people and achieving exposure for the country.
- There is a process of nation building and integration together with a need for improved health and social control.
- The process chosen is elitist, where disproportionate support for one sport is used to achieve world recognition.
- Examples of this include Kenyan Athletics, West Indian Cricket, Nigerian Boxing, Indonesian Badminton and Brazilian Soccer.
- Success has led to other sports being expanded in each country.
- And elitist principles being at least partly relaxed.
- As success in a sport has led to exposure on the world stage.
- And broader status being given to the significance of sport as a political vehicle.

ADVANCED (G8) COUNTRIES

611

COMMERCIAL		POLITICAL
	SCARCITY	
Commercial Vehicle		Political Vehicle
Private Sponsorship	HIGH STATUS	State Sponsorship
Professionalism		Nationalism
Sport as an Institution		Sport as a Social Situation
American Dream		Shop Window

ISSUES

MASS PARTICIPATION IN SPORT

612

recreative ← **SPORT FOR ALL** → sportive

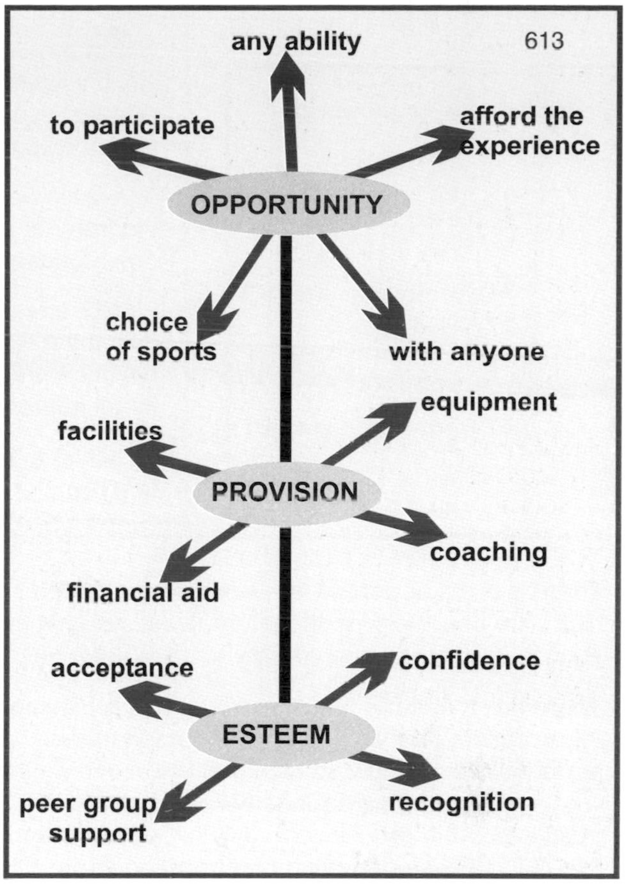

ETHNIC FESTIVALS UK

| TRADITIONAL (historical) | LOCAL (functional) |
| POPULAR (social) | ISOLATED (geographical) |

MAJOR CHARACTERISTICS

occasional
localised
festival
folklore
limited rules
violent
unique features

EXAMPLES

Highland games   Mob games
    Lakeland games   Wrestling

613

any ability

to participate   afford the experience

OPPORTUNITY

choice of sports   with anyone

equipment

facilities

PROVISION

coaching

financial aid

acceptance   confidence

ESTEEM

peer group support   recognition

614

MASS PARTICIPATION

| CHILDREN and YOUTH | ADULT | ELDERLY |

| curriculum equalities | leisure centre access | off-peak facilities |

| extra-curricular opportunities | competition and club access | life-time sports |

| structured outdoor experiences | open country pursuits | Tourist opportunities |

attendance ← **SPECTATOR** → media

615

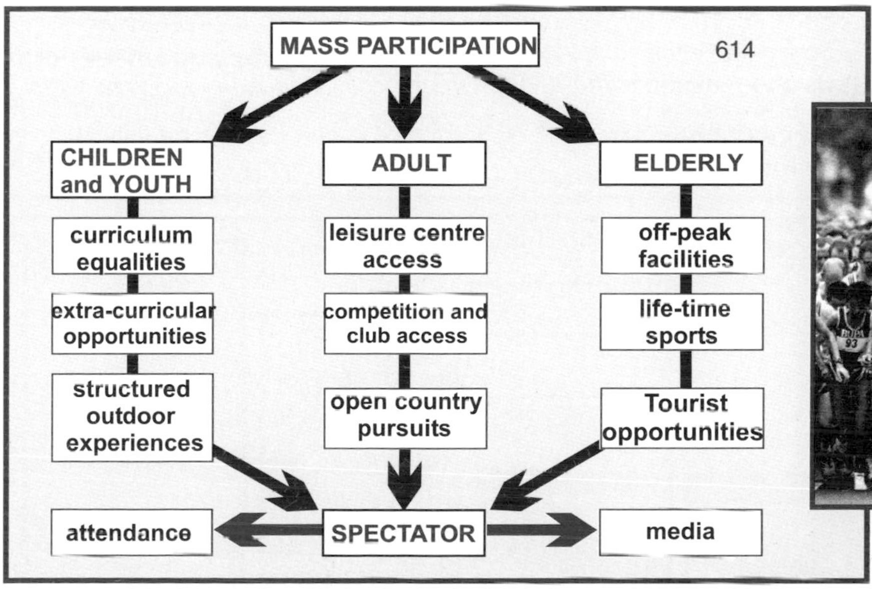

CULTURAL DETERMINANTS

IDEOLOGICAL	HISTORICAL	ENVIRONMENT	POLITICAL	SOCIOECONOMIC
participation ethic	self help	urbanisation	democracy	social ranking
equal opportunity	class status	moderate climate	welfare state	gender ranking
voluntarism	riparian owners	countryside in	decentralised	division of labour
individualism	sporting and	easy reach	administration	mode of production
romance of the	spectating tradition			comparative
countryside				influence

performance pyramid
616

- Excellence — stage 4
- Performance — stage 3
- Participation — stage 2
- Foundation — stage 1

EXCELLENCE
- A poor tribal society is likely to select a single sport with which to identify itself.
- One which is natural to the people, cheap to develop and unsophisticated, for example, marathon running in Ethiopia.
- An emerging country may start like that, as in Kenya, but broaden their programme as a result of role model success and exposure to the world.
- Their focus now is on nation-building and integration.
- Finally, advanced countries (for example the G8 top industrialised countries) like the UK, Australia, France and USA would be looking for a much broader pyramid of opportunity, provision for all and self-esteem for all minorities to participate.
- To achieve these targets disproportionate funding for sport is necessary for Olympic success.

EXCELLENCE IN SPORT - The Issue :
- There is a major debate in a world which places sport high as a barometer of the international political and economic success of a country.
- There are a number of different ways of achieving this.
- All recognise that the international standards of performance are now so high that disproportionate funding has become a fundamental necessity.
- In all cases the process can only be achieved through a pyramid process of getting promising performers to the top.
- But the shape of that pyramid depends on the extent to which elitism is operating, through necessity or design.

2. performer
4. official
1. activity
3. administrator
5. spectator

endeavour
prowess
fairplay
pleasure   617

EXCELLENCE and PROFESSIONALISATION
- The significance of extrinsic and intrinsic values leads to a balance between professional administrative standards and required levels of sportsmanship.
- Each of the five levels of participation shown in diagram 617 above need to be fully professionalised to establish excellence.

THE ACTIVE SPORTS DEVELOPMENT MODEL (2002)

SCHOOL PE AND EXTRA-CURRICULAR PROGRAMMES

MINI GAMES

TOPS PROGRAMMES

COMMUNITY PROGRAMMES

YOUTH CLUBS

PARTNERSHIP YOUTH GAMES

TALENT CAMPS

WORLD CLASS START

or equivalent programme

STAGE 1
LOCAL SCHEMES

local competition

coaching courses

STAGE 2
CLUB DEVELOPMENT

regular coaching

skills awards

competition

STAGE 3
ASSESSMENT

assessment days

selection process

STAGE 4
DEVELOPMENT SQUADS

advanced coaching / performance enhancement

only limited competition

REPRESENTATIVE SPORT AT COUNTY AND REGIONAL LEVELS
ADULT SPORTS CLUBS AND COMPETITIONS

Information

EXCELLENCE in SPORT continued

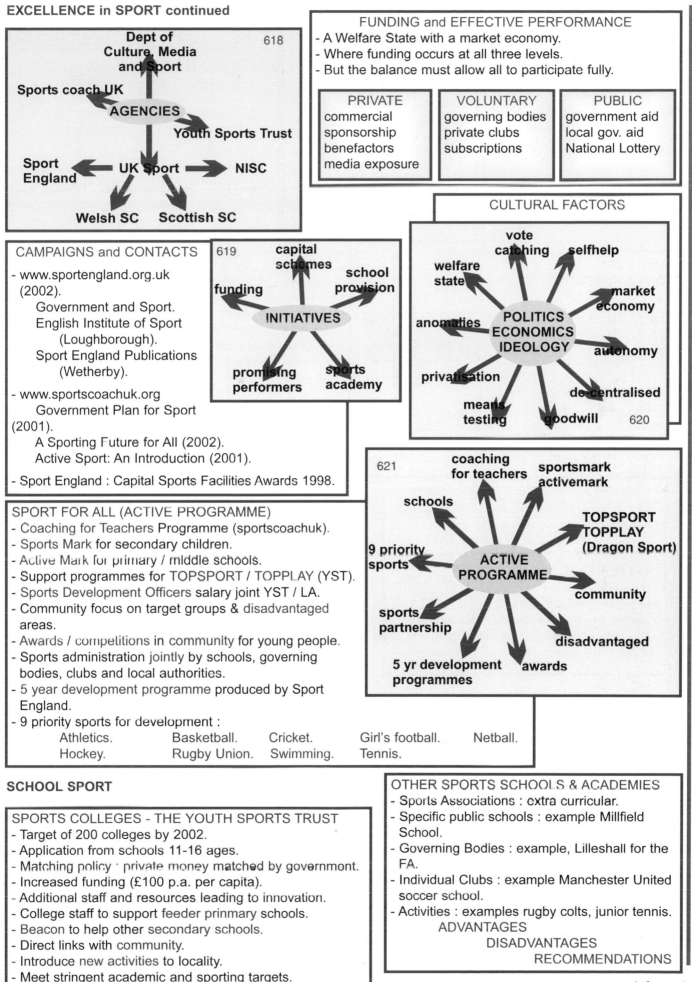

Dept of Culture, Media and Sport 618

Sports coach UK

AGENCIES

Youth Sports Trust

Sport England

UK Sport → NISC

Welsh SC   Scottish SC

FUNDING and EFFECTIVE PERFORMANCE
- A Welfare State with a market economy.
- Where funding occurs at all three levels.
- But the balance must allow all to participate fully.

PRIVATE	VOLUNTARY	PUBLIC
commercial sponsorship benefactors media exposure	governing bodies private clubs subscriptions	government aid local gov. aid National Lottery

CAMPAIGNS and CONTACTS

- www.sportengland.org.uk (2002).
  - Government and Sport.
  - English Institute of Sport (Loughborough).
  - Sport England Publications (Wetherby).
- www.sportscoachuk.org
  - Government Plan for Sport (2001).
  - A Sporting Future for All (2002).
  - Active Sport: An Introduction (2001).
- Sport England : Capital Sports Facilities Awards 1998.

619

INITIATIVES
- capital schemes
- school provision
- funding
- promising performers
- sports academy

CULTURAL FACTORS

POLITICS ECONOMICS IDEOLOGY
- vote catching
- selfhelp
- welfare state
- market economy
- anomalies
- autonomy
- privatisation
- de-centralised
- means testing
- goodwill   620

SPORT FOR ALL (ACTIVE PROGRAMME)
- Coaching for Teachers Programme (sportscoachuk).
- Sports Mark for secondary children.
- Active Mark for primary / middle schools.
- Support programmes for TOPSPORT / TOPPLAY (YST).
- Sports Development Officers salary joint YST / LA.
- Community focus on target groups & disadvantaged areas.
- Awards / competitions in community for young people.
- Sports administration jointly by schools, governing bodies, clubs and local authorities.
- 5 year development programme produced by Sport England.
- 9 priority sports for development :

Athletics.	Basketball.	Cricket.	Girl's football.	Netball.
Hockey.	Rugby Union.	Swimming.	Tennis.	

621

ACTIVE PROGRAMME
- coaching for teachers
- sportsmark activemark
- schools
- TOPSPORT TOPPLAY (Dragon Sport)
- 9 priority sports
- community
- sports partnership
- disadvantaged
- 5 yr development programmes
- awards

SCHOOL SPORT

SPORTS COLLEGES - THE YOUTH SPORTS TRUST
- Target of 200 colleges by 2002.
- Application from schools 11-16 ages.
- Matching policy : private money matched by government.
- Increased funding (£100 p.a. per capita).
- Additional staff and resources leading to innovation.
- College staff to support feeder primary schools.
- Beacon to help other secondary schools.
- Direct links with community.
- Introduce new activities to locality.
- Meet stringent academic and sporting targets.

OTHER SPORTS SCHOOLS & ACADEMIES
- Sports Associations : extra curricular.
- Specific public schools : example Millfield School.
- Governing Bodies : example, Lilleshall for the FA.
- Individual Clubs : example Manchester United soccer school.
- Activities : examples rugby colts, junior tennis.
  - ADVANTAGES
  - DISADVANTAGES
  - RECOMMENDATIONS

Information

6.8 Contemporary Studies

SCHOOL SPORT (continued)

SPORT DEVELOPMENT OFFICERS (SDOs)

- Mainly sport graduates.
- Shaping extracurricular sport in schools.
- Appointed by Local Authorities.
- Funded jointly by Local Authority and Youth Sports Trust.

SCHOOL SPORT COORDINATORS (SSCs)

- Qualified PE specialists.
- Shaping PE and sport in primary schools.
- Part of 'Beacon' Initiative.
- Mostly appointed to Sports Colleges to help other schools.

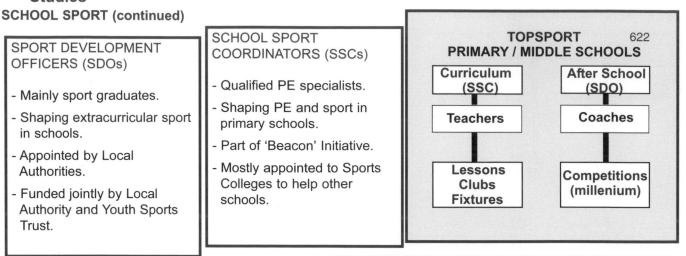

TOPSPORT 622
PRIMARY / MIDDLE SCHOOLS

Curriculum (SSC)	After School (SDO)
Teachers	Coaches
Lessons Clubs Fixtures	Competitions (millenium)

SPORT & MINORITIES

623

GENDER - RIGHTS or PRIVILEGES?

- Modern feminist movements have advanced the rights of women in sport, but this is still resisted by many men and women.

- Only a minority of games involve women on equal terms and combat sports like boxing and wrestling for women are generally deemed undesirable.

GENDER - the HISTORICAL PERSPECTIVE

- Victorian attitudes to women led to females being excluded from rational sport on the grounds that it was too manly and could endanger childbirth.
- Fashions among the upper and middle classes prevented freedom of movement.
- Prevailing attitudes discouraged women from vigorous activity, any activity which brought their femininity into question, such as competition, sweating, displaying their bodies.
- Upper class women excluded themselves from this and developed selective sports on their own private land and in private schools.
- Lower class women were obliged to work to supplement their husband's wages as well as bring up their families and so had no time for sport.

624

AGE

YOUNG

- It is clearly necessary that young children must start to specialise if they are going to reach the top in certain sports.
- They are open to abuse, losing their chance to experience a range of sports.
- They are not physically ready for some training regimes and skills.
- Young people's bodies cannot always stand the years of stress.
- And they can become burnt out while still young.

ELDERLY

- The presumption is that to be elderly is to be senile and incapable of physical activity.
- Sport for the elderly is most valuable to them and their morale.
- Many sports (governing bodies) are improving their veteran policy.
- Access is a major problem, but non-peak periods during the day are used.
- The main problem is the esteem of elderly females brought up as non-participants in sport.
- Aerobics has grown in popularity with this group of women.

Information

SPORT and MINORITIES (continued)

RACE and ETHNIC DIFFERENCES
- The Asian community from Kenya have made considerable social advances, but have not regarded sport as a career route.
- Many from the Indian sub-continent have been too busy surviving and coping with the language.
- In some areas, however, Asian soccer and cricket leagues are producing good players.
- Many Asians are Moslems and this limits female participation in sport.

625

RACE and BLACK ISSUES
- With rational sport being established on class grounds in the 19th century, all subsequent immigrant groups have been initially excluded.
- The West Indian (Afro-Caribbean) ethnic community brought cricket with them and while not being immediately attracted to classroom work, showed considerable interest and talent in sport.
- Some of this is a reflection of America and also early role models in boxing and cricket.
- Afro-Caribbean sportspeople now have a substantial place in soccer, athletics and basketball.
- There are very few soccer spectators from this ethnic background, probably due to resistance from existing fans and the fear of racism.
- Afro-Caribbean females are very interested and talented at sport.

DISABILITY

DISABILITY
- There has always been a conflict of attitude between ability and disability in the context of sport.
- Opportunity is often limited by the attitudes of the able-bodied.
- And also limited by the self-esteem of many who suffer from impairments.
- The main problem which is being tackled is access, where public sport facilities are now required to have ramps and wide doorways to allow wheelchair access.
- The Paraplegic Games and numerous marathons have highlighted their potential success at world level.

DISABILITY
IMPAIRMENTS :
- Loss of faculty or use of part of the body.
DISABILITIES :
- Loss of ability in certain activities due to impairment.
HANDICAP :
- Physical and social barriers as a result of disability.
TYPES :
- Mental, visual, hearing, C.P., les autres, quadriplegic, paraplegic, amputees.

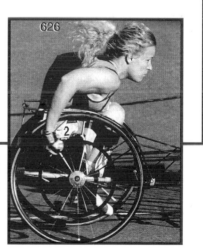
626

SPECIFIC ISSUES
DRUGS and SPORT

TYPES of DRUGS	EFFECTS
Stimulants	Increase alertness, reduce fatigue, increase competitiveness and hostility.
Narcotics / Analgesics	Management of severe pain.
Anabolic Steroids	Increase muscle strength and bulk, promote aggressiveness.
Diuretics	Reduce weight quickly, reduce concentration of substances by diluting urine, masking agent.
Peptide & Glycoprotein Hormones & Analogues	Growth hormone and regulation of red blood cell production (example : rEPO, HGH).
Creatine & Supplements	Not drugs but health risks with excessive use.

TESTING PROCEDURES

- Random tests.
- Admission to all sports and performers.
- Sophisticated procedures.
- Which drugs are being taken?

PUNISHMENT

- Temporary or permanent bans of performers.
- Punishment of coaches and ability to identify guilty officials.
- Punishment of governing bodies and Governments.

Information

DRUGS IN SPORT (continued)

CONCERNS ABOUT DRUGS in SPORT

Performance Enhancement
- Part of the win ethic and the right to excel.

Health Risk
- There has been little research into long-term damage.

Cheating
- It isn't fair for the unscrupulous to take advantage.

Illegal
- Some drugs are against the law, others against sporting regulations.

Role models
- Young people can be attracted to these unethical, dangerous drugs because their heroes take them, thus ceasing to be only a personal decision.

The SPORTSMAN as a BILLBOARD
- In 2002 David Beckham was worth more than £3.6m.
- £2.3m of this was for endorsements, appearances and exhibitions.
- Clothing, equipment, lifestyle.
- He got the rest for actually playing football.

ADVERTISING and the SPORTS STAR

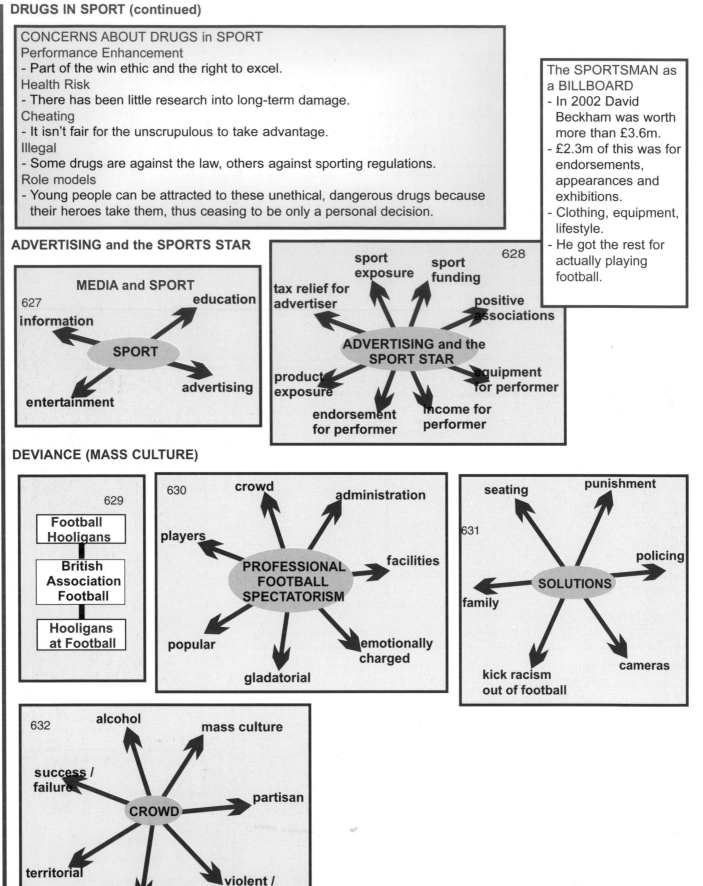

MEDIA and SPORT

627
- information
- education
- SPORT
- entertainment
- advertising

ADVERTISING and the SPORT STAR

628
- sport exposure
- sport funding
- tax relief for advertiser
- positive associations
- product exposure
- equipment for performer
- endorsement for performer
- income for performer

DEVIANCE (MASS CULTURE)

629
- Football Hooligans
- British Association Football
- Hooligans at Football

PROFESSIONAL FOOTBALL SPECTATORISM

630
- crowd
- administration
- players
- facilities
- popular
- emotionally charged
- gladatorial

SOLUTIONS

631
- seating
- punishment
- policing
- family
- cameras
- kick racism out of football

CROWD

632
- alcohol
- mass culture
- success / failure
- partisan
- territorial
- violent / disruptive
- media impact

Bob Davis

Information

INTRODUCTION MINORITY ACTIVITIES
POPULAR RECREATION

Outdoor Pursuits

701
Combats

Field Sports
702

703 Gymnastics

Pub games 705
Skittles

704

POPULAR CHARACTERISTICS	SOCIAL SETTING (pre-industrial)
occasional, violent, occupational, wagering, local, courtly / popular, rural, ritual / festival, uncoded.	feudal, limited travel, markets, harsh laws, cottage industry, sacred or profane, illiteracy.

PUBLIC SCHOOL LINKS

Climb
713

Fight

718
Hare & hounds

Gymnasium 712

PUBLIC SCHOOL CHARACTERISTICS	KEY DEVELOPMENTAL FEATURES
sons of gentry, boarding, fee paying, non-local, trustees, spartan.	championships, expertise, girl schools, old students, moral integrity, physical endeavour, oxbridge melting pot, written rules.

RATIONAL RECREATION

716
Outdoor pursuit

717
Boxing

Fox hunt 714

715
Gymnastics

718 Pub games bowls

RATIONAL CHARACTERISTICS	SOCIAL SETTING
respectable, ritual, regulations, regulated, written rules, regular, roles, referees, regionalised, recreational.	agrian, industrial / urban revolutions, middle class emergence, factory system, fixed wages, development of railways, spread of board schools, YMCA and sport.

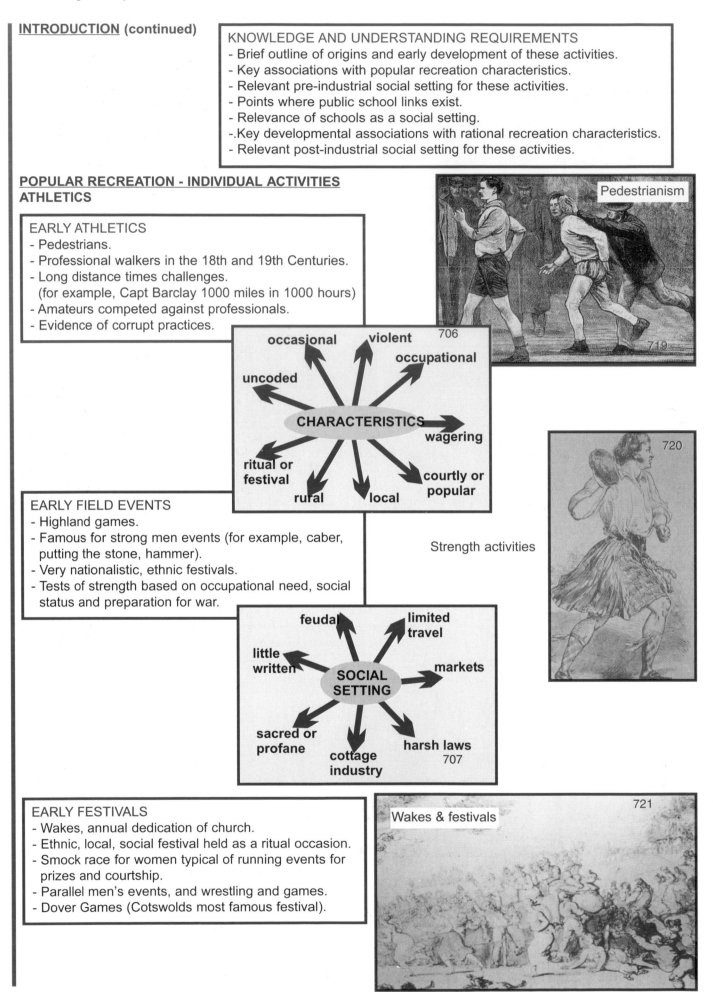

INTRODUCTION (continued)

KNOWLEDGE AND UNDERSTANDING REQUIREMENTS
- Brief outline of origins and early development of these activities.
- Key associations with popular recreation characteristics.
- Relevant pre-industrial social setting for these activities.
- Points where public school links exist.
- Relevance of schools as a social setting.
- .Key developmental associations with rational recreation characteristics.
- Relevant post-industrial social setting for these activities.

POPULAR RECREATION - INDIVIDUAL ACTIVITIES
ATHLETICS

EARLY ATHLETICS
- Pedestrians.
- Professional walkers in the 18th and 19th Centuries.
- Long distance times challenges.
  (for example, Capt Barclay 1000 miles in 1000 hours)
- Amateurs competed against professionals.
- Evidence of corrupt practices.

Pedestrianism
719

occasional   violent   706
uncoded   occupational
CHARACTERISTICS   → wagering
ritual or festival
rural   local   courtly or popular

720

EARLY FIELD EVENTS
- Highland games.
- Famous for strong men events (for example, caber, putting the stone, hammer).
- Very nationalistic, ethnic festivals.
- Tests of strength based on occupational need, social status and preparation for war.

Strength activities

feudal   limited travel
little written
SOCIAL SETTING   → markets
sacred or profane
cottage industry   harsh laws
707

EARLY FESTIVALS
- Wakes, annual dedication of church.
- Ethnic, local, social festival held as a ritual occasion.
- Smock race for women typical of running events for prizes and courtship.
- Parallel men's events, and wrestling and games.
- Dover Games (Cotswolds most famous festival).

Wakes & festivals
721

BATHING and SWIMMING

CLEANLINESS
- As there was no tapped water, the river was used.
- It was healthy for citizens and prevented illness and absence from work.

RECREATION
- Free time was limited, but if the weather was good, bathing in the rivers was popular.
- It depended on the water being clean.

SPORT
- More free time meant more swimming time, and higher standards of swimming and diving.

SURVIVAL
- The river was a most dangerous place, particularly during floods.
- Children, workers and sportsmen needed to learn to swim.

722

WATERFRONT ACTS

RIVER TOWNS
- Defence, occupation, communication, food, cleanliness.

FISHING
- Much depended on free time and wealth of fishermen.
- Gentry had land, time, transport and wealth for game fishing.
- Peasantry limited to town water.

BOATING
- Dual use of boating and shooting skills led to pleasure boating with gigs for hire.

SAILING
- Occupational and recreative skills essential.
  Mainly on estuaries and sheltered bays.

RIVER BANKS
- Water meadows central for recreation.
- Flooding prevented crops and building.
- Games, horse racing, prize fighting and athletic festivals held annually.

706

occasional — violent — occupational — uncoded — CHARACTERISTICS — wagering — ritual or festival — rural — local — courtly or popular

723

ROWING

feudal — limited travel — little written — SOCIAL SETTING — markets — sacred or profane — cottage industry — harsh laws
707

724

BOATING
- Developed into two main features; recreative boating was possible for people to hire gigs and row themselves or be rowed.
- Ferries, on the other hand were water taxis, particularly on the Thames to carry people across or along the river.

DOGGETT COAT AND BADGE
- This was an annual competition between watermen in the final year of their apprenticeship.
- It was held on the 1st of August from 1714 and still exists today.

POPULAR RECREATION - GAMES
INVASION GAMES

INVASION GAMES

- Mob football, hurling and mob hockey were only some of the primitive and violent invasion games played at Shrovetide.
- It was often a street game, part of an old statute allowing the lower classes to let off steam, once a year.
- It can still be seen at Ashbourne, Derbyshire, and the Haxey Hood Game, Hurling and the Hallaton Bottle Game are variations of it.

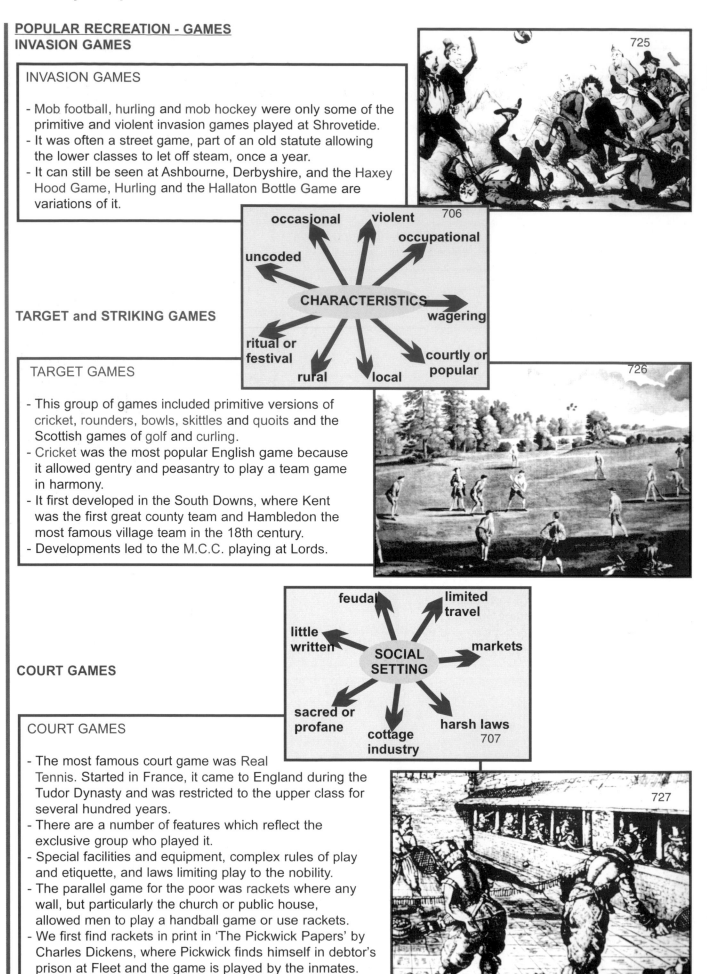

706

CHARACTERISTICS

- occasional
- violent
- occupational
- uncoded
- wagering
- ritual or festival
- rural
- local
- courtly or popular

TARGET and STRIKING GAMES

TARGET GAMES

- This group of games included primitive versions of cricket, rounders, bowls, skittles and quoits and the Scottish games of golf and curling.
- Cricket was the most popular English game because it allowed gentry and peasantry to play a team game in harmony.
- It first developed in the South Downs, where Kent was the first great county team and Hambledon the most famous village team in the 18th century.
- Developments led to the M.C.C. playing at Lords.

SOCIAL SETTING

- feudal
- limited travel
- little written
- markets
- sacred or profane
- cottage industry
- harsh laws

707

COURT GAMES

COURT GAMES

- The most famous court game was Real Tennis. Started in France, it came to England during the Tudor Dynasty and was restricted to the upper class for several hundred years.
- There are a number of features which reflect the exclusive group who played it.
- Special facilities and equipment, complex rules of play and etiquette, and laws limiting play to the nobility.
- The parallel game for the poor was rackets where any wall, but particularly the church or public house, allowed men to play a handball game or use rackets.
- We first find rackets in print in 'The Pickwick Papers' by Charles Dickens, where Pickwick finds himself in debtor's prison at Fleet and the game is played by the inmates.

PUBLIC SCHOOL ATHLETICISM
CHARACTERISTICS
of the PUBLIC SCHOOL SYSTEM

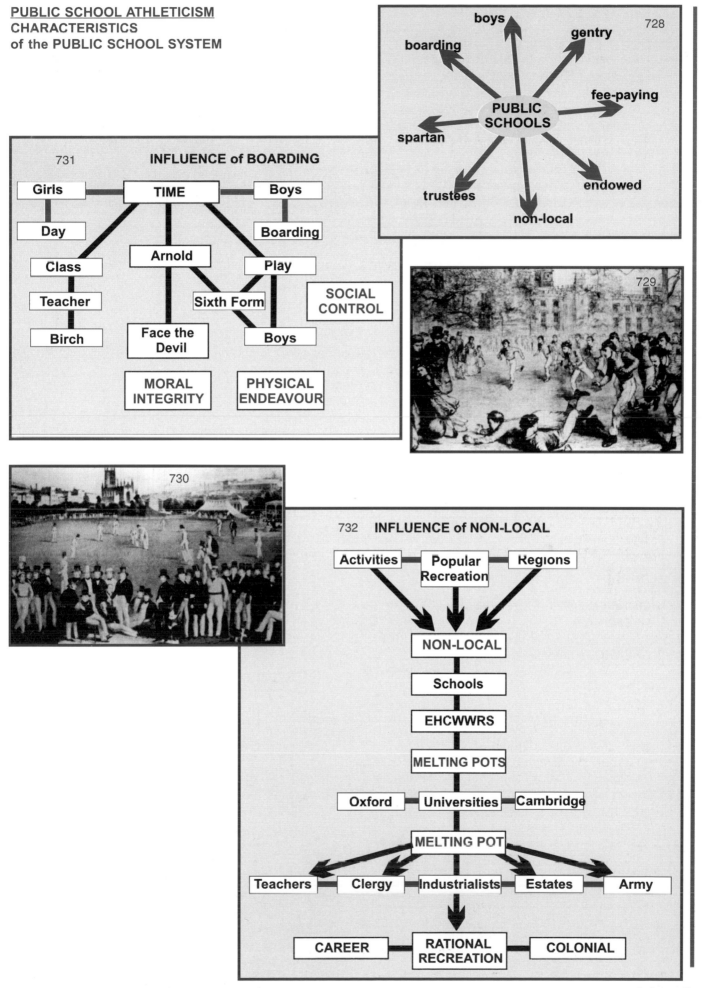

728

boys

boarding

gentry

PUBLIC SCHOOLS

fee-paying

spartan

endowed

trustees

non-local

731   **INFLUENCE of BOARDING**

| Girls | TIME | Boys |

Day

Boarding

Class

Arnold

Play

Teacher

Sixth Form

SOCIAL CONTROL

Birch

Face the Devil

Boys

MORAL INTEGRITY

PHYSICAL ENDEAVOUR

729

730

732   **INFLUENCE of NON-LOCAL**

Activities — Popular Recreation — Regions

NON-LOCAL

Schools

EHCWWRS

MELTING POTS

Oxford — Universities — Cambridge

MELTING POT

Teachers — Clergy — Industrialists — Estates — Army

CAREER — RATIONAL RECREATION — COLONIAL

PUBLIC SCHOOL ATHLETICISM - TECHNICAL AND SOCIAL DEVELOPMENT

Stage 1 - INITIAL BOYS DEVELOPMENTS
- Cricket started, but with established rules.
- Mob Football, differed in each school :
  - Eton, Field and Wall Game,
  - Rugby, handling game,
  - Harrow and Charterhouse, dribbling game.
- Local conditions determined structure.
- Rackets and Fives :
  - Started on walls of the Old School at Harrow,
  - Fives started at Eton, Rugby and Winchester,
  - Courts different in each case.

733

Stage 2 - IMPACT OF LIBERAL HEADMASTERS
- Dr Thomas Arnold and others enacted reforms to produce responsible Christian Gentlemen.
- With concept of Godliness and Manliness (1820's - 1850's) :
  - Broader curriculum.
  - Reduced flogging.
  - Playground control by Sixth Form.
  - Exclusion of field sports and poaching.
- Games encouraged as a vehicle of social control :
  - Regular play.
  - Written rules.
  - Codes of honour and loyalty to school established.
- Expansion leading to House System and House competitions being established.

729

Stage 3 - FULL EXPRESSION OF ATHLETICISM
- Physical Endeavour and Moral Integrity : central features of sport in public schools as part of Muscular Christianity.
- Support from Heads in gentry and middle class schools.
- Assistant masters as Oxbridge blues taught and played games.
- Wide programme of athletics, swimming, gymnastics and games.
- Organised interschool fixtures as Public School Championships.
- Old Boys took cult of athleticism into society and encouraged working class rational sport.
- Figure 736 shows the annual Eton v Harrow cricket match at Lords.

VALUES LINKED WITH ATHLETICISM

734

promoting health

promoting vigorous habits

competitive experience

PHYSICAL

toughening up society

correcting overstudy

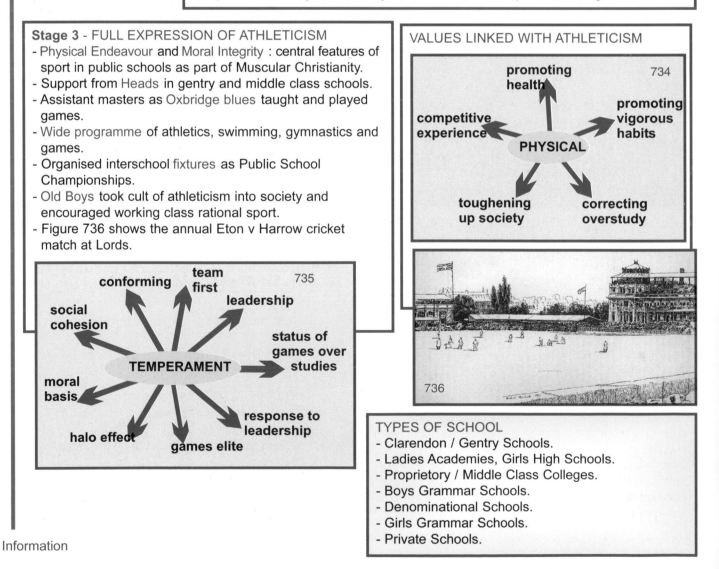

736

735

conforming

team first

leadership

social cohesion

status of games over studies

TEMPERAMENT

moral basis

response to leadership

halo effect

games elite

TYPES OF SCHOOL
- Clarendon / Gentry Schools.
- Ladies Academies, Girls High Schools.
- Proprietory / Middle Class Colleges.
- Boys Grammar Schools.
- Denominational Schools.
- Girls Grammar Schools.
- Private Schools.

IDENTIFY KEY INDIVIDUAL ACTIVITIES with TOM BROWN'S SCHOOLDAYS
ATHLETICS

HARE AND HOUNDS
The senior boys were going for the Barby Run. Tom and his friends decide to run too, but without permission.
The hares were set off and the pack followed with Tom and Co. behind. Tom and friends got lost and returned very late, bedraggled.
The Head told them off for breaking the rules, but did not flog them because they had shown courage and initiative.

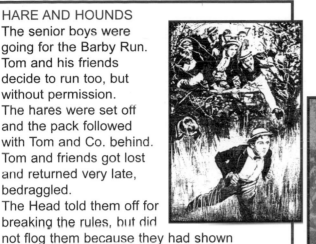

SPORTS DAY AT RUGBY SCHOOL
- Sports day was the result of the school valuing athleticism.
- On that day, the head showed parents his school at its athletic best.
- Boys supported their house, and witnessed physical endeavour, comradeship, and moral integrity.
- The steeplechase was brought onto the school field for sports day.

SWIMMING

POACHING
The boys loved to go swimming and there were several different bathing places.
They also liked fishing, but were only allowed on one bank.
The bailiff caught Tom poaching and took him to Dr Arnold.
Tom admitted his guilt, but asked that East's rod should not be taken.
The bailiff agreed, but Tom was flogged by the Head next morning.

BATHING AND SWIMMING
- RUGBY SCHOOL: the river Avon was used, Tom Brown includes an explanation of bathing places to suit ability of swimmers. Water was rented by Arnold.
- HARROW SCHOOL: the pool known as the 'duck puddle' developed from a natural facility to an advanced provision for swimming.

ROWING

ROWING
- The phrase 'wetbob' and 'drybob' reflected the division of athletic focus into rowing and games.
- Most major public schools were near to rivers.
- The availability of boats to hire developed into school rowing clubs.
- The most important feature of a rowing eight was team effort, and this was extended to the House and School.
- Linked with this development was the importance of being able to swim.

Information

IDENTIFY KEY PUBLIC SCHOOL GAMES with TOM BROWN'S SCHOOLDAYS

Remember that this is fiction. It is what Thomas Hughes felt about his schooldays at Rugby under the headship of Dr Thomas Arnold.
It is thought that Tom Brown was in fact representing Thomas Hughes' adventures while at school. Hughes had a great respect for Dr. Arnold, but believed much more strongly in the value of sport as a character building experience as he belonged to a group of Muscular Christians.

FOOTBALL

It was the day of the football match on Big Side. Tom told East he had played the game with village lads, but East said Rugby played real football. East was playing and was injured. When the ball came towards goal, Tom raced on and dived on it. Big Brook asked if he was hurt and then said that he was made of the right stuff.

RUGBY

- Only Rugby among the Clarendon Schools played a handling / tackling game of football.
- Eton, Harrow and others played a dribbling (foot) game.
- Perhaps it was because 'Web-Ellis picked up the ball and ran with it'.
- More likely, it was the quality of the playing field.
- The first written rules for both Rugger and Soccer, were written at the schools.

CRICKET

- The game of Cricket had rules of play before the expansion of the game in the public schools.
- As an organised game, it was more readily acceptable to school authorities.
- The time available to play and practice, the quality of the playing fields and the availability of teachers and professionals to coach led to very high standards in the schools.

THE CRICKET

Tom eventually reached the Sixth Form and was made Captain of Cricket. The final match was against the M.C.C. It was a good match, but Tom put Arthur in earlier than normally.
A young master suggested that Tom had risked the match by doing this, but Tom said that the result mattered little, but Arthur would remember this all his life. Tom also suggested that cricket was more than a game, that it was an institution. Arthur thought it was life itself.

COURT GAMES

The development of informal partner games was common to most public schools.

FIVES
- Fives Courts were built against the walls of Eton, Winchester and Rugby Schools, this was copied by other schools.

RACQUETS
- Harrow was the first to play and develop this game, and this was copied by others.

REAL TENNIS
- It is thought that only Eton had a Real Tennis court.

GIRLS SCHOOLS

GIRLS SCHOOLS
- Girls schools looked to be less 'muscular' and chose games less popular with boys schools.
- Hockey and Lacrosse were played in the winter and Lawn Tennis in the summer.
- See figure 744 of Lacrosse at St Leonard's School.

RATIONAL RECREATION - INDIVIDUAL ACTIVITIES
ATHLETICS

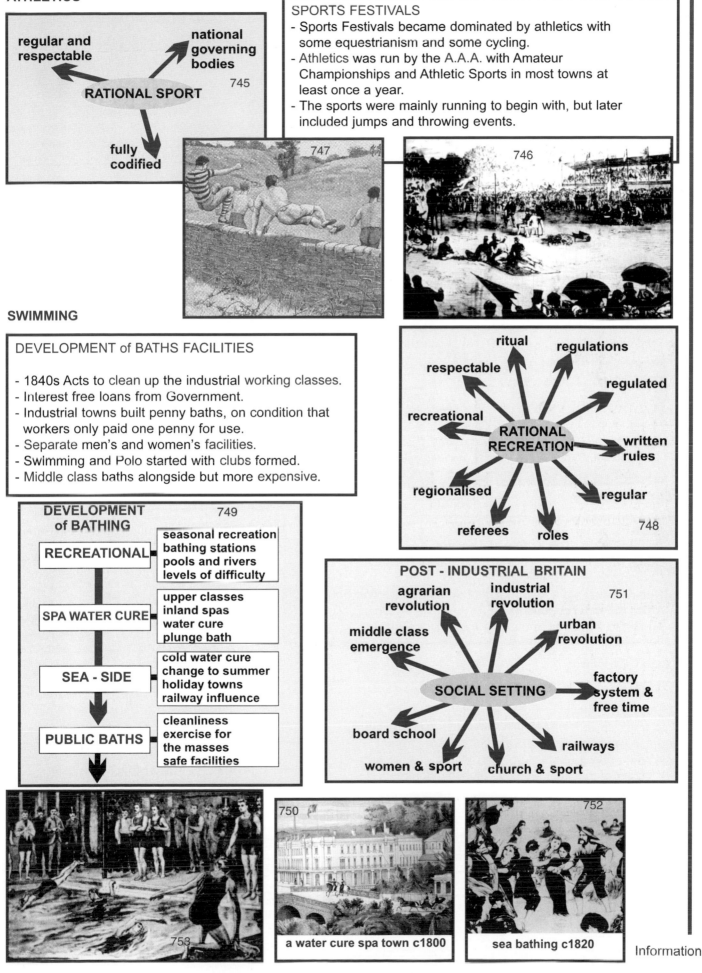

regular and
respectable

national
governing
bodies

RATIONAL SPORT   745

fully
codified

SPORTS FESTIVALS
- Sports Festivals became dominated by athletics with some equestrianism and some cycling.
- Athletics was run by the A.A.A. with Amateur Championships and Athletic Sports in most towns at least once a year.
- The sports were mainly running to begin with, but later included jumps and throwing events.

747

746

SWIMMING

DEVELOPMENT of BATHS FACILITIES

- 1840s Acts to clean up the industrial working classes.
- Interest free loans from Government.
- Industrial towns built penny baths, on condition that workers only paid one penny for use.
- Separate men's and women's facilities.
- Swimming and Polo started with clubs formed.
- Middle class baths alongside but more expensive.

ritual   regulations

respectable   regulated

recreational   **RATIONAL RECREATION**   written rules

regionalised   regular

referees   roles   748

DEVELOPMENT of BATHING   749

RECREATIONAL — seasonal recreation / bathing stations / pools and rivers / levels of difficulty

SPA WATER CURE — upper classes / inland spas / water cure / plunge bath

SEA - SIDE — cold water cure / change to summer / holiday towns / railway influence

PUBLIC BATHS — cleanliness / exercise for the masses / safe facilities

POST - INDUSTRIAL BRITAIN

agrarian revolution   industrial revolution   751

middle class emergence   urban revolution

SOCIAL SETTING   factory system & free time

board school

women & sport   church & sport   railways

753

a water cure spa town c1800   750

sea bathing c1820   752

Information

RATIONAL RECREATION - INDIVIDUAL ACTIVITIES (continued)

THE REGATTA and ROWING
- Aquatics became very respectable.
- Rowing is controlled by the A.R.A. and is exclusive to the upper / middle classes.
- Swimming was now run by the A.S.A. and had its own amateur championships. It has developed from the Spa Movement and the Public Baths which were built to clean up the working classes.
- Sailing became very popular among the most wealthy members of Victorian society, headed by the Americas Cup.
- Canoeing, (John MacGregor) was popular on most rivers.

754

RATIONAL RECREATION - GAMES
INVASION GAMES

RUGBY
- The R.F.U. was established in 1871 and separated from the association game.
- Strictly amateur, northern clubs split to establish a professional rugby league.

756

SOCCER
- The F.A. was established in 1863 and the F.A. Cup as a national competition.
- This was dominated by Old Boys teams, until professional northern clubs made it the Peoples' Game.

755

HOCKEY
- Mob hockey was re-organised by cricket clubs in the Thames Valley who wanted to play a winter game.
- Girls high schools played hockey, hence women playing.

757

TARGET GAMES

CRICKET
- Became the national game of England.
- Rules were revised by the M.C.C. and the County Championships established.
- Test matches were held regularly, with Australia and South Africa the main opponents.
- Amateurs improved to rival the professional players.

COURT GAMES

LAWN TENNIS
- The middle classes developed Lawn Tennis as an alternative to real tennis. It was initially played in gardens, but if these were too small, private clubs were formed.
- Women played because of the privacy.
- Wimbledon became the championship centre.

758

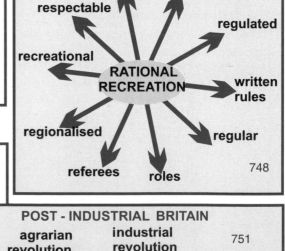

ritual
regulations
respectable
regulated
recreational
RATIONAL RECREATION
written rules
regionalised
regular
referees
roles
748

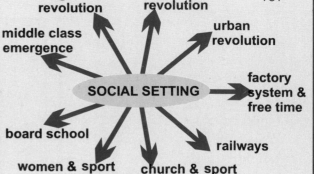

POST - INDUSTRIAL BRITAIN
751
agrarian revolution
industrial revolution
middle class emergence
urban revolution
SOCIAL SETTING
factory system & free time
board school
railways
women & sport
church & sport

Information

SOCIAL SETTING OF RATIONAL SPORT

SOCIAL CLASS AND SPORT
- The gentry had already achieved a full sports programme with their preferred activities and plentiful leisure time.
- The emerging urban middle classes took these gentry sports and reorganised them according to amateur codes which excluded financial rewards.
- The industrial working classes had little time for sport, but when it was rationalised and seen to be a vehicle for social conditioning.
- Social Christians and industrialists encouraged the development of organised sport for the workers, who largely existed in urban poverty, see picture to right.
- There was considerable delay before women had the same opportunities.

WORK AND FREE-TIME

- The cottage industry had been a family affair where the timing of when to work was dictated by the amount to be done.
- Factory developments meant that the human element was controlled by machinery, as shutting off the machines meant loss of production.
- Factory work time started with a 72 hour week over six days, with Sunday a day of rest stipulated by sabbatharianism.

- This meant that the workers had no free time unless they were unemployed and then they had no money.
- The Saturday Half Day and the Early Closing Movement gave workers time for organised sport.

- Women were paid a quarter of what men got for the same work, and therefore did not have the union strength to obtain the Saturday half day.
- Benevolent employers built sports facilities for their workers.

URBANISATION AND LEISURE

- As towns grew, particularly the industrial towns, the countryside became farther away and so urban leisure facilities became a social necessity.
- Arboretums were initially built for the middle classes, but gradually public parks were also opened for walking in and later for sports.

- The centres of older cities were rebuilt removing the slums and building shopping and business centres.
- With back-to-back housing near the factories and mills, entrepreneurs realised that professional football clubs would bring in a lot of revenue from the gate money
- These were built near the town centres.

- The pollution to the rivers running through the industrial towns, destroyed fishing opportunities for the working classes.

to Brighton and back for 3s 6d - 1859

COMMUNICATIONS AND TRAVEL
- The use of the stagecoach opened up sport for the gentry, but meant that the lower classes were limited to local holidays and sports.
- With the coming of the railways, the middle classes gained access to the seaside and were able to travel to neighbouring towns for sport.

- The lower classes could not afford to go by rail regularly, nor did they have the time and so the excursion trip became the annual seaside visit for the lower classes.

- The roads deteriorated during the popularisation of the railways.
- However, with the advent of middle class cycle touring, the roads were improved.
- Gradually, the gentry and the lower classes with their second-hand bikes, managed to travel to the countryside by cycle.

- Literacy was limited until printing.
- The popular press and the pocket editions became available and compulsory education led to a literate working class.
- It was as a result of these changes that the sporting press was born.

CHURCH AND SPORT
- Major changes occurred in the Church's attitude to sport in the late 19th century.

- Muscular Christianity led to a large number of church clubs.
- Y.M.C.A.- a major influence on sport for young clerks.

Information

DEVELOPMENT OF OUTDOOR ADVENTUROUS ACTIVITIES
THE MOUNTAIN EXPERIENCE

MOUNTAIN ACTS

- Mystery of the mountains.
- Occupational use by shepherds who became guides.
- Alpinists visited (the Alps) to reach the top, preferably in the snow.
- Botanists climbing in difficult places for rare plants.
- Rock Climbers, attempting the most difficult routes. The Lake District, Highlands and North Wales opened up.

mountain tourists 1874

WINTER EXCITEMENT

WINTER ACTS

- Ice Fairs : held on frozen rivers during winter as festival occasions.

- Speed Skating : very popular in Holland and on the Fens of England.
- Became professionalised.

- Figure Skating : started on the Serpentine in Hyde Park (London) once skates had edges.

- Skiing : Nordic skiing is very old, but the English started Alpine skiing.

CYCLING

BONE SHAKER
- A pretend horse.
- Young gentlemen showing off.
- A gimmick only.

DEVELOPMENTS
- Gentry preferred horses until Queen Victoria's daughters started a craze.

- Cycle Touring Club (CTC) established.

- Middle class men in towns formed clubs which excluded women initially.
- Too expensive for lower classes until the second-hand trade started.

PENNY FARTHING
- Large wheel for speed.
- Too dangerous for women and old people.
- Tricycle was an alternative.
- Used for racing on the roads and on the track.

ROVER SAFETY
- Cog and chain ended need for large wheel.
- Safer for women and elderly.
- Not as fast until gears invented.

ELEMENTARY SCHOOLS - DRILL, P.T. and P.E.

THE MODEL COURSE AND MILITARY DRILL. 1902.
- The Boer War went badly for Britain and school P.T. was blamed.

- The War Office imposed a syllabus on all elementary schools with soldiers doing the instruction.
- It was designed to increase 'fitness to fight' :
    - to improve discipline for work and war,
    - to help children to withstand hardship,
    - to become familiar with military weapons.
- The content was set exercises by numbers and included marching and drill with staves, acting as rifles.

- Boys and girls were involved and the teaching method was by direct commands Army style.

768

PHYSICAL TRAINING SWEDISH STYLE.
- Within two years the Model Course was thrown out and replaced by a Ministry syllabus based on Swedish lines and taught by teachers.
- The objectives now hinged on sound educational principles of the day and a careful observation of scientific principles.
- The exercises were systematic and consisted of tables related to different parts of the body.
- The first syllabus of this type was in 1904, with new syllabuses issued in 1909 and 1919.
- The teaching method was still formal teaching set class exercises in large groups in a hall / outside.

769

THE 1933 SYLLABUS.
- In the 1919 Syllabus, the enlightened step of encouraging play activities for children under seven was introduced.
- The 1933 syllabus retained this and added more games and play activities for older children.
- The major change which was made was the introduction of gymnastic skill in addition to the physical exercises of earlier syllabuses.
- Lots of moves like cartwheels and rolls were introduced as well as the use of apparatus where it was available.
- In addition to class activities, children were taught to work in group corners, giving them more independence and variety.

770

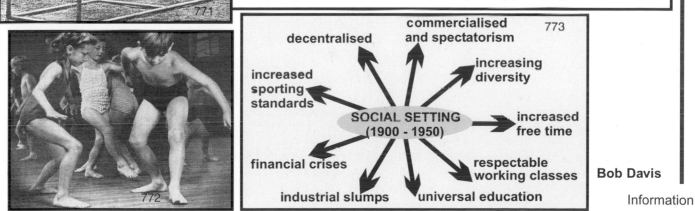
771

MOVING AND GROWING and PLANNING THE PROGRAMME.
- Following the 2nd World War (1939-45) teachers were looking for new 'educational' ways of teaching.
- During the war exciting frame apparatus had been used in assault courses for soldiers and schools adapted these.
- There was also a desire for children to be creative and invent their own movement patterns.
- With the post-war building programme, all primary schools had halls with fixed apparatus and so children were able to produce skilled sequences on the floor and also complex apparatus patterns.

772

773

decentralised

commercialised and spectatorism

increasing diversity

increased sporting standards

SOCIAL SETTING (1900 - 1950)

increased free time

financial crises

respectable working classes

industrial slumps

universal education

Bob Davis

Information

Information

COMPARATIVE STUDIES

THE COMPARATIVE PERSPECTIVE

COMPARATIVE STUDY
involves the study of :
- Structures and mechanisms operating in a number of different social settings (i.e. countries).
- Comparing and accounting for similarities and contrasting differences in those social settings and the range of activities within those social settings.

You may have to :
- List or exemplify.
- Rationalise, justify, or account for such examples.
- Compare and account for similarities with other social and organisational frameworks.
- Contrast and account for differences in such frameworks.
- Consider the implications of such policies and relationships.

THE AREAS OF STUDY FOR EACH COUNTRY
- The nature of government and the level of its involvement in sport.
- The organisational and administrative features governing sport, physical recreation and physical education (both governmental and non-governmental).
- Issues arising out of the relationship between the above activities, their organisational structure and the social setting in which they operate.
- The social, historical, and geographical influences which have affected and still do affect the nature of the above activities in each of the countries or social settings given in the syllabus.

COUNTRIES CHOSEN
- Note that for the UK, relevant topics will have been part of social or contemporary studies (all systems and social structures covered in detail).
- Some syllabuses will include countries other than those shown here, in which case the general methods and approach to study should be used, headings and topics to be covered in similar depth.

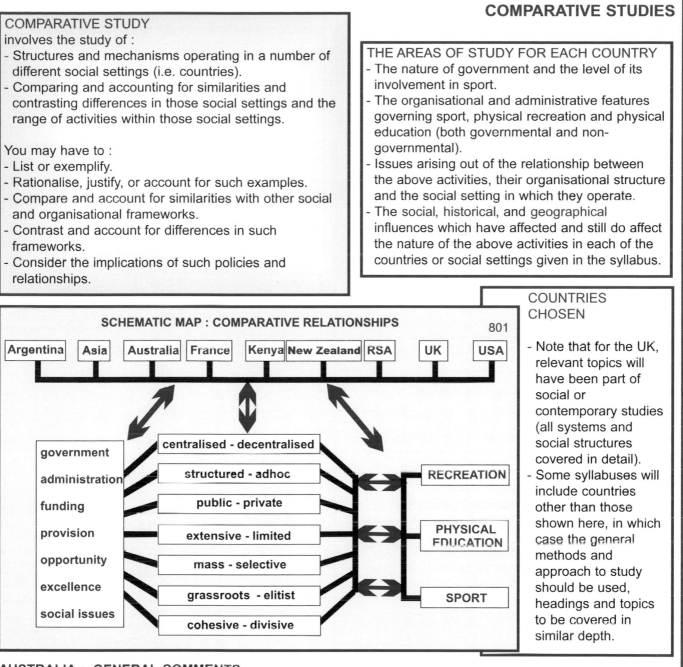

SCHEMATIC MAP : COMPARATIVE RELATIONSHIPS   801

Argentina | Asia | Australia | France | Kenya | New Zealand | RSA | UK | USA

government
administration
funding
provision
opportunity
excellence
social issues

centralised - decentralised
structured - adhoc
public - private
extensive - limited
mass - selective
grassroots - elitist
cohesive - divisive

RECREATION
PHYSICAL EDUCATION
SPORT

AUSTRALIA : GENERAL COMMENTS

SPORT and RECREATION as part of the AUSTRALIAN LIFESTYLE
- Most Australians live in urban areas and do not rely on the 'outback' for their recreation in the way that we often imagine to be the case.
- The diversity of terrain and climate ensures that opportunities exist for the most diverse range of activities.
- Outdoor Education and Recreation developments do not compare with the long established Summer Schools and 'Wilderness Trails' in the U.S., or the 'Classes Transplantée' and 'Centres de Vacance' in France.
- The Outward Bound Trust, well known in the UK, has been established in Australia since the 1960's, and in most Australian States outdoor education is now on the curriculum in schools.

CULTURAL ROOTS
- Common cultural roots with the UK by virtue of both its colonial origins & immigrants from the UK.
- Hence the growth of such institutions as 'Timbertops' (Geelong Grammar School), operating very similarly to Gordonstoun School in Scotland.
- More recently, a broader influence was introduced by more recent immigrants from both Europe, and most recently, Asia.
- Many Australian sports clubs were founded by immigrant groups.and games were often marred by ethnic rivalries.
- It is now illegal for clubs (example : 'Melbourne Croatia') to have names signifying ethnic origins.

AUSTRALIA : GENERAL COMMENTS - continued

CULTURAL LINKS
- The relationship between climate and coast is similar to parts of France and the West Coast of the USA and the lifestyle based on 'sun, sea and surf'.
- Colonial links with the UK are seen in team sports, particularly rugby and cricket.
- The heavy industrial base of the North of England has exported some of its recreational culture.
- This is seen most clearly in sports such as Rugby League (and to some extent soccer).
- The yearning for the country or the mountains as an escape from industrial grime has not been transplanted from the UK since much of Australia's early economy was pastorally based.
- The major sports were all spawned during the first wave of colonisation.
- A recent development has been the influence of professionalism and commercialism.
- Born of the 'pacific rim' influence of the USA and 'pay TV.'
- Both rugby codes have been particularly affected.

OUTDOOR RECREATION IN AUSTRALIA

CONTROL of OUTDOOR RECREATION
- The Department of the Environment & Heritage ('Environment Australia' or DEH) has centralised administrative control over Australia's vast tracts of wilderness, desert, and scenic beauty.
- Divisions within 'Environment Australia' include :
· Coasts & Oceans, Heritage, Industry, Inland waters,
· Land management, Meteorology, Parks and reserves
- Each State has its own Departments of Environment / Tourism which oversee developments and policies within its boundaries and parks.
- Other areas of beauty are managed by the respective State Departments of Conservation, Forests and Land.

NATIONAL PARKS
- This term can be confusing as each State in Australia is in effect an individual country.
- National parks are therefore managed and controlled by the State in which they exist rather than by the Federal Government.
- An exception to the above is the Great Barrier Reef.
- This is managed by the Great Barrier Reef Marine Park Authority (GBRMPA) under the direct control of the Federal Government, rather than a State Department.
- There are well-established codes of behaviour for visitors to national parks and other areas of scenic and natural beauty.
- All agencies in Australia make much use of information technology and the Internet in making such information available.

ABORIGINAL CULTURE
- Has not been allowed to contribute to the development of Australian sports and recreations.
- Aboriginal involvement in 'Australian Sports' is not unknown but opportunity is not universal.
- All State Governments now have departments whose purpose is to provide opportunity for participation and to develop programmes of integration for the aboriginal people.

ROLE-MODELS
- Are emerging from indigenous / ethnic groups and show greater opportunity and increased participation by such groups.

802

PARALLEL with the NATIVE NORTH AMERICAN
- Who, like his Aboriginal counterpart was almost wiped out by the colonising invader.
- The process of :
    - 'decimate'
        - 'isolate'
            - 'discriminate'
                - 'ignore'
                    - 'pacify'
                        - 'provide for'
                            - 'include'
is evident in both cultures, and cannot yet be said to be complete.
- Inclusion of native races and their cultures may be seen as the cleansing of conscience in regard to the genocide (as now perceived) during the respective periods of colonisation.

PHILOSOPHY of OUTDOOR RECREATION
- Both Australia and the USA are 'young societies'.
- Derived to some extent from colonial links with Britain.
- Both countries have since undergone large-scale immigration and are therefore multi-cultural societies to a greater degree than Britain.
- And to a much greater degree than France.
- Most Australians are 'city dwellers' and have an affinity with recreations within the built environment.
- The exception to this is their affinity for the beach and its associated recreations (most Australians live within an hour's drive of the coast).

803

AUSTRALIA - OUTDOOR EDUCATION

OUTDOOR EDUCATION
- Mirrors that in Britain and the USA, with provision made for programmes but no clear requirement to carry them out.
- Australian schools offer Outdoor Education programmes within a range of 'electives' which are often not compulsory.
- Compare the USA with wide provision (but no compulsion) for outdoor experience in its summer camps.
- However, Australia is beginning to make wider provision, and the Australian College of Education in Canberra now runs undergraduate programmes in this field.
- Implementation is up to individual schools.
- There is an increasing recognition to the affinity of the Aboriginal people for the outdoors.
- Special programmes are organised for Aboriginal students, and respect for their cultural heritage is being adopted within programmes of outdoor education.

DIVERSITY
- We tend to associate Australian outdoor sports and recreations with the sun and the sea.
- But the country is in fact a continent and encompasses a range of climatic conditions.
- Australian skiers and alpinists can train all-year-round without leaving Australia.
- The growth of such activities as 'triathlon' and other related sports gives examples of activities derived from the combination of good climate and technology.
- Together with the 'healthy outdoor' philosophy of the surfer.

ORIGINS
- Physical Education system is close to the UK.
- Colonial roots, Muscular Christianity, public and grammar schools led to similarities to UK up to the 1914-18 war.
- The current comprehensive school system resembles the USA (and more lately the UK).
- Public school tendency towards religious foundations reflects France.
- Secularisation of the State system similar to France, and the USA.

PHYSICAL EDUCATION IN AUSTRALIA

STRUCTURE of DEVOLUTION of SPORT in AUSTRALIA
804

- **FEDERAL MINISTER** Youth, Sport, Recreation
  - **ASC** Australian Sports Commission
    - **AIS** Australian Institute for Sport
  - **Education Minister**
    - **ACHPER**
      - **State Education and PE Bodies**
  - **DEST**
    - **State Sports Bodies**
      - **'Active Australia'** Formerly 'Aussie Sport'
- **teachers** — **schools** — **coaches**

DEVELOPMENT
- Physical education is the responsibility of each individual State, with federal input through ACHPER.
- Involvement at National level is also shared by the Federal Minister of Education.
- Whose responsibility includes :
  - The inspection of schools on behalf of the Federal Government.
  - The Department of Environment, Sport and Territories (DEST) which works through the State Ministries of Sport and their institutes to develop initiatives such as 'Active Australia' and school sport programmes.
- SEPEP is a programme of sports awareness, including the concept of sportsmanship and 'fair play', training and officiating rather than simply a programme of sports participation.
- The federal Aussie system is different from the type of federal system in operation in the USA.
- The Australian Council for Health, Physical Education and Recreation (ACHPER) plays a central role in the development of physical education programmes for schools and the community Moneghetti report (Victoria 1993) initiated review of PE in schools.

FURTHER DEVELOPMENTS
- PASE (Physical and Sport Education), developed in Victoria.
- Contrast with developments in the UK.
- PE and Sport (in Aus) are being placed on the curriculum for all pupils within compulsory programmes.
- Sport is recognised as having value in its own right, rather than simply serving as a vehicle for 'education through the physical'.

- 'Aussie Sport' was designed as a programme for the development of junior sport whereas 'Active Australia' is a framework for all the population I.e. 6-60.
- 'Aussie Sport' was a targeted programme, and consisted of Sport to upper primary and lower secondary kids (only sport or modified sport).
- 'Active Australia' is a complete framework of participation for all ages.

PE EXAMS and CURRICULUM in AUSTRALIA

STRUCTURE of STATE PE PROVISION

806

DEPARTMENT of SCHOOL EDUCATION
(Sport and Physical Education Section)

ACHPER State Branch

PE Programme Development

districts

schools

'Active Australia' 'Youth Sport'

'School Sport'

PE EXAMS
- Physical Education (HSC) is examined in Australian schools.
- Compares with the examinations in PE at 'A' level in UK and at baccalaureate level in France.
- No equivalent to this in the USA, which bases its assessment of ability on performance outcome and continuous testing and measurement.
- In Victoria this examination is now known as the VCE (Victorian Certificate of Education).
- All Australian States (with variations) have compulsory physical education modules, in some cases with additional 'electives' across a range of related topic areas, such as Exercise Science, or Outdoor / Adventure Education.

SPORT IN AUSTRALIA

DEVELOPMENT
- Australians traditionally measure their world sporting status by Olympic and Commonwealth Games performance, and test matches in both rugby codes and cricket.
- Poor performances in the 1976 Olympics led to changes which have forged the present-day administrative and organisational structures.
- The Australian Sports Commission (ASC) is the overall controlling authority.
- Australian Institute of Sport (AIS) and the ASC both have their headquarters in Canberra.
- The AIS has branches in different parts of Australia (Adelaide contains the cricket HQ).
- Each State has its own Institute or Academy of Sport independent from but closely linked with the National AIS.
- Programmes such as 'Sportleap', 'Sportsearch' and 'Active Australia' are run at national, state and local level in order to identify and foster potential talent.
- 'Active Australia' embraces the Disability Education Programme including 'Willing & Able' for Australia's athletes, and international training and assistance for disabled athletes from other countries.

ORIGINS of SPORT in AUSTRALIA

807

rugby league · soccer · cricket · rugby union

immigration

colonialism · hockey

SPORT · pacific rim influences · commercialism

sporting excellence

indigenous sport

Arrafura Games

Sepaktakraw

SPORTS SCHOOLS
- Traditionally very few, and those that have existed have largely been in the private sector.
- Such schools now exist in the public sector in all States, parents' groups or local sponsorship fund the special sport programmes.

PROFESSIONAL SPORT
- High potential earnings.
- Career possibilities within recreation sector.
- Wide range of sports now professional.
- High media and popular profile for professional sportsperson.

AUSTRALIAN SPORT

808

DEST
Dept of Environment States & Territories

ASC
Australian Sports Commission

AIS
Australian Institute for Sport

Individual Sport Academies of Excellence

National Sporting Organisations (NSO)

Australian Sports Drug Agency (ASDA)

women in sport

National Aboriginal Sport Foundation

State Sporting Academies

State sporting organisations

local clubs and performers

Australian Coaching Council ACC

National Coaching Accreditation Scheme NCAS

National Coaching Scholarship

Information

FRANCE : GENERAL COMMENTS

CULTURAL INFLUENCES
- Courtly and aristocratic influences in sport and recreation meant that until the Revolution a pattern of recreation similar to England existed in France.
- Following the revolution, sport in France was influenced by militarism and nationalism (born during the Napoleonic period), and by the Olympianism of de Coubertin.
- Gymnastics had a strong influence, and the work of Clias at Joinville was similar to developments in England and (by others) in the former British colony of America.
- PE in French schools is still known as 'La Gym'.
- Both France and Britain have indigenous minorities striving to re-establish their own cultures (Bretons, Basques, Catalans - Cornish, Welsh and Scottish).
- Comparable with the indigenous populations of both Australia and the USA.
- Nationalism and sport are closely interwoven into the French culture (the influence of the Revolution, and reinforced by de Gaulle in the post-war period), this has never been so in England.
- Similarity exists with historical events in the USA.
- All three countries (France, UK, USA) have distinct 'regional separatisms' which come together under the national flag for major international sporting occasions.

STRUCTURE of ADMINISTRATION in FRANCE   809

MINISTRY (issues policy and exerts central control)

Régions (22)

Départments (96)

Arrondissements (324)

Cantons (3549)

Communes (36385)

DEVELOPMENTS
- Although not as large as the United States or Australia, France is large enough to have climatic and topographical variety which supports a wide range of sports and recreations.
- The attraction of its winter sports facilities in both the Alps and the Pyrénées bring visitors from all over the world for both recreational and sporting purposes.
- A feature of French recreational patterns is the holi day month of August, producing an exodus to the coast on a large scale and 'Le Camping Francais' (compare Australia and the West Coast of USA).
- Failure in the Rome Olympics (1960) saw de Gaulle institute changes to the structure of sporting organisation hence the highly subsidised support of its national programmes and the 5-point plan (refer to page 8.7).

THE FRENCH POLITICAL (PRESIDENTIAL) SYSTEM
- Many political parties.
- Including extreme right-wing nationalism.
- Produced a centralised system of government reflected in the organisation of sport, recreation and physical education.
- Sport is heavily subsidised.
- The French system is heavily influenced by Paris to the disadvantage of the regions.
- This is changing with the development of commercial sponsorship alongside central funding.
- France participates internationally on an increasing scale, both rugby codes are well established in the South but become truly 'National' when 'le cockerel' appears on players' shirts.
- Soccer has blossomed since World (1998) and European Cup (2000) Victories, but France's oldest established 'international event' is the Tour de France cycle race.

OUTDOOR RECREATION IN FRANCE

SIZE
- France has approximately the same population as the UK but twice the land area.
- This encompasses a much broader climatic and topographical range.
- Winter sports and recreations are firmly established, as are the coastal resorts (particularly in the South Ð 'Le Midi') in the summer months.
- The widely spread nature of the society stretches communications.
- Many traditional recreations are strongly 'regionalised' because of this.
- Breton wrestling for example, takes place in the North, whilst Pélote (Provence) and bull fighting are established in the South.
- Numerous rivers and an extensive coastline mean that water-based activities have always had a place within the French recreational culture.

CONTROL
- France's 22 'Régions' take responsibility for what elsewhere might be described as 'National Parks'.
- This policy includes the preservation of the rural countryside and historic monuments and buildings.

PHILOSOPHY of OUTDOOR RECREATION
- The philosophy is of being at one with nature, the fresh air and the simplicity of a rural existence.
- This was shared with the naturalism movement of the English middle and upper classes of the second half of the 19th century.
- This philosophy was guided by the middle class ethic of spiritual and physical purity which also emerged in England at the same time.

Information

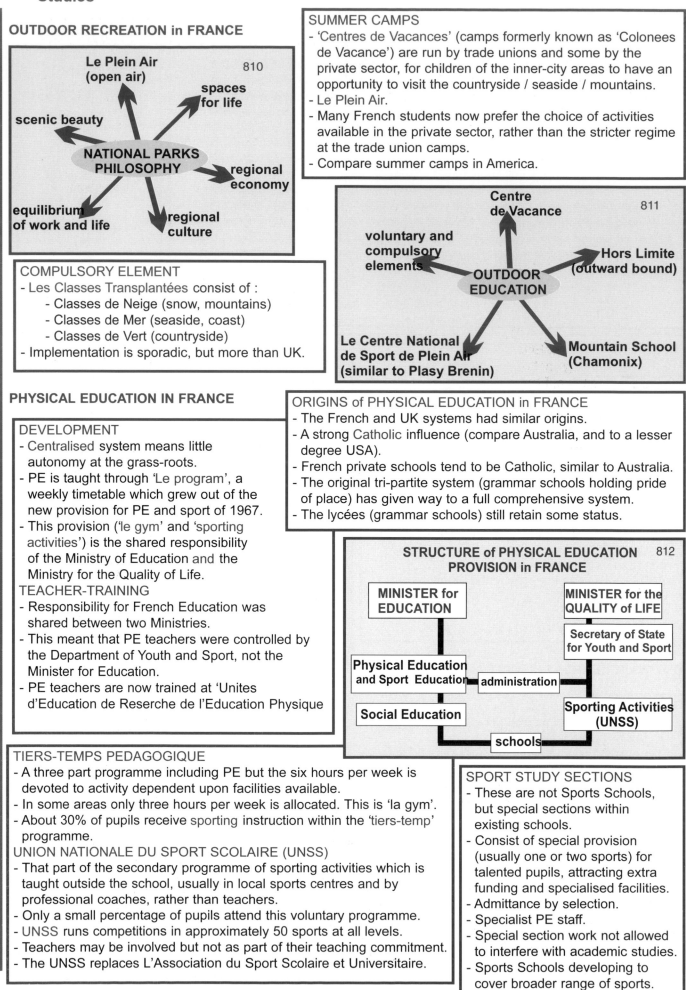

OUTDOOR RECREATION in FRANCE

Le Plein Air (open air) 810

scenic beauty · spaces for life · NATIONAL PARKS PHILOSOPHY · regional economy · equilibrium of work and life · regional culture

COMPULSORY ELEMENT
- Les Classes Transplantées consist of :
  - Classes de Neige (snow, mountains)
  - Classes de Mer (seaside, coast)
  - Classes de Vert (countryside)
- Implementation is sporadic, but more than UK.

SUMMER CAMPS
- 'Centres de Vacances' (camps formerly known as 'Colonees de Vacance') are run by trade unions and some by the private sector, for children of the inner-city areas to have an opportunity to visit the countryside / seaside / mountains.
- Le Plein Air.
- Many French students now prefer the choice of activities available in the private sector, rather than the stricter regime at the trade union camps.
- Compare summer camps in America.

Centre de Vacance 811

voluntary and compulsory elements · OUTDOOR EDUCATION · Hors Limite (outward bound) · Le Centre National de Sport de Plein Air (similar to Plasy Brenin) · Mountain School (Chamonix)

PHYSICAL EDUCATION IN FRANCE

DEVELOPMENT
- Centralised system means little autonomy at the grass-roots.
- PE is taught through 'Le program', a weekly timetable which grew out of the new provision for PE and sport of 1967.
- This provision ('le gym' and 'sporting activities') is the shared responsibility of the Ministry of Education and the Ministry for the Quality of Life.

TEACHER-TRAINING
- Responsibility for French Education was shared between two Ministries.
- This meant that PE teachers were controlled by the Department of Youth and Sport, not the Minister for Education.
- PE teachers are now trained at 'Unites d'Education de Reserche de l'Education Physique

ORIGINS of PHYSICAL EDUCATION in FRANCE
- The French and UK systems had similar origins.
- A strong Catholic influence (compare Australia, and to a lesser degree USA).
- French private schools tend to be Catholic, similar to Australia.
- The original tri-partite system (grammar schools holding pride of place) has given way to a full comprehensive system.
- The lycées (grammar schools) still retain some status.

STRUCTURE of PHYSICAL EDUCATION PROVISION in FRANCE 812
MINISTER for EDUCATION · MINISTER for the QUALITY of LIFE · Secretary of State for Youth and Sport · Physical Education and Sport Education · administration · Sporting Activities (UNSS) · Social Education · schools

TIERS-TEMPS PEDAGOGIQUE
- A three part programme including PE but the six hours per week is devoted to activity dependent upon facilities available.
- In some areas only three hours per week is allocated. This is 'la gym'.
- About 30% of pupils receive sporting instruction within the 'tiers-temp' programme.

UNION NATIONALE DU SPORT SCOLAIRE (UNSS)
- That part of the secondary programme of sporting activities which is taught outside the school, usually in local sports centres and by professional coaches, rather than teachers.
- Only a small percentage of pupils attend this voluntary programme.
- UNSS runs competitions in approximately 50 sports at all levels.
- Teachers may be involved but not as part of their teaching commitment.
- The UNSS replaces L'Association du Sport Scolaire et Universitaire.

SPORT STUDY SECTIONS
- These are not Sports Schools, but special sections within existing schools.
- Consist of special provision (usually one or two sports) for talented pupils, attracting extra funding and specialised facilities.
- Admittance by selection.
- Specialist PE staff.
- Special section work not allowed to interfere with academic studies.
- Sports Schools developing to cover broader range of sports.

SPORT IN FRANCE

ORIGINS
- 'Olympianism'. De Coubertin (initiator of the modern Olympic movement) was a French aristocrat.
- Modern structure of Sport in France is based on whether sports are 'Olympic' or 'non-Olympic'.

YOUTH SPORT LINKS
- Maisons des Jeunes et Culture make provision for sport as part of central policy.
- Municipal groups (for example, the Fire Services) promote a range of recreational activities ('sapeurs-pompiers'), which includes inter-town competition and outdoor experiences.
- Tennis and golf have grown enormously in the last ten years.
- Easy access to facilities reflects a centralised policy which provides them on the basis of social need which reflects an acknowledgement of the value of the recreative process, as opposed to provision aimed purely at the production of excellence.

DEVELOPMENT
- All sport is funded through the National Olympic and Sports Committee.
- This is divided into two sections :
    - Top class (international) sport ('Olympic' and 'non-Olympic').
    - Sport for All (regional level and downward).
- Sport is controlled centrally by the Ministry of Youth and Sport through regional and departmental (district) directorates.
- The directorates have no autonomy and exist to carry out Ministry objectives.
- Sports organisations are divided into 'Olympic' and 'non-Olympic'. Rugby transferred to Olympic status in preparation for 2000 Olympics.
- 'Multisport' federations and the federations of university and school sport make up the four major administrative threads of French sport.
- The success of France in international sport has now attracted commercial sponsorship to both individual sports and the central organisation that supports international and Olympic teams.

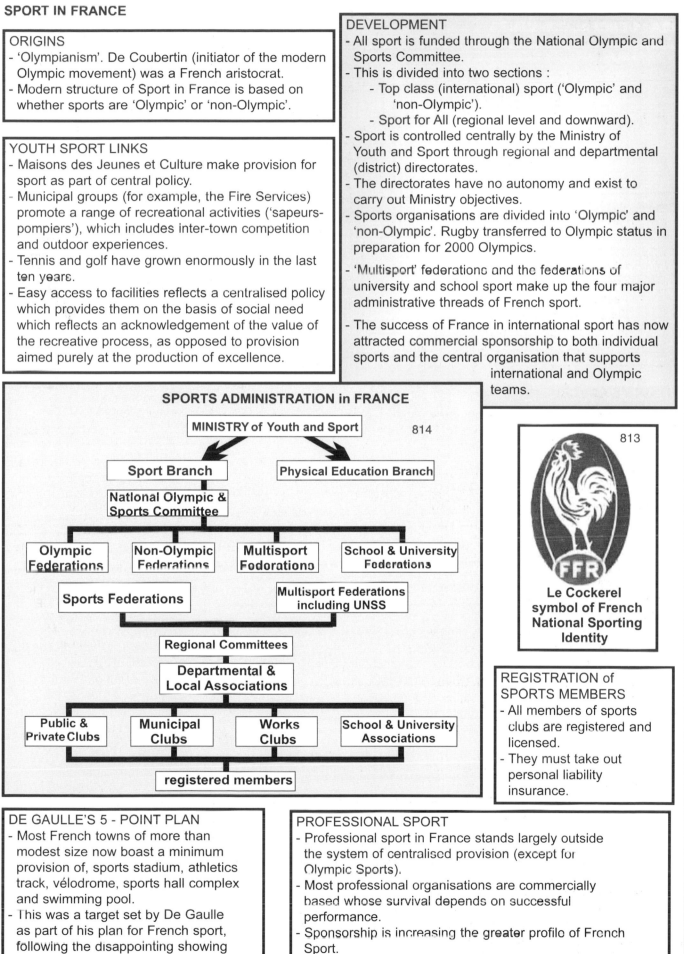

SPORTS ADMINISTRATION in FRANCE

MINISTRY of Youth and Sport   814

Sport Branch   Physical Education Branch

National Olympic & Sports Committee

Olympic Federations | Non-Olympic Federations | Multisport Federations | School & University Federations

Sports Federations   Multisport Federations including UNSS

Regional Committees

Departmental & Local Associations

Public & Private Clubs | Municipal Clubs | Works Clubs | School & University Associations

registered members

813

Le Cockerel symbol of French National Sporting Identity

REGISTRATION of SPORTS MEMBERS
- All members of sports clubs are registered and licensed.
- They must take out personal liability insurance.

DE GAULLE'S 5 - POINT PLAN
- Most French towns of more than modest size now boast a minimum provision of, sports stadium, athletics track, vélodrome, sports hall complex and swimming pool.
- This was a target set by De Gaulle as part of his plan for French sport, following the disappointing showing at the 1960 Olympiad.

PROFESSIONAL SPORT
- Professional sport in France stands largely outside the system of centralised provision (except for Olympic Sports).
- Most professional organisations are commercially based whose survival depends on successful performance.
- Sponsorship is increasing the greater profile of French Sport.

USA : GENERAL COMMENTS

CULTURAL INFLUENCES
- Comparable with Australia, both countries have suppressed the influence of an indigenous culture in sport and recreation (and across the social and political spectrum).
- Also influenced by British colonial presence.
- And (similar to Australia) by policies of mass immigration.
- The War of Independence, and the Civil War (compare with French and Russian revolutions).
- USA is a federal state (compare Australia).
- USA has wide topographical and climatic diversity (compare Australia and to a lesser degree France).

THE DECENTRALISED STATE
- The USA is the least centralised in terms of administration and responsibility is devolved to state and local level wherever possible.
- The capitalist ethic has meant that independence of individual organisations is highly valued.
- Federality in the USA is expressed for international sporting events (the Olympics, the soccer World Cup and other World Championships).
- And for National legislation (for example, 'Title IX' - equal opportunities for women).
- Currently, federal funding is still substantial, but commercial sponsorship is increasing as the USOC and government accept that this is commonplace elsewhere.

815

The image of women as cheer leaders contrasts with the philosphy of Title IX legislation

STACKING
- Ensures the preservation of the White Anglo-Saxon Protestant (WASP) power base, with Vietnamese at the bottom of the pile on the 'last in' principle. This is also reflected in roles in sport, and only relatively recently have we seen black quarterbacks playing American football and black coaches on the sidelines.
- TV, professionalism and advertising have helped break down these barriers in the US as well as in Australia and elsewhere.
- But blacks and other ethnic groups are not allowed to rise to a level where they can exert control and generally do not become more than well-paid 'gladiators'.
- This is the 'glass ceiling' syndrome, which also applies to women.
- Blacks and ethnic minorities in the UK, and Aborigines in Australia are generally ascribed a more lowly status by society (in spite of legislation aimed at countering this), and although France has 'l'egalitarianism' written into its constitution, there are some groups, including Algerians, who would feel that they are still a political (and sporting) minority.

ISOLATIONISM
- All the major sports in the US (except for Track & Field) are 'contrived', indigenous sports.
- Their 'World Series' mentality is applied to sports that are not 'World Sports'.
- Hence US 'sports moguls' retain both control and the certainty of American success.
- The level of specialisation achieved within these sports is such that, as commercial interests orchestrate a projection of these sports onto the world stage, US teams are almost guaranteed to be ahead of their rivals.
- NBC have reported very low viewing figures for the 2000 Olympics. It seems that Americans also prefer major sport to occur in the USA - not elsewhere!

OUTDOOR RECREATION IN THE USA

CONTROL
- America's natural resources are centrally controlled by the Department of the Interior.
- The use of land and water space for recreational purposes is the responsibility of a whole range of Departments (Bureau).
- Influence of presidents Wilson and Roosevelt.

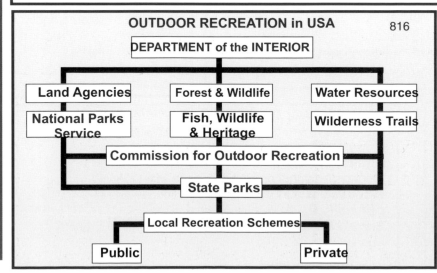

OUTDOOR RECREATION in USA 816

DEPARTMENT of the INTERIOR

Land Agencies | Forest & Wildlife | Water Resources

National Parks Service | Fish, Wildlife & Heritage | Wilderness Trails

Commission for Outdoor Recreation

State Parks

Local Recreation Schemes

Public | Private

SIZE
- USA has land area of 3.5 million sq. miles.
- Comparable with Australia but almost 15 times its population.
- Size and diversity helps recreation within a far superior communications infrastructure.

Information

OUTDOOR RECREATION IN THE USA - continued

PHILOSOPHY
- USA is a 'young nation', created by adventurers and pioneers of the great outdoors (compare Australia).
- USA has wilderness areas (much less than Australia).
- Large proportion of population access these areas.
- Outdoor recreation embraces a much wider range of activity than the 'sea-shore' (as in Australia).
- Outdoor education is seen as very important but is delivered to school age young people through 'summer camps' rather than school programmes.

NATIONAL PARKS
- Federal Law through the National Park Service controls America's great National Parks.
- These are distinct from State Parks, which are administered by the States in which they lie.
- The 'frontier spirit' which forged America is seen as an important ethic which should continue to be part of the cultural heritage of all Americans.
- Contrast with 'equilibrium of work and life' philosophy of French National Parks.

OUTDOOR EDUCATION
- Occurs more regularly outside schools.
- However, schools are often involved in placing students on State-run summer camp programmes.
- State authorities (aided by Federal funding) make provision for young people of limited means to attend State summer camps.
- Many camps are run privately and much kudos is derived from attendance at a 'prestige' venue.
- These camps are intended to introduce young Americans to nature and to each other.
- Some are founded on an educational basis, whilst others are purely for holidays / recreation.
- Socialisation is seen as an important part of the process as is a fostering of the competitive spirit.
- 'Fat camps' and 'puny camps' would seem to serve the purpose of isolation, rather than integration for the young people forced to attend them.
- Compare with the French system for the 'outdoor experience'.
- Much greater statutory provision exists in USA and France than either the UK or Australia.

PHYSICAL EDUCATION IN THE USA

ORIGINS
- Western European influences.
- German and Scandinavian (largely Swedish) systems of physical education.
- A mixture of public / private (education) provision.
- Bi-polarisation between church and secular institutions (compare UK, France and Australia).

DEVELOPMENT
- Physical Education in the United States is run at local level by Local District School Boards.
- Who have the responsibility devolved down to them from the State Board of Education.
- And who, in turn, pass on day-to-day control to the Principal of each school.
- Policy is devolved down to the Local School Board only and NOT to the individual school.
- Therefore, unlike the PE teacher in the UK (who is responsible for his / her own teaching programme), the 'Phys Ed.' Teacher in the US is often responsible for teaching a programme devised by the Director / Superintendent of Physical Education in Schools at Local School Board level.
- However, some School boards (for example, those in Washington DC) allow considerable flexibility for teachers to devise their own programmes.
- Compares most closely with that in France, since teachers there have little or no flexibility to utilise their own professional judgement in determining the content of the programme they teach.
- French schools implement a National programme, but USA schools have a Local programme.

STRUCTURE of SCHOOL PE 817

- STATE EDUCATION BOARD
- Local / District School Boards
- Director / Superintendent of PE
- High / Elementary School Principal
- School Dept of Physical Education
- Individual Teacher

BIPOLAR STRUCTURE of PE and SPORT in USA HIGH SCHOOLS 818

- DIRECTOR of HEALTH and PHYSICAL EDUCATION
  - Director of Physical Education
    - Physical Education Staff
    - Physical Education Classes
  - Director of Athletic Programme
    - Head Coaches (various sports)
    - Coaches / Assistant Coaches
  - Student Body — Student Teams

- In the USA, the Director of Health and Physical Education often has overall control over the 'Athletic Programme' and the physical education programme.
- He / she will appoint appropriately to the two major posts :
  - The 'Educator'
  - The Coach
- With distinct and separate roles.

PHYSICAL EDUCATION IN THE USA - continued

BACKGROUND
- Some coaches may teach 'Phys Ed' to make up their time (or indeed an academic subject) but they are paid as coaches and 'job security' depends upon sporting and not academic success.
- Some 'Phys Ed' teachers may coach but this is more common in Junior High Schools than in their senior counterparts.
- This 'bi-polar' emphasis produces conflicts as to which aspect of a student's life should take precedence, with academic performance often losing out.
- In the USA, where High School and College sport reign supreme, professional clubs have to wait their turn for the recruitment of school age sportspeople.

SPORT IN THE USA

ORIGINS
- Colonial influence (compare Australia), note French colonial influence to the north.
- Mass immigration from Europe (late nineteenth and early 20th centuries).
- Emerging middle classes transplanted the sporting ethos of the English aristocracy / middle classes to the universities Cornell, Harvard, Princeton and Yale (Ivy League).
- This produced American (or 'grid-iron') football and compares to the 'Oxbridge' ethos in the UK.
- Innovators such as James Naismith presented basketball as a rationalised, acceptable recreation for the working classes, controlled by a middle-class, white élite.
- Institutions such as the Church / YMCA have had a major influence on the growth of US sport.
- The growth of Mass Education and the eventual influence of mass access to recreation.

DEVELOPMENT :
- Except for baseball and ice-hockey, sport in USA has developed through the collegiate system of sporting excellence.
- Here 'outcome' has largely ridden roughshod over 'process' (the end justifies the means).
- There are three co-existent cultures :
  - The Lombardian ethic : winning is all that counts. This is outcome led heightened by the needs of professionalism and a society that only acknowledges winners.
  - The Radical ethic : winning is important but not at all costs. The 'process' has intrinsic value, which outweighs the extrinsic outcome (for example, educational, personal enrichment, development of co-operative social skills).
  - The Counter-culture ethic : the process (or experience) is all that matters. This culture derides competition as pure selfish posturing.

COMPARISON of USA with other COUNTRIES
- Contrast with France where academic interests have always been given the higher priority.
- Similar to France where the majority of school sport under the UNSS system is supervised by paid coaches (working entirely outside the school system).
- In Australia, school sport is still run by teachers at school level but in conjunction with help from outside agencies, particularly in an administrative capacity.
- In the UK, school sport is run and organised by teachers with little outside help.
- Wilkinson Report (UK) removes promising schoolboy footballers from school sport altogether, basing them at Premier League centres of excellence. The FA now runs the national schools under 15 side, not teachers. This would never happen in the USA, where school and college sport reign supreme, and professional clubs have to wait their turn.

ETHNIC ISSUES
- Baseball, without the same 'college roots' as other sports, gave opportunities to a range of ethnic sportsmen long before it was feasible in football and basketball.
- Black influence in sport has grown since the 'civil rights' successes of the sixties and seventies.
- Hispanic influences are strongest in baseball but the influence of the Vietnamese, has still to be felt.
- The White Anglo-Saxon Protestant (WASP) group remains the source of power and influence, utilising wealth and social status to prevent other groups from climbing the ladder (the glass ceiling).

STRUCTURE
- Collegiate Sport has two 'divisions': the National Collegiate Athletic Association (NCAA) and the National Association of Inter-Collegiate Athletics (NAIA).
- The former powerful Amateur Athletic Union (AAU) was replaced by individual sports governing bodies in 1977/8 and the former Association of Inter-Collegiate Athletics for Women (AIAW) was absorbed into the NCAA in 1981.

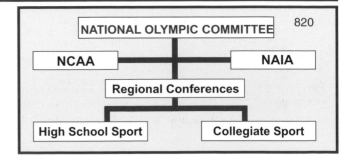

Information

PROFESSIONAL SPORT IN THE USA

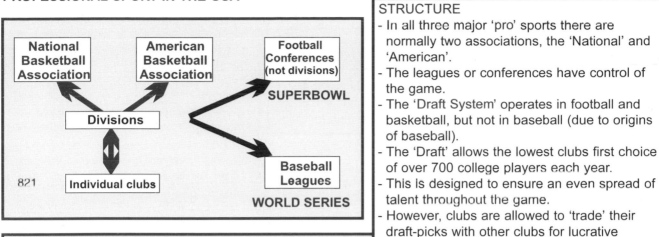

STRUCTURE

- In all three major 'pro' sports there are normally two associations, the 'National' and 'American'.
- The leagues or conferences have control of the game.
- The 'Draft System' operates in football and basketball, but not in baseball (due to origins of baseball).
- The 'Draft' allows the lowest clubs first choice of over 700 college players each year.
- This Is designed to ensure an even spread of talent throughout the game.
- However, clubs are allowed to 'trade' their draft-picks with other clubs for lucrative amounts, thus rather defeating the object of the system.

OTHER ISSUES in USA SPORT

- The 'female performer' in USA high school / college / professional sport is the cheer-leader!!
- The female gymnast or track athlete has to serve both functions.
- Access to professional sport is almost always via the college sports system (football and basketball but not baseball and ice hockey).
- Because of this, private sports clubs do not exist in the numbers we have in the UK. 'Little Leagues' and 'Minor Leagues' however do exist in both ice hockey and baseball, and provide feeders to pro-leagues.
- American 'Pro' sport is financed by sponsorship, TV money, and the personal wealth of 'team owners'.
- The only real federal money that makes its way into sport is that used to finance US Olympic teams and their development.

ARGENTINA : GENERAL COMMENTS

HISTORICAL AND CULTURAL INFLUENCES

- Argentina was colonised by Spain and this has influenced both population and culture.
  Independence was not gained until early in the 19th century and the political situation has stabilised only very recently, (Laws of Basic Consensus, 1993) following the war in the Falkland Islands (Malvinas).
- The first significant attempts to make any central provision for sport and recreation occurred during the 'Peronist' period of the 1950s but were reversed during the rule of the subsequent military 'junta'.

POPULATION

- The population of Argentina is mainly of European origin, with the native (mestizo) population very poorly treated.
- 'Amerindians' (mixed race) make up the population.
- British influence was felt in sport and education towards the end of the 19th century.
- Cabicates négras (black little heads) are the most disadvantaged indigenous native group.

OUTDOOR RECREATION IN ARGENTINA

PROVISION ?

- As in many other emergent cultures, the concept of recreation for the mass of the population is relatively new. Argentina (like Kenya and South Africa) has the recreational ethic of a European middle class culture overlying the former rural and occupation-related recreations of its indigenous populations.
- Such activity centres upon Argentina's grasslands and plains, its mountains and the coastal strip of its eastern seaboard.
- Equestrian activity embraces the élite activity of polo and the horsemanship of the gaucho.
- 'Imported' activities such as Pelota are popular in recreational and sporting formats.
- Alpine-based recreations have traditionally been the preserve of the middle classes but the development of cheaper transport now allows broader access to remote areas.

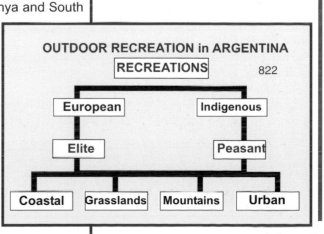

OUTDOOR RECREATION in ARGENTINA

PHYSICAL EDUCATION IN ARGENTINA

BACKGROUND
- Early developments in PE occurred in the private schools and in and around the city of Buenos Aires.
- Prior to the 'Laws of Basic Consensus' there was no 'nationally effective' programme of physical education in Argentina's schools.
- The National Institute of Physical Education was created in 1985.

SPORT IN ARGENTINA

STRUCTURE OF SPORT
- The Asociaci—n Deportiva Estudjantil (ADE) organises sport in private schools' and state school sport is centred around the province of Buenos Aires.
- In other provinces sport is provided by sports clubs not schools.
- Elite sport was organised by the Confederacion Atletica de Deportes (CAD) but in 1989 this became the Secretaria de Deportes de la Nacion (National Secretariat of Sport) and is responsible directly to the national president.
- In theory its aim is to co-ordinate community, educational, high performance (including professional) and Olympic sport.
- In practice, it awards scholarships to gifted athletes and organises Olympic preparation and selection in conjunction with the Comite Olimpico Argentino.
- Professional sport is well established in Argentina. The country has a population that is 85 per cent urban, hence large centres of population to support professional sport.
- Football, basketball and (more recently) rugby are well supported.
- Many Argentine professionals however, travel to Europe or North America where sporting salaries are far higher than at home.

CONTENT
- The contents of the PE programme are part of the General Basic Education (EGB) and consist of four learning blocks:

- Block 1 : The body & movement with gymnastics as the main medium of learning.

- Block 2 : Bodily health and well-being in the world around us: the acquisition of simple and complex skills.

- Block 3 : Motor games and 'play' to integrate personality, expression and develop motor skills.
- Move towards playing and understanding adult games with appropriate rules.

- Block 4 : The application of knowledge of the body, abilities and motor skills to spontaneous and regulated games.
- Hygiene and consideration for the body and those of others.
- Conservation of the surroundings.

KENYA - GENERAL COMMENTS

SOCIAL AND CULTURAL INFLUENCES
- Similar to other former colonies with sport, recreation & physical education developed by largely Christian and 'Empire' influences, which overlaid ancient tribal cultures.
- Independence (1963) has seen development in selected sports and activity largely centred in a few urban centres.
- Infrastructure development is very poor and recreational provision is made largely for the wealthy and tourist classes.

THE ECONOMY
- A very poor economy based on agriculture and 'foreign' interests own much of its production (e.g. coffee).
- Such exploitation means that profit goes elsewhere and this has serious implications for a government, which:
  - Is very much affected by tribal conflicts.
  - Is struggling to make any real provision for much of its population due to lack of revenue.
- There are areas affected by drought and malnutrition with very poor school attendance in some regions.

OUTDOOR RECREATION IN KENYA
(including outdoor education)

RECREATIONS
- Historically, recreations tend to reflect life-styles and preparation for life as a warrior influenced the fighting and weapon-orientated activities for boys.
- Girls tended to mimic their elders also but dance was (and still is) an important cultural aspect of recreation for both sexes.
- Modern recreational patterns influence only those in the (minority) urban areas who can afford them but most of the population still largely rural in situation and lifestyle.

CONSERVATION - NATIONAL PARKS
- The former colonial lifestyle that popularised the hunting of game and safaris, is still catered for and this now embraces issues of both conservation and élitism.
- The national parks (e.g. The Massai Mara) are utilised by the few rich Kenyans who can afford the expensive lifestyle along with wealthy tourists who bring in a large proportion of the country's foreign currency earnings.
- Lack of revenue means that little provision for recreation is made outside of the major centres such as Nairobi and Mombassa.

PHYSICAL EDUCATION IN KENYA

PROVISION OF PE
- The development is typical of former colonial countries with PE being developed within the private sector in (largely) religious foundations.
- Provision outside the private sector was (and still is) poor and current programmes are poorly implemented outside the major urban areas.
- Poor attendance contributes to this but lack of finance means that in practice the nature of (facility) provision in many schools relies on the tradition of Harambee (collection) amongst parents.
- The state provides the initial buildings and pays the staff but little else.

SCHOOL SPORT
- Reasonably well supported and is administered through the country's fifty-five regions.
- This structure is reflected in the nature of sporting competition in which there are district, regional and national championships.
- This is largely in 'European sports' such as soccer, cricket and netball.
- There is little provision for indoor sport outside of the private sector.
- There is considerable strength in track and field athletics and soccer is highly popular.

SPORT IN KENYA

STRUCTURE and PARTICIPATION
- Sport in Kenya today is run from the office of the Vice President and Ministry of Home Affairs, Heritage and Sports, which also has a huge brief encompassing many other areas.
- Basketball and cricket both have a strong following but athletics is the most successful and soccer the most popular sport.
- All these sports have strong professional links.
- Golf is played largely by 'well to do' Kenyans and visiting tourists.

OLYMPIC SPORT
- The Kenyan National Olympic Committee (NOCK) is an independent organisation, free from government control.
- It is privately funded and controls all amateur as well as Olympic sport.
- The Kenya National Olympic Association and the Kenya Amateur Athletic Association were both founded in 1952 in the days when the country was still a British colony.

SOUTH AFRICA (RSA) - GENERAL COMMENTS

CULTURAL INFLUENCES
- The cultural roots of sport are set the days of the British Empire and colonialism, with the muscular Christian ethic being a prime influence.
- A major difference between South Africa and Kenya is that South Africa has considerable mineral wealth.
- Also, (until very recently) independence left a white 'European' culture in power.
- Sporting cultures have been firmly set in the European context and native populations were so completely marginalised that only the recent overthrow of apartheid has begun to change things.
- One outcome of this is that soccer is now the game of the masses whilst rugby remains the province of the former white groups.

OUTDOOR RECREATION IN SOUTH AFRICA

STRUCTURES
- SANREC develops community recreational programmes with a network of nine Provincial Committees (PRORECS) which administer its programmes within each province.
- The SANGALA project consists of :
    - Community Sangala - the whole community.
    - Training Sangala - training community leaders.
    - Corporate Sangala - middle and senior management in both private and public sectors.
    - Senior Sangala - encourages physical activity among senior citizens.
    - Street Sangala - life-skills project for homeless children.
- RSA has fifty-three national parks or protected areas including the world famous Kruger National Park.
- These areas have been the preserve of the privileged whites but also attract foreign tourists and currency.

ACCESS AND PROVISION
- Programmes sponsored by SANGALA (South African National Games and Leisure Association) are the beginning of a long process of empowerment of ordinary people in access to and provision for recreation that will take some time to develop fully.

- The SANGALA programmes are the result of co-operation between SANREC and the Department of Sport and Recreation and were launched in 1996 with the aim of involving all South Africans in healthy recreational activities as part of the nation-building process.

Information

PHYSICAL EDUCATION IN SOUTH AFRICA

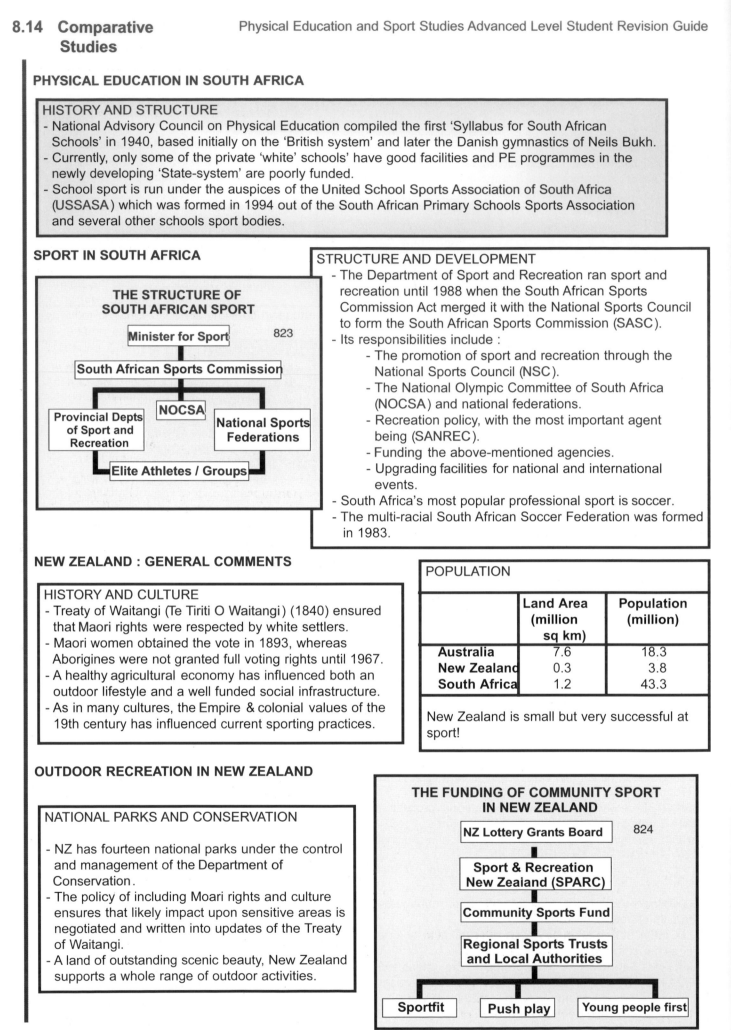

HISTORY AND STRUCTURE
- National Advisory Council on Physical Education compiled the first 'Syllabus for South African Schools' in 1940, based initially on the 'British system' and later the Danish gymnastics of Neils Bukh.
- Currently, only some of the private 'white' schools' have good facilities and PE programmes in the newly developing 'State-system' are poorly funded.
- School sport is run under the auspices of the United School Sports Association of South Africa (USSASA) which was formed in 1994 out of the South African Primary Schools Sports Association and several other schools sport bodies.

SPORT IN SOUTH AFRICA

THE STRUCTURE OF SOUTH AFRICAN SPORT

Minister for Sport 823

South African Sports Commission

NOCSA

Provincial Depts of Sport and Recreation

National Sports Federations

Elite Athletes / Groups

STRUCTURE AND DEVELOPMENT
- The Department of Sport and Recreation ran sport and recreation until 1988 when the South African Sports Commission Act merged it with the National Sports Council to form the South African Sports Commission (SASC).
- Its responsibilities include :
  - The promotion of sport and recreation through the National Sports Council (NSC).
  - The National Olympic Committee of South Africa (NOCSA) and national federations.
  - Recreation policy, with the most important agent being (SANREC).
  - Funding the above-mentioned agencies.
  - Upgrading facilities for national and international events.
- South Africa's most popular professional sport is soccer.
- The multi-racial South African Soccer Federation was formed in 1983.

NEW ZEALAND : GENERAL COMMENTS

HISTORY AND CULTURE
- Treaty of Waitangi (Te Tiriti O Waitangi) (1840) ensured that Maori rights were respected by white settlers.
- Maori women obtained the vote in 1893, whereas Aborigines were not granted full voting rights until 1967.
- A healthy agricultural economy has influenced both an outdoor lifestyle and a well funded social infrastructure.
- As in many cultures, the Empire & colonial values of the 19th century has influenced current sporting practices.

POPULATION

	Land Area (million sq km)	Population (million)
Australia	7.6	18.3
New Zealand	0.3	3.8
South Africa	1.2	43.3

New Zealand is small but very successful at sport!

OUTDOOR RECREATION IN NEW ZEALAND

NATIONAL PARKS AND CONSERVATION

- NZ has fourteen national parks under the control and management of the Department of Conservation.
- The policy of including Moari rights and culture ensures that likely impact upon sensitive areas is negotiated and written into updates of the Treaty of Waitangi.
- A land of outstanding scenic beauty, New Zealand supports a whole range of outdoor activities.

THE FUNDING OF COMMUNITY SPORT IN NEW ZEALAND

NZ Lottery Grants Board 824

Sport & Recreation New Zealand (SPARC)

Community Sports Fund

Regional Sports Trusts and Local Authorities

Sportfit

Push play

Young people first

Information

PHYSICAL EDUCATION IN NEW ZEALAND

HEALTH AND PE
- This area of the NZ curriculum is compulsory for all students up to Year 10.
- The programme is centred upon the Maori word 'hauora' (a sense of well-being).
- This reflects the inclusion of the country's native culture.
- Many of the key terms are expressed in the Maori language as well as in English.
- There are eight stages of learning within seven 'key areas', which are :
  - Mental health.
  - Sexuality education.
  - Food and nutrition.
  - Body care and physical safety.
  - Physical activity.
  - Sport studies.
  - Outdoor education.

THE NZ SECONDARY SCHOOLS SPORTS COUNCIL
- Set up in 1992.
- Its regional structure helps promote a wide range of sporting activities in the country's schools.
- The council's regional directors also act as administrators of the 'Sportfit' programme.
- This is one of the initiatives sponsored by the Hillary Commission.
- Which encourages the young people of New Zealand to become actively involved in sport and recreation.

SPORT IN NEW ZEALAND

SPORT AND RECREATION COMMISSION (SPARC)
- The principal provider of funding and services to New Zealand sport is the SPARC (Sport and Recreation Commission) through the NZ Lottery Grants Board.
- A private organisation established by Act of Parliament in 2002.
- Its role embraces the broad spectrum of sport and recreation, including the funding of programmes of excellence and combines the former roles of the NZSF (New Zealand Sports Foundation) and the Hillary Commission (formed in 1987 to oversee NZ sport).
- This is similar to the role of the ASC and AIS in Australia.
- The country's rugby teams are legendary but there has also been success on the athletics track, the cricket field and in cycling in a country that values sport very highly.

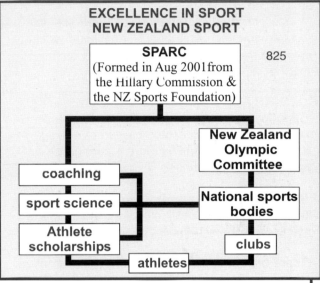

EXCELLENCE IN SPORT NEW ZEALAND SPORT

SPARC (Formed in Aug 2001 from the Hillary Commission & the NZ Sports Foundation) — 825

- coaching
- sport science
- Athlete scholarships
- athletes
- New Zealand Olympic Committee
- National sports bodies
- clubs

ASIA - GENERAL COMMENTS

CULTURE
- Many parts of South and East Asia were influenced by British colonialism or the influence of British trading communities.
- This included the sub-continent of India, and of course, China, which was never colonised but became a centre of trading activity from 1840 until early in the 20th century.
- Japan and Korea retained their own cultures.
- China re-established its own cultural heritage with the formation of the 'People's Republic' in 1949.

DEVELOPMENTS
- Developments in sport and recreation have come as a result of the globalising influence of international sport.
- Due to growth of modern communications technology and international markets for western goods and lifestyles.
- Many commercial concerns now utilise south east Asia as both part of an expanding global market and a source of cheap labour.

OUTDOOR RECREATION IN ASIA

RECREATION
- Chinese and Japanese culture have both traditionally valued recreation.
- Recently, both India and Pakistan have made considerable efforts to develop a centralised infrastructure.
- Examples :   - India - Sports Authority of India.
              - Pakistan - Pakistan Sports Board.
- In both cases government funding is provided despite poor economies & huge social problems.

MASS SPORT
- Mass sport in Japan has a definite 'Olympic' flavour.
- The Japanese Olympic Committee and the Japanese Amateur Sports Association organise activities for the whole community, including the Junior Sports Club (founded in 1962).
- There are nine branches throughout Japan with sports meetings organised at local and regional level for the 1.5 million members.
- In N. Korea, the Children's Games and National Games reflect the political overtones found in China with its 'workplace sport' & mass exercise programmes.

PHYSICAL EDUCATION IN ASIA

PE PROGRAMMES
- Vary across this region and reflect differing cultures and / or political persuasions.
- China and N. Korea have centralised systems which are highly structured.
- India and Pakistan have embryonic state systems which are poorly funded.
- Elsewhere there is a mixture of 'British schools' (examples : Hong Kong & Singapore) teaching PE as it occurs in the UK.
    - Local systems still very much based on 'the games ethic' - little or no formalised teaching.

SPORT IN ASIA

CULTURE AND POLICY
- Sport in Asia consists of a mixture of ancient activities that have in some cases been overlaid by colonial influence and by more recent global sporting trends in others.

- Most cultures now have policies of excellence but their focus is often upon globally popular sports rather than those reflecting indigenous activities.

- There are some exceptions to this generalisation.
- China particularly promotes its own culture in addition to that of the global sporting arena.

STRUCTURES
- Japan - Ministry of Education, Science & Culture, ('Monbusho') Physical Education Bureau, Boards of Education. Great emphasis of sport for life.
- China - the State Physical Education & Sports Commission : Provincial Physical Education Commissions. Very highly structured.
- India - Dept. of Education : Central Board of Secondary Education.
    - Specific syllabus - but not fully implemented.
- North Korea - Education Committee : Physical Culture & Sports Guidance Committee.

ECONOMICS
- Most Asian economies now centrally fund and support programmes of excellence.
- Not always based on effective mass participation programmes.
- The clear aim here is to gain short-term success without the infrastructure and cost associated with programmes of excellence based on full participation.
- Highly organised sporting structures also exist in schools - sometimes at the expense of effective programmes of physical education.

- In India, Pakistan, China and N. Korea there is strong military influence in both sports participation and facility / programme provision.

Frank Galligan

THE OLYMPIC GAMES - A CASE STUDY IN GLOBAL SPORT

HISTORY OF THE ANCIENT GAMES
- The Games of the ancient world (known collectively as Panhellenic Games) are the earliest well-recorded civilised athletic festivals.
- The Games of Olympia the best known of these.
- Others were :
  - The Pythian Games (Delphi)
  - The Isthmian Games (Isthmia)
  - The Nemean Games (Nemea)
- These were known as 'Crown Games' as victors received a laurel or other crown rather than money.
- The first recorded victor, in the Stade of 776BC was Koroibus of Elis, who was (unusually) a baker.
- Other events included :
  The Diaulos.
    The Dolichos.
      Wrestling.
        Pankration.
          Boxing.
            The Pentathlon.
              The Race in armour (Hoplite or Hippolite)
- Boys events were sometimes held but never girls.

HISTORY PRE 20TH CENTURY
- The Cotswold 'Olympik' Games, were begun by Robert Dover in 1612.
- The Wenlock Olympian Games held at Much Wenlock by William Penny Brooks in 1850.
- The Gog MaGog Olympik Games (1620) are the earliest recorded 'Olympic' resurgence.
- Other events included the Olympian Festivals of the National Olympian Association in the 1860s 70s and 80s and the Liverpool Olympic Festivals held for a short time in the 1860s and 70s.
- De Coubertin visited English public schools (including Rugby) and was impressed with English games and Thomas Arnold.
- He believed that it was the character developed by exercise and games that was the key to the re-building of France after the Franco-Prussian War.
- De Coubertin's Olympic dream came into being on Easter Sunday 1896 when 311 athletes from 13 countries contested nine sports.

AMATEURISM AND SOCIAL CLASS
- The issue of professionalism was contentious in Olympic sport.
- It revolved not just around whether sportsmen were paid but whether they were gentlemen.
- Early Olympians would have been white, middle or upper class and wealthy.

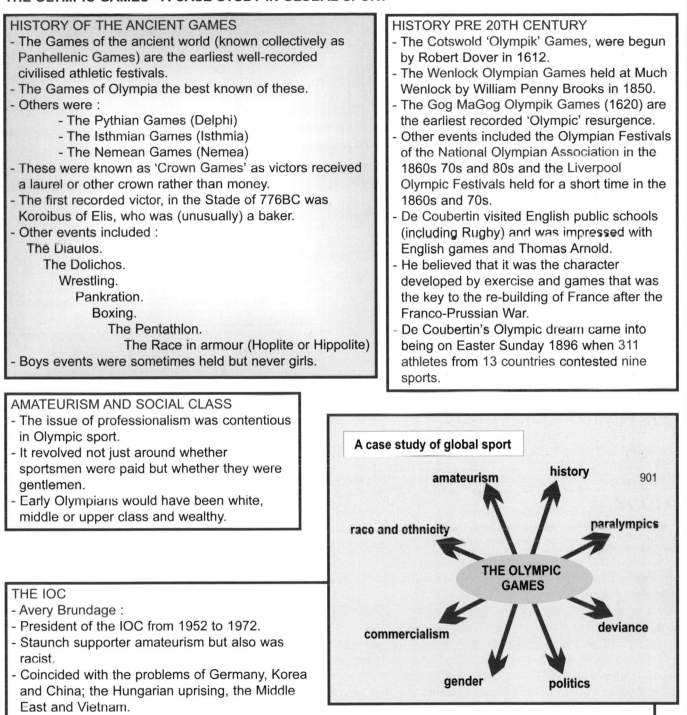

A case study of global sport

THE OLYMPIC GAMES

amateurism   history   901
race and ethnicity   paralympics
commercialism   deviance
gender   politics

THE IOC
- Avery Brundage :
- President of the IOC from 1952 to 1972.
- Staunch supporter amateurism but also was racist.
- Coincided with the problems of Germany, Korea and China; the Hungarian uprising, the Middle East and Vietnam.
- Associated with the 'Black Power' salute of Mexico 1968 and his statement 'the Games must go on' after the massacre of the Israeli athletes at Munich in 1972.
- Attempted to persuade the free world not to boycott the Berlin Games of 1936 (was criticised for this).

- Juan Antonio Samaranch :
- President from 1980 until 2001.
- Had to deal with political boycotts and the growth of professionalism in sport.
- Integrity of the IOC and its commissioners was challenged and his own conduct as President scrutinised.
- Presided over the return of South Africa to the Olympics and the holding of Olympics in Seoul.

- Jaques Rogge (Belgium). succeeded Samaranch in July 2001.

RACE AND ETHNICITY IN THE OLYMPICS

THE OLYMPIC CREED
- States that athletes should be free to participate irrespective of race, colour or creed.
- Mass access to sport requires that constraints upon cultural and sub-cultural groups should be removed.
- In order for minority groups to have equality they must also have access and provision.

- Access can be denied by :
    - A numerically superior culture.
    - Self-imposed cultural constraint.
    - Economic / topographical limitations.
- The major issue therefore is the exclusion of racial minorities from existing opportunity, or the failure to extend provision to all.

- Olympic Solidarity programmes and the various IOC commissions are responsible for education and provision in areas of need.
- Funded by income from television rights.

STACKING AND CENTRALITY
- These concepts reflect the cultural values within nation groups.
- The WASP culture of Britain, the USA and Europe was initially reflected in the Olympic movement.
- But the IOC is a now more cosmopolitan body with over 100 delegates from all over the World.

- The IOC is also a 'self-perpetuating club' without democratic accountability, but this is about to change.

- The concepts of stacking and centrality exist in nearly all cultures and is caused by the inclination of the most powerful group to perpetuate its own well being and values.

- One result of this is the 'glass ceiling', which refers to the invisible bar to advancement for ethnic and gender groups.

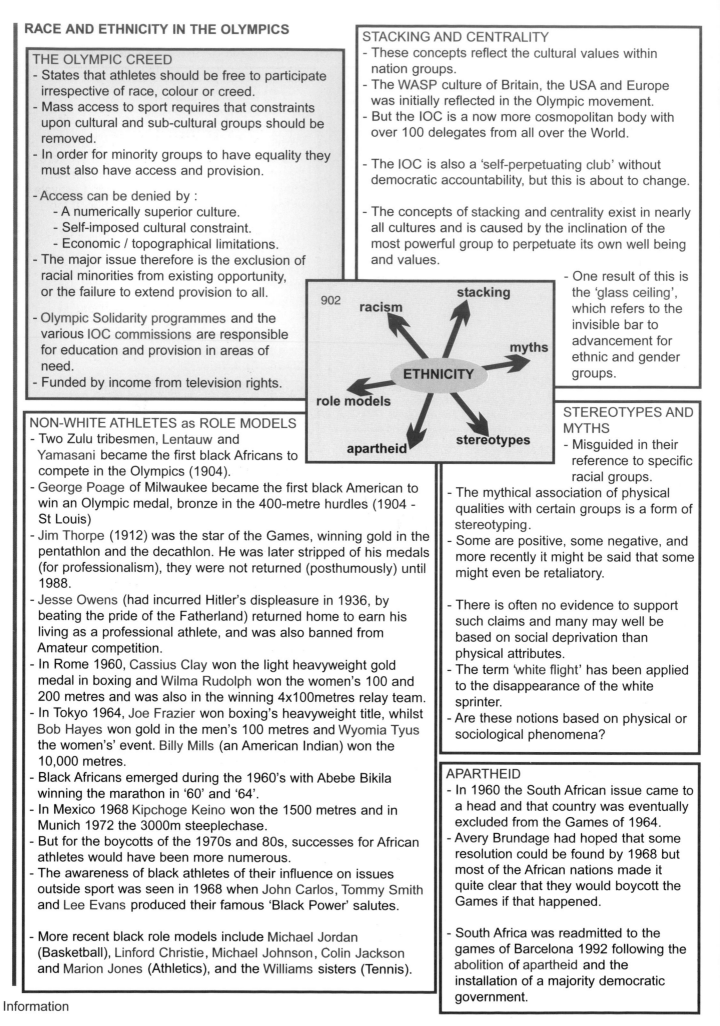

NON-WHITE ATHLETES as ROLE MODELS
- Two Zulu tribesmen, Lentauw and Yamasani became the first black Africans to compete in the Olympics (1904).
- George Poage of Milwaukee became the first black American to win an Olympic medal, bronze in the 400-metre hurdles (1904 - St Louis)
- Jim Thorpe (1912) was the star of the Games, winning gold in the pentathlon and the decathlon. He was later stripped of his medals (for professionalism), they were not returned (posthumously) until 1988.
- Jesse Owens (had incurred Hitler's displeasure in 1936, by beating the pride of the Fatherland) returned home to earn his living as a professional athlete, and was also banned from Amateur competition.
- In Rome 1960, Cassius Clay won the light heavyweight gold medal in boxing and Wilma Rudolph won the women's 100 and 200 metres and was also in the winning 4x100metres relay team.
- In Tokyo 1964, Joe Frazier won boxing's heavyweight title, whilst Bob Hayes won gold in the men's 100 metres and Wyomia Tyus the women's' event. Billy Mills (an American Indian) won the 10,000 metres.
- Black Africans emerged during the 1960's with Abebe Bikila winning the marathon in '60' and '64'.
- In Mexico 1968 Kipchoge Keino won the 1500 metres and in Munich 1972 the 3000m steeplechase.
- But for the boycotts of the 1970s and 80s, successes for African athletes would have been more numerous.
- The awareness of black athletes of their influence on issues outside sport was seen in 1968 when John Carlos, Tommy Smith and Lee Evans produced their famous 'Black Power' salutes.

- More recent black role models include Michael Jordan (Basketball), Linford Christie, Michael Johnson, Colin Jackson and Marion Jones (Athletics), and the Williams sisters (Tennis).

STEREOTYPES AND MYTHS
- Misguided in their reference to specific racial groups.
- The mythical association of physical qualities with certain groups is a form of stereotyping.
- Some are positive, some negative, and more recently it might be said that some might even be retaliatory.

- There is often no evidence to support such claims and many may well be based on social deprivation than physical attributes.
- The term 'white flight' has been applied to the disappearance of the white sprinter.
- Are these notions based on physical or sociological phenomena?

APARTHEID
- In 1960 the South African issue came to a head and that country was eventually excluded from the Games of 1964.
- Avery Brundage had hoped that some resolution could be found by 1968 but most of the African nations made it quite clear that they would boycott the Games if that happened.

- South Africa was readmitted to the games of Barcelona 1992 following the abolition of apartheid and the installation of a majority democratic government.

COMMERCIALISM AND THE IOC

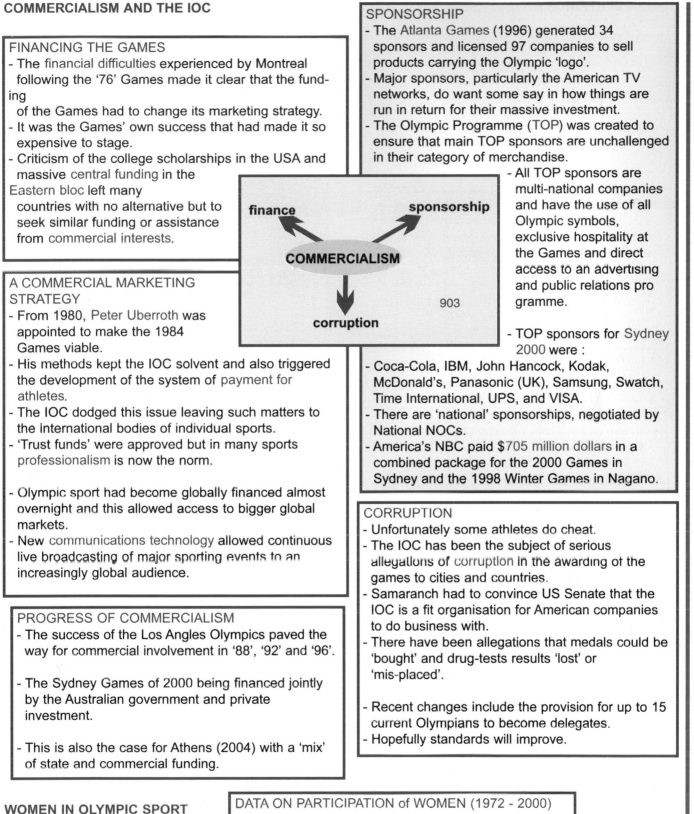

FINANCING THE GAMES
- The financial difficulties experienced by Montreal following the '76' Games made it clear that the funding of the Games had to change its marketing strategy.
- It was the Games' own success that had made it so expensive to stage.
- Criticism of the college scholarships in the USA and massive central funding in the Eastern bloc left many countries with no alternative but to seek similar funding or assistance from commercial interests.

A COMMERCIAL MARKETING STRATEGY
- From 1980, Peter Uberroth was appointed to make the 1984 Games viable.
- His methods kept the IOC solvent and also triggered the development of the system of payment for athletes.
- The IOC dodged this issue leaving such matters to the international bodies of individual sports.
- 'Trust funds' were approved but in many sports professionalism is now the norm.

- Olympic sport had become globally financed almost overnight and this allowed access to bigger global markets.
- New communications technology allowed continuous live broadcasting of major sporting events to an increasingly global audience.

PROGRESS OF COMMERCIALISM
- The success of the Los Angles Olympics paved the way for commercial involvement in '88', '92' and '96'.

- The Sydney Games of 2000 being financed jointly by the Australian government and private investment.

- This is also the case for Athens (2004) with a 'mix' of state and commercial funding.

SPONSORSHIP
- The Atlanta Games (1996) generated 34 sponsors and licensed 97 companies to sell products carrying the Olympic 'logo'.
- Major sponsors, particularly the American TV networks, do want some say in how things are run in return for their massive investment.
- The Olympic Programme (TOP) was created to ensure that main TOP sponsors are unchallenged in their category of merchandise.
  - All TOP sponsors are multi-national companies and have the use of all Olympic symbols, exclusive hospitality at the Games and direct access to an advertising and public relations programme.

- TOP sponsors for Sydney 2000 were :
- Coca-Cola, IBM, John Hancock, Kodak, McDonald's, Panasonic (UK), Samsung, Swatch, Time International, UPS, and VISA.
- There are 'national' sponsorships, negotiated by National NOCs.
- America's NBC paid $705 million dollars in a combined package for the 2000 Games in Sydney and the 1998 Winter Games in Nagano.

CORRUPTION
- Unfortunately some athletes do cheat.
- The IOC has been the subject of serious allegations of corruption in the awarding of the games to cities and countries.
- Samaranch had to convince US Senate that the IOC is a fit organisation for American companies to do business with.
- There have been allegations that medals could be 'bought' and drug-tests results 'lost' or 'mis-placed'.

- Recent changes include the provision for up to 15 current Olympians to become delegates.
- Hopefully standards will improve.

COMMERCIALISM
finance — sponsorship — corruption

903

WOMEN IN OLYMPIC SPORT

DATA ON PARTICIPATION of WOMEN (1972 - 2000)

Year	Sports	Events	NOCs	Women
1972	8	43	65	1056
1976	11	49	66	1247
1980	12	50	54	1125
1984	14	62	94	1567
1988	17	86	117	2186
1992	19	98	136	2708
1996	21	108	169	3626
2000	28	120	199	4254

| **WOMEN IN OLYMPIC SPORT (continued)**

HISTORY OF WOMEN'S PARTICIPATION
- The first opportunity for women came with golf and tennis in 1900, archery in 1904, figure skating in 1908 and swimming in 1912.

- De Coubertin believed that as there had been no women at the ancient Greek Games they should still be prevented from taking part.

- In 1900, Britain's Charlotte Cooper was the first female gold medallist - in the tennis singles.
- The opening of the track and field athletics events to women in 1928 at Amsterdam was highly significant and due to the diligence and persistence of a Frenchwoman, Alice Milliat.

- Mildred 'Babe' Didrickson won two gold medals and a silver in the 1932 Los Angeles Games.
- At these Games there were 1,300 male competitors, but only 120 women!
- Fanny Blankers-Koen won four gold medals in the 1948 Games in London, still unsurpassed at a Games.

HISTORY OF WOMEN'S PARTICIPATION
- Since 1964, the women of eastern Europe have made the biggest impact, not always for the best of reasons.
- Since 1989 (and glasnost and the fall of the Berlin Wall) Eastern European domination of women's sport has declined as state support and the state sponsored structures which underlay those countries' 'shop window' philosophy were dismantled.

- Women's access to sport is a reflection of the culture in which they live.
- In some fundamentalist Muslim countries, women are barred from participation and some pressure groups feel that their countries should be excluded from Olympic competition.

- Thirty-four countries in 1992 and twenty-seven countries in 1996 did not send female competitors to the Games.
- By Sydney 2000 this had fallen to only nine countries.

THE POWER OF THE SPORTING FEMALE
- Marketability means power.
- Although much resistance has been overcome, some women athletes also have to break down more localised resistance before they can enjoy the same freedoms.

- The women of Morocco, led by Nawal El Moutawakel (400m hurdles winner 1988) have begun to overcome the resistance of a religious culture which discourages women from engaging in public display.

- Generally, the image and power of female athletes is growing but the failure of some women stars to attract equal sponsorship to men remains an issue.

DENIAL OF ACCESS
- Women have traditionally been denied access to Olympic sport on four levels :
  - Global.
  - Institutional.
  - Cultural.
  - Domestic.

WOMEN IN THE IOC
- Pirjo Haggman of Finland was appointed in 1981 and Britain's Dame Mary Glen-Haig in 1982.
- HRH The Princess Royal was appointed in 1984.
- A number of women have been appointed since.
- But men still outnumber women heavily.

FURTHER DEVELOPMENTS
- Even though women were included in athletics in 1928, the 1936 Games saw only four sports providing women's events.

- There was a significant increase in the number of women in London in 1948.
- Twenty years later in Mexico there were still only eight women's sports.

- Numbers increased again following the 1976 Games in Montreal but even at the Games of 1996 there were 97 events open to women in 24 sports, whereas the total events open to men was 163.

THE MODERN SPORTING FEMALE
- The overwhelming constraints placed upon early sporting women were those of modesty, propriety and restraint.
- A young Olga Korbut, called into the Soviet team in Munich in 1972, changed all that with a daring and flirtatious floor sequence.

- Others: Nelli Kim, Vera Cĭslavskĭ and Nadia Comaneci, plus a host of others from the eastern bloc moved gymnastics - and women's sport - out of the age of the 'gymslip'.

- Marion Jones and the Williams sisters are perhaps the most recent 'Olympic stars' with Britain's Paula Radcliffe hopefully set to join them in 2004.

Information

POLITICAL USES OF THE OLYMPICS

POLITICAL AND OLYMPIC IDEALS
- The Olympic Charter opposes any political abuse of sport but such events are not new.
- The 1916 Games were cancelled due to World War 1 and invitations to the Games of 1920 were withdrawn from Austria, Bulgaria, Germany, Hungary and Turkey.
- The 1940 Games were cancelled and invitations not sent to Germany or Japan for the Games in 1948.
- The development of the 'East German machine' grew out of the use of sport by the former GDR as a tool of display / propaganda.
- The Soviet system was also politically motivated.
- The latest arrivals are the gymnasts, swimmers and distance-runners of the People's Republic of China.

PROTEST
- 1968 saw the first participation of the GDR and the protest of the 'Black Power' salute.
- Terrorism at the 1972 Games and the need for greater security removed the freedom and openness for which the Games had stood.
- There was political opposition to Britain's participation in Moscow in 1980 and the US government directed the withdrawal of its team from the same Games.
- This led to the withdrawal of USSR and other Soviet bloc countries from the Los Angeles Games of 1984.

OLYMPIC BIDS AND POLITICS - HOW THE GAMES ARE AWARDED

BIDDING PROCEDURE
- This is concluded six years before a Games takes place but bids must be lodged at least two years earlier.
- Any number of cities may bid but the IOC will only accept one bid from any member country, a decision made by its own NOC.
- The members of the IOC take a vote, and the city with a clear majority is successful but if there is no clear majority, the least popular city is eliminated.
- Further rounds of voting then take place, with one city being eliminated each time.
- There are now more bids for any Games than was the case up to Montreal in '76 and British bids for '92 and '96 had 20 and 25 opponents respectively.
- The Winter Games of 2002 had ten bids and this forced the IOC to change the process so that cities were first of all reduced to four by selection prior to any voting.
- It is the bidding process that has attracted criticism, with accusations of IOC delegates allegedly acquiring gifts, cash and other 'favours' in return for their votes.
- Four Commissioners have been removed from office and a further six have resigned.
- The length of service for a commissioner has been reduced from life to eight years but as this is renewable many critics still feel that the IOC is still a 'self-perpetuating' institution.

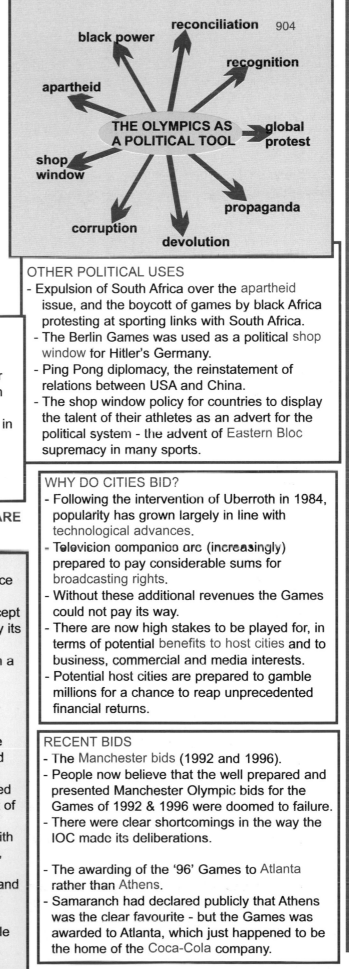

THE OLYMPICS AS A POLITICAL TOOL — reconciliation, black power, recognition, apartheid, global protest, shop window, corruption, propaganda, devolution — 904

OTHER POLITICAL USES
- Expulsion of South Africa over the apartheid issue, and the boycott of games by black Africa protesting at sporting links with South Africa.
- The Berlin Games was used as a political shop window for Hitler's Germany.
- Ping Pong diplomacy, the reinstatement of relations between USA and China.
- The shop window policy for countries to display the talent of their athletes as an advert for the political system - the advent of Eastern Bloc supremacy in many sports.

WHY DO CITIES BID?
- Following the intervention of Uberroth in 1984, popularity has grown largely in line with technological advances.
- Television companies are (increasingly) prepared to pay considerable sums for broadcasting rights.
- Without these additional revenues the Games could not pay its way.
- There are now high stakes to be played for, in terms of potential benefits to host cities and to business, commercial and media interests.
- Potential host cities are prepared to gamble millions for a chance to reap unprecedented financial returns.

RECENT BIDS
- The Manchester bids (1992 and 1996).
- People now believe that the well prepared and presented Manchester Olympic bids for the Games of 1992 & 1996 were doomed to failure.
- There were clear shortcomings in the way the IOC made its deliberations.
- The awarding of the '96' Games to Atlanta rather than Athens.
- Samaranch had declared publicly that Athens was the clear favourite - but the Games was awarded to Atlanta, which just happened to be the home of the Coca-Cola company.

DEVIANCE AND THE OLYMPICS

DEVIANCE
- The reasons why rules are framed are not uniform and agreed.
- Deviant behaviour refers to those who will find a way around the rules however they are framed.

- Deviant behaviour falls into one or more of the following categories :
    - Institutional.
        - Group specific.
            - Individual.
- And is either :
    - Voluntary.
        - Co-operative.
            - Enforced.
- Sports bodies develop strategies to limit deviance - anti-doping, drug control, red carding, yellow carding, penalties - backed up by specific and detailed rules.

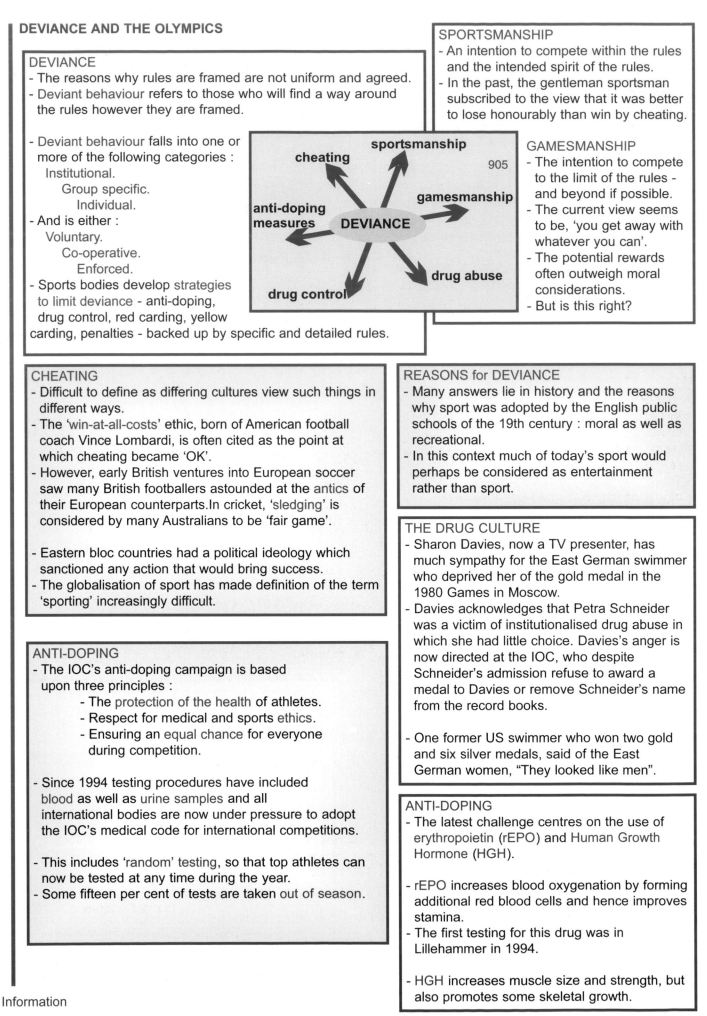

SPORTSMANSHIP
- An intention to compete within the rules and the intended spirit of the rules.
- In the past, the gentleman sportsman subscribed to the view that it was better to lose honourably than win by cheating.

GAMESMANSHIP
- The intention to compete to the limit of the rules - and beyond if possible.
- The current view seems to be, 'you get away with whatever you can'.
- The potential rewards often outweigh moral considerations.
- But is this right?

CHEATING
- Difficult to define as differing cultures view such things in different ways.
- The 'win-at-all-costs' ethic, born of American football coach Vince Lombardi, is often cited as the point at which cheating became 'OK'.
- However, early British ventures into European soccer saw many British footballers astounded at the antics of their European counterparts. In cricket, 'sledging' is considered by many Australians to be 'fair game'.

- Eastern bloc countries had a political ideology which sanctioned any action that would bring success.
- The globalisation of sport has made definition of the term 'sporting' increasingly difficult.

ANTI-DOPING
- The IOC's anti-doping campaign is based upon three principles :
    - The protection of the health of athletes.
    - Respect for medical and sports ethics.
    - Ensuring an equal chance for everyone during competition.

- Since 1994 testing procedures have included blood as well as urine samples and all international bodies are now under pressure to adopt the IOC's medical code for international competitions.

- This includes 'random' testing, so that top athletes can now be tested at any time during the year.
- Some fifteen per cent of tests are taken out of season.

REASONS for DEVIANCE
- Many answers lie in history and the reasons why sport was adopted by the English public schools of the 19th century : moral as well as recreational.
- In this context much of today's sport would perhaps be considered as entertainment rather than sport.

THE DRUG CULTURE
- Sharon Davies, now a TV presenter, has much sympathy for the East German swimmer who deprived her of the gold medal in the 1980 Games in Moscow.
- Davies acknowledges that Petra Schneider was a victim of institutionalised drug abuse in which she had little choice. Davies's anger is now directed at the IOC, who despite Schneider's admission refuse to award a medal to Davies or remove Schneider's name from the record books.

- One former US swimmer who won two gold and six silver medals, said of the East German women, "They looked like men".

ANTI-DOPING
- The latest challenge centres on the use of erythropoietin (rEPO) and Human Growth Hormone (HGH).

- rEPO increases blood oxygenation by forming additional red blood cells and hence improves stamina.
- The first testing for this drug was in Lillehammer in 1994.

- HGH increases muscle size and strength, but also promotes some skeletal growth.

DEVIANCE AND THE OLYMPICS (continued)

THE IOC AND DRUG CONTROL
- The first drug-related death (the Danish cyclist Knud Jensen) occurred in the 1960 Games in Rome.
- The IOC's current interpretation includes the deliberate and inadvertent use of performance-enhancing substances.
- The establishment of a medical control system, responsible for drug testing, has been operative since the 1968 Games.

PARALYMPICS

IMPAIRMENT CLASSIFICATIONS
- Cerebral Palsy (CP-ISRA).
- Spinal Cord Lesion, Spina Bifida and Polio (ISMWSF).
- Athletes with Blindness (IBSA).
- Les Autres or Amputations (ISOD).

HISTORY
- In 1944 Dr. Ludwig Guttmann opened a spinal injuries centre at Stoke Mandeville Hospital.
- He pioneered a new approach to rehabilitation centred on sport.
- The Paralympics movement began life as an organised sports competition for war veterans with spinal cord injury in 1948.
- Within a short time competitors from Holland were also taking part.
- In 1960 a Games on the Olympic pattern was organised and in 1976 in Toronto competition was expanded to include other disability groups.
- The Games were initially an independent event but have shared the main Olympic venue since Seoul in 1988 and Albertville in France for the Winter Games.
- It was not until 1988 that a commitment was made by the IOC to assist the IPC with the organisation of the Games.

THE IOC AND DRUG CONTROL
- IOC Medical Commission involves establishing all routines and practical aspects of collecting urine samples and ensuring that they are securely transported to the accredited laboratory for that Games.
- The Commission works closely with the International Sporting Federations as well as the accredited laboratory.
- IOC rules do not prevent further sanctions against guilty parties by the international federations of individual sports.

- Ben Johnson, the discredited Olympic sprinter of the 1988 Games was reinstated following his original ban for steroid abuse only to be found guilty again and banned for life in 1993.

MARKETING AND IMPAIRMENT
- The first 'Olympic Games for the Disabled' took place in Sweden in 1980, and the first use of the term 'Paralympics' was at the Games in Seoul in 1988.

- Samaranch supported the disabled movement, but he felt that too close an association with disabled sport might harm the market potential of the Games.
- There were apparently three allegations :
  - He did not want the title 'The Olympic Games for the Disabled' used, for marketing reasons.
  - He would not allow the Olympic flag or symbols to be used.
  - The IPC were not to ask for inclusion of disability events in the main Olympic programme.

- The Paralympics now has its own symbol (three teardrops).
- Wheelchair events were held (on a demonstration basis) in the track and field programme in Sydney 2000.

LINKS WITH THE OLYMPIC MOVEMENT
- The number of athletes involved has increased from 400 in 1960 to just over 3000 in Atlanta in 1996, and 3,824 from 123 countries in Sydney in 2000.

- The general opinion is that the Sydney organisers gave disability sport the stage it deserved.
- Clearly, venues are now shared with the 'big brother' Games of much longer standing and since 1988 the IOC has, at least officially, acknowledged and embraced the Paralympics.

Frank Galligan

SUMMARY OF GLOBAL FACTORS

The following four pages chart the factors and issues which affect global sport, and form a summary for the nine countries / areas chosen for study in this text.

Themes	Australia	France	USA	UK
Topography and Climate	Huge land area. Varied physical features. Varied climate.	Large land area. Varied physical features. Varied climate.	Huge land area. Varied physical features. Varied climate.	Lack of size and defined climate reduces range of available sports.
Historical Influences	British colony. British, European, Asian immigrants.	Colonial power. Colonial, North African immigrants.	British colony. Afro-Caribbean, European, Hispanic immigrants.	Colonial-industrial empire. Reformist influences.
Political Systems	British then Socialist Federal Government.	Revolution to social democracy.	British, then capitalist Federal Government.	Democratic bicameral parliamentary system.
Cultural Influences	Suppression of Aboriginal culture and subsequent Asian cultures (stacking).	Embracing of former colonial cultures : (l'egalitarianism).	Suppression of native, black, hispanic and east European cultures.	Diminution of class divide has reduced middle class dominance of sport.
Philosophical Approach	Mixed capitalist / socialist ethic.	Intellectualised socialism.	Capitalist ethic : WASP syndrome.	Blurring of capitalist socialist ethics. Minority inclusion.
Economic System	Agriculture based but embracing new technologies and its position on Pacific Rim.	Mixed economy drained by heavy social programme and subsidies.	Profit motive rules. Produces some 'winners' but many 'losers'.	Move from heavy to technological economy creating leisure and unemployment.
Education	State education within federal system. Some private schools mainly R.C. Devolved to State level.	National Education very centralised. Private system mainly RC schools. Little devolution of power.	State education within federal system. Small private system. Devolution to local School Boards.	State education system but significant and influential private sector.
PE Teachers	Few specialists in primary sector. Teachers also coach but with good support structure.	Specialists only in the secondary sector. Limited involvement in school sports. This is done through UNSS.	Some PE teachers involved in coaching. Specialist staff coach sport at High School level.	'Laissez faire ' approach has required 'all purpose' roles of PE teachers.
Sports Schools	Growing number of these schools. Largely self-funded. Traditionally in the private sector.	Formerly only 'sports study sections' but 'sports schools' now being introduced. Funded centrally.	Few sports schools as such but 'win ethic' ensures that all schools aim for sports excellence.	A few private (for example, Millfield, Kelly College). Some state schools have 'designated status' as sport schools.
Power Base	Generally, still the white Western groups.	Paris retains its hold via a centralised bureaucracy.	The WASP males hold power. Based on wealth and social status.	Diminishing aristocracy replaced by ascendant middle class meritocracy.
Centralisation	Two levels of centralised control : federal, state.	Most centralised via Ministry of Youth & Sport (no devolution).	Least centralised. Complete devolution to grass roots.	Some centralised control via QANGOs. No centralised policy.
Stacking	In evidence, with East Europeans, Asians, Aboriginals in that order.	In practice, North Africans (especially Algerians) at the bottom of the pile.	Very much in evidence, Vietnamese now last in line.	Some deprivation on ethnic or poverty grounds has this effect.

Argentina	Kenya	South Africa	Asia	New Zealand
Huge land area Varied physical Features Varied climate.	Large land area : varied physical features : varied climate inc. drought.	Large land area Varied physical features: good but varied climate.	Huge variation in the physical geography / features: huge land-mass to small islands.	Land area and climate roughly equal to that of Britain : varied topography.
Former Spanish colony, much British influence in industry, education and sport.	Former British colony: Independent since 1963.	Former British colony White colonial influences, Ethnic dispossessions.	Some British colonies : others (e.g. China) 'colonised' by British trade and commerce.	Former British colony / cultural heritage. Maori people & culture included within its democracy.
Spanish - then various 'national' & military governments until free elections following the Falklands war.	Independence : to social democracy. Conflict between European and older tribal cultures.	British, then nationalist (Apartheid) gov't. Recent adoption of democratic principles.	Ancient / dynastic cultures overlaid (varying degrees) by British trade / colonial expansion. Diverse political models.	Constitutional democracy. Treaty of Waitangi (1864) established the equal rights and ancient customs of Maori.
85% 'European' population and culture. 'Amerindians' and 'mephistos' make up the rest.	European colonialism overlaying ancient tribalism: factionalism based on ancient tribal differences.	Suppression of native, black, and Asian cultures.	Attempted suppression of ancient cultures without success. Assimilation of outside cultures - driven by capitalist ethic.	Full inclusion of ancient (Maori) culture within political and social frameworks.
Militarist influences still present but on the decline.	Democracy but ridden with inter-tribal conflict.	Capitalist ethic overlain by recent adoption of social democracy.	Ancient 'spiritual' values often govern attitudes to sport in the modern world.	British colonial values have been adapted to accommodate aggressive competitive tendencies.
Agriculture and mining and mineral wealth : Poorly managed by a series of governments.	Very poor agricultural economy with many farmers exploited by 'western interests'.	Huge reserves of natural resources but re-distribution and ownership an issue.	Varies from centralist (China & N. Korea) to capitalist (Japan) and from agricultural to industrial / technological.	Largely agricultural economy with reliance upon both British and Pacific rim markets.
State education within federal system : some private schools : mainly R.C. Devolved to provincial level.	National education system but poorly funded : also private system - many church schools.	State system devolved to nine 'provinces' but poorly funded in contrast to established private system.	State education exists in all cultures but with much variation: for example : heavily 'politicised' in China, N. Korea.	National education system - centralised with control devolved to nine regional authorities: private system (largely religious bodies).
Newly established in both primary & sec sectors. Teachers do some coaching but most sport taught at 'junior' club level.	Some specialists in the secondary schools and also in the private sector. Involved in sport but limited facilities.	High level of teaching in private schools but not in State system: very poor facilities, even in some private 'white' state schools.	Specialists in all sectors in China, North Korea and Japan but not elsewhere. Poor provision elsewhere.	Specialists in primary & secondary sectors: heavy emphasis on school sport: Highly structured PE programmes.
No: see comments above.	No, but some private schools are strong.	Not as yet but new infrastructure still developing.	Highly significant in China but developing in India and in N. Korea.	Recent developments with the formation of SPARC : High level of school sport is the norm.
Generally, those of Spanish / Western. European origins.	Many European (colonial) business interests and small native group.	Currently changing: whites still have much influence economically.	Central political control in China, Pakistan and N. Korea with significant military influence.	Former 'Colonial' influences predominate but indigenous groups have significantly more input than elsewhere.
Centralised structure is being developed.	Little centralisation.	Slowly developing a centralised structure.	Yes in China & N Korea. Yes for elite sport in India and Pakistan.	Yes, established fully from 1976 onwards.
Still in evidence, with 'Mestizos' and 'Cabicates Négras' at the bottom of the pile.	White Europeans with indigenous tribal cultures 'stacked' below them.	Officially this no longer exists but in practice many indigenous groups are considerably disadvantaged.	Most evident in India and Pakistan.	Tribal groups have 'pecking order' but Europeans and former colonials have power.

Themes	Australia	France	USA	UK
Government Funding	Federal Government devolves power and funding to each State. Growing private sector funding.	Heavy government involvement in sport. Centralised funding and control.	Little involvement at government level. State bodies pass power to grass roots level. Much private funding.	UK Sport controls lottery funding - for capital projects and athlete income. No direct government control over policy.
National Initiatives	Poor performance at 1976 Olympics caused Government intervention - set up AIS and ASC.	Poor performance at 1960 Olympics caused De Gaulle's 5 point plan, and setting up of Sports academies.	No outstanding failures, but highly motivated by Soviet success 60's to 80's. None specific.	Failure at 1996 Olympics heightens debate on National Sporting Academy.
Mass Participation	Federally sponsored programmes run at State and local level., for example, 'Active Australia'. 'Willing and Able' caters for disabled people. 'Women sport' urges women into sport.	'Sport pour Tous' aims to encourage a multi-sport approach through the family means within everyone's reach.	No 'federal' plans. 'Little league' sport caters for kids. Adult programmes run by men's and women's organisations and as part of school or college programmes.	Major initiatives 'Sport for All', 'Top Sport'. Thought to be insufficient. NGBs run schemes (for example, athletics, swimming, gymnastics).
Elite Sport	ASC and AIS control national programmes and élite development. State academies foster talent within a State and work with the AIS on programmes. Such as 'Sportsleap' and 'Sportsearch'.	National centres of excellence (INSEP). Regional sports and PE centres have developed programmes and there is a centre for Research and Technology. Some undergraduates can use sporting achievements as part of their degree.	The 'Lombardian' ethic (win at all costs) sits at the heart of sport in the US. Élitism is at the heart of most sporting activity, and is, in effect, a programme for excellence.	Amateur (participation) ethic being replaced by money led outcome or professional approach.
Poverty	Officially not a bar to access. Funding allows scholarships to academies of sport. Some groups still feel excluded.	Heavily funded programmes for talent identification allow access to all. Funding spreads down to local levels of provision.	The sports scholarship is the only access to sports programmes. In effect the only programmes for excellence.	Insufficient centralised funding and 'diversionist' allocation policies produce insufficient provision in most needy areas.
Gender Issues	Currently very much an issue. 'Womensport Australia' is a loud political voice. Women have greater % of medals than men at major Games.	Equality exists by right. However, not always so in practice. Social / family pressures have restricted participation but recent role-models have broken new ground.	'Title IX' a major boost for women. But the 'matriarchal' society is not too keen to 'divert' women from their 'real purpose'. Men complain that funding is taken away from them.	Policies for 'equality' exist, but lack of centralised system inhibits implementation.
Athletes with Disabilities	Australia has a superb programme of development for disabled sportspersons via 'Active Australia' and 'Willing and Able'.	The notion of equality exists in legislation but sadly not always in practice.	Active assimilation policies exist. The 'Atlanta experience' upset many disabled athletes, provision allegedly very poor, but increased in the run-up to the Sydney Olympics.	Growing awareness and participation levels but much left to voluntary associations. Lack of a clear centralist approach.

Argentina	Kenya	South Africa	Asia	New Zealand
Central Gov't devolves (limited) power and funding to provinces.	Central provision in theory but poor economy limits support.	Much broader provision under new gov't. but massive task ahead.	Full Gov't funding in China / N Korea. Partial funding in Japan. Elite sport only in India and Pakistan.	Government funding in all areas.
Yes in Physical Education and Olympic Sport. Other areas developing slowly.	Largely in Athletics. Little development in other areas.	SANREC funding of SANGALA programme.	China - full range of Gov't funded programmes. Japan - National Children's Games. India - Boys Sports Companies (Army).	'Sportfit' 'Pushplay' 'Thirty minutes'.
Developing provision by the Secretaria de Deportes de la Nacion but this is developing very slowly with most growth in the province of Buenos Aires. (see below)	Growth of professional sport has stimulated interest in athletics, soccer and basketball but little in the way of effectively funded mass participation programmes.	Traditionally, little or no provision for 'mass' sport : however, SANGALA & other programs are slowly changing this	Traditional pro-grammes in China and Japan - also N. Korea (worker sport etc.) but now developing in India, Pakistan and elsewhere in Asia : Women in certain reli-gious groups find there is much resistance to their participation.	'Sport & Recreation New Zealand' (SPARC - from Aug 2002) spon-sor programmes such as 'Sportfit', 'Thirty Minutes' and 'Push-play', all designed to encourage mass par-ticipation and an active lifestyle.
The Secretaria de Deportes de la Nacion and the Argentine Olympic Association make provision for the funding of élite sport. The 'Secretaria' is also responsible for mass sport but its work is very ineffective thus far.	Nation-building ethic and limited central funding dictate that a limited range of sports is catered for. The Kenyan Olympic committee is funded voluntarily - not by government.	Prior to the demise of Apartheid, South Africa selected its élite performers from a small privileged group of 'whites' : New policies now embrace 'all' - but will take some time to be effective.	Élite sport in China long established as part of political model : India (SAI) and Pakistan (PSB) much more recent : Structures in place in Japan and N. Korea but in rather differing political scenarios.	Well-funded and developed by the SPARC in conjunction with the NZOC where appropriate. New Zealand has a small population base and achieves very highly despite this drawback.
High unemployment (20%) and presence of disadvantaged groups (see stacking) means that poverty is an issue in Argentina.	High levels of poverty, particularly in rural areas. Drought and resultant famine cre-ate major problems for government.	High levels of poverty in 'township' and other marginalised groups. Vast natural mineral wealth benefits only a small privileged few.	Not an issue in China, or N. Korea, nor in Japan, but India and Pakistan have economic problems with access and funding, and some groups are excluded on the basis of culture or religion.	Poverty is not a major issue in new Zealand. Indigenous cultures have traditionally not been excluded : in stark contrast to the situation in Australia.
Not (yet) a major issue. Provision in women's sport is made for those who are already 'advantaged' and others do not yet have a powerful enough voice.	Cultural resistance to change. Many Kenyan women find family objections - which only subside when prize money is seen to be an alternative to poverty.	Exist on two levels : - cultural resistance within ethnic groups - selection policies are still 'skewed' towards social élite	Japan and China have policies of equality in the case of women athletes. This however is not yet the case in India and Pakistan, particu-larly in some religious groups.	New Zealand women, including Maori women are equal in terms of legislation, general practices and opportunity.
Provision was made in the 'Peronist' period but subsequently declined. The 'Laws of Basic Consensus' have yet to really address this issue.	No apparent policy in sport. Some funding from IOC initiatives and some participation from the few who may have independent means.	The South African Sports Commission funds disability sport & sends competitors to the Paralympic Games through Disability Sport South Africa (DISSA) grass roots provision is limited.	Again, the centrally funded programmes of China provide for disability sport but the ethic (nor the funding for it) has not yet spread to some parts of Asia.	Disability sport is centrally funded in the same way as able-bodied sport (SPARC).

SYNOPTIC QUESTION & ANALYSIS FRAMEWORK

ASSESSMENT PROCEDURE

THE QUESTIONS
- Each of the Examining Boards have been required to include synoptic questions in their A2 examination.

- There are a number of different potential formats to be considered and candidates should check the specification and revision material of their particular board.

- All questions must link AS module(s) with A2 module(s) and include reference to applied performance.

- Due recognition must be given to compulsory and optional modular content.

MARK ALLOCATION
- The allocation of marks vary with each Board.
- There is a requirement that the synoptic assessment will be 20% of the overall assessment total.

- Boards may allocate synoptic marks from one or two final units which may include a performance unit or an assignment.

- Boards have the right to mark the synoptic question using content marks, banded criteria or a combination of the two.

THE APPROACH
- Thematic approaches may be :
A. General questions involving full range of compulsory modules with choice of options (AQA).
B. Subject based, such as the Olympic Games, amateurism, etc. with multi-disciplinary analysis (Edexcel).
C. Science based and may include physiological / biomechanical / psychological content (OCR).
D. Socio-cultural basis involving contemporary studies with historical / comparative content (OCR).

- Questions may be essay type (Edexcel), or structured (OCR and AQA).

- All boards require that candidates write their answers in structured continuous prose.
- The sample answers contained in the CDROM have been presented in bullet points, do not use this style in your own examinations.

AQA
- AQA Synoptic Assessment is in two parts, A2 Module 6 - Synoptic Coursework Assignment, and :
- A2 Module 5 Section B.
- The current structure of this assessment has retained the principle of involving a review of the two scientific disciplines of physiology and psychology as they function in a socio-cultural framework.
- This all-inclusive analysis is eased by a choice of answering three from four thematic questions, where each is valued at 12 marks.
- Assessment is made using a knowledge mark scheme rather than by banded criteria.

EDEXCEL
- Currently, the Edexcel Board has retained the principle of involving a review of the previous study of all units in their synoptic assessment.

- It is placed in A2 Unit 4 and involves two Sections.

- Section B :
- A Synoptic Analysis of Trends in International Sport through Global Games.

- The candidate is required to answer one question from a choice of four.
- Focus is on contemporary, comparative study of issues related to global games and, therefore, involves socio-cultural analysis, but the specification makes the point that candidates 'will be required to apply their knowledge of scientific factors that elite performers may use in preparation for global competition'.

EDEXCEL

- Section C :
- A Synoptic Analysis of Scientific Principles in the Development of Performance.

- The candidate is again required to answer one question from a choice of four.
Focus is on physiological, psychological and/or mechanical analysis, but also includes sociological strategies.
The inclusion of the latter allows candidates with less confidence in scientific analysis to answer the question with a socio-cultural focus.

- Each question is valued at 25 marks and a marking profile is based on banded criteria which recognise Relevance, Content and Structure & Style.

Information

OCR
- The candidate is required to answer one question from a choice of two.
- Each question requires you to answer two parts (based on AS and A2 content).

Question 1 has a scientific focus.

- This question identifies the significance of having a scientific background when linking Anatomy and Physiology or Skill Acquisition (compulsory elements from AS), and Exercise Physiology or Biomechanics or Sport Psychology (optional elements from A2).

Question 2 has a sociocultural focus.

- This question identifies the significance of Contemporary Issues (compulsory element from AS), and Historical or Comparative Studies (optional elements from A2).

- The mark allocation is 45 marks.

- Each part carries 13 marks for relevant informative knowledge and advanced knowledge.

- The remaining 19 marks are allocated to synoptic analysis, which is marked against banded grade criteria to be found in the OCR syllabus specification.
- These marks are allocated for links between AS elements and A2 elements in both directions, for the application of theoretical knowledge to practical situations, and for grammar / prose techniques.

Bob Davis
Jan Roscoe
John Honeybourne

Index

T

tangible rewards	4.9
target games	7.4, 7.10
target heart rate	2.8
teacher training	8.6
temperature regulation	1.13, 2.3, 2.4
tendons	1.1, 1.2, 2.10
tennis	7.10
The Fight	7.1
Thorndike's laws	4.4
thresholds	2.1, 2.10
thrombosis / stroke	2.15
tidal volume (TV)	1.12, 1.13, 2.11
Tiers Temps Pedagogique	
	8.6
tissue respiration	1.11, 1.12
Title 1X	8.8, 9.10
Tom Brown's schooldays	
	7.7, 7.8
TOPPLAY	6.7
toppling	3.7, 3.9
TOPSPORT	6.7
total metabolic rate	2.4
training programmes	2.12, 2.14, 2.15
trait	5.1
trait anxiety	5.10
Treaty of Waitangi	8.14, 9.9
triadic model	5.3
trial and error	4.3, 4.7
tribal culture	6.4
turbulent flow	3.5
type A personality	5.1
type B personality	5.1

U

UK sport	6.7
UNSS	8.6, 9.8
urbanisation and leisure	
	7.11

V

validity	2.7
Vanderswaag	6.1
variable practice	4.11
variance	2.4, 2.8
vascular response to exercise, short-term	
	1.14
vascular shunt	1.10
vasoconstriction	1.9, 1.10, 1.14
vasodilation	1.9, 1.10, 1.14
vasomotor control	1.10, 1.14
VCE	8.4
Vealey	5.6
vector	3.1, 3.2
$\dot{V}E$	1.12, 2.11
velocity	3.1, 3.2, 3.6
velocity time graphs	3.1
venoconstriction	1.9, 1.10
venomotor control	1.10

venous return	1.10
ventilation rate	1.12, 1.13
ventricular systole	1.8
verbal guidance	4.12
vicarious experiences	5.6
visual guidance	4.12
vital capacity (VC)	1.12, 2.11
$\dot{V}O_{2max}$	2.6, 2.11, 2.12, 2.13, 2.14
vortex flow	3.5

W

warm-up	1.6, 1.10, 2.8, 2.10, 2.12
WASP	8.8, 8.10, 9.2, 9.8
waves summation	1.4
weight	3.3, 3.7
weight training	2.8, 2.12
Wenlock Games	9.1
white fibres	1.6
white fibro cartilage	1.1
whole method	4.10
Wilkinson Report	8.10
'willing and able'	8.4, 9.10
Wingate test	2.7
winter sports	7.12
women in sport	8.8, 9.10, 9.11
work	2.1, 2.2, 3.7
work and free time	7.11
work efficiency	2.2
wrestling	8.5

Y

yellow elastic cartilage	1.1
YMCA	7.11, 8.10
Youth Sports Trust (YST)	
	6.7

Z

zero transfer	4.9